Action Research
Living Theory

D0207356

Action Research
Living Theory

Jack Whitehead and Jean McNiff

S SAGE Publications

London • Thousand Oaks • New Delhi

SAGE Publications Ltd
1 Oliver's Yard
55 City Road
London EC1Y 1SP

SAGE Publications Inc.
2455 Teller Road
Thousand Oaks, California 91320

SAGE Publications India Pvt Ltd
B-42, Panchsheel Enclave
Post Box 4109
New Delhi 110 017

British Library Cataloguing in Publication data

A catalogue record for this book is available
from the British Library

ISBN10 1 4129 0854 X   ISBN13 978 1 4129 0854 2
ISBN10 1 4129 0855 8 (pbk)   ISBN13 978 1 4129 0855 9 (pbk)

Library of Congress Control Number 2005932717

Typeset by C&M Digitals (P) Ltd., Chennai, India
Printed on paper from sustainable resources
Printed in Great Britain by TJ International, Padstow, Cornwall

Contents

Introduction

This book is about the practice and theory of action research. It is written for practitioner action researchers who are committed to improving their learning, and offering explanations for how and why they are doing so. Specifically it is written for those on formal accredited courses and their lecturers, and also for those at a more advanced stage of their workplace enquiries, who wish to engage with ideas about the practicalities of doing action research, and about its theoretical underpinnings.

The book is a guide to the most pressing topics in the field, including the little addressed yet probably most urgent issue of how it is possible to assess quality in action research, so that it can generate theory whose validity can be tested against publicly communicable standards of judgement. This is especially urgent in light of many governments' policies regarding the future directions of educational research, how it should be funded, and the potential implications for education. Currently, funding for educational research tends to go to those institutions that have demonstrated quality research output. In the UK, funding goes to those with the highest grades in the national research assessment exercise. These institutions tend to be those whose research is clearly within the social sciences. The possible continuation of the social sciences as the dominant paradigm in educational research carries deep implications for the likely continued positioning of practitioners as participants in higher-education-led research, rather than researchers and theorists who are conducting their own practice-based research in their own right.

This situation is of concern, especially in light of the current increased openness to practitioner research, as demonstrated in recent funded initiatives such as the Best Practice Research Scholarships in the UK. Yet while practitioner research is generally held in high regard for its contributions to quality practice, it is not yet held in equal regard for its potential contributions to quality theory. Part of the reason is that its methods for assessing quality have not yet been fully worked out, and in some cases not even addressed. The new openness to practitioner research is therefore offset by a caution that perhaps practitioners are still not capable of doing quality research or generating theory because they are not fully conversant with the appropriate methods for judging the quality of their own work, and, given that the topic is seldom raised in the practitioner research literature, it would seem of low priority. So if practitioners themselves do not take care in addressing these core issues, the wider educational research community could be forgiven also for not taking them seriously.

The matter is now urgent, and especially so in light of this recently published statement by the 2008 Research Assessment Exercise (2005):

> Where researchers in higher education have undertaken applied and practice-based research that they consider to have achieved due standards of excellence, they should be able to submit it to the RAE in the expectation that it will be assessed fairly, against appropriate criteria.

The published RAE criteria state that best quality research should demonstrate quality 'that is world-leading in terms of originality, significance and rigour'. This presents a key opportunity for practitioner researchers. The practitioner research community needs now to do serious work on identifying its own criteria and standards of judgement to show both that they know what quality means in action research and also that they are capable of articulating those standards and producing theories that stand the test of the standards in achieving originality, significance and rigour. Practitioners themselves need to define and articulate the standards of judgement they use to evaluate their own work, and make these standards of judgement available to the wider educational research community for the assessment of practitioners' accounts, so that shared agreement can be reached about how accounts should be judged on their own terms within the still dominant paradigm of the social sciences.

This book engages with these issues. We explain, through offering an account of our own action research, how we address the issues both of how we do action research, and of how we assess the quality of our own research and original theories so that we can test their validity and legitimacy against the critical scrutiny of the wider research community who read this book. We hope by doing this that we encourage public debates about what is at stake in doing action research and how its quality can be judged. We depart from conventional social science criteria and standards of judgement, and we identify new forms that, we believe, are more appropriate for judging the quality of practitioner action research, namely, the idea that we can transform the values that inspire our work and give meaning to our lives into specifically critical living epistemological standards of judgement by which we judge the quality of our living theories of practice. We explain these ideas throughout, in our usual accessible language, with copious examples of how this is already being achieved in contemporary work.

This was always meant to be a pedagogical text, in which we set out the practices and principles of action research, addressing mainly practitioners on higher degree courses or at a more advanced level in their workplace studies. Yet we have always maintained that the best way of teaching something is to show how you do it yourself. Practical examples seem to work best, and, given that action research is eminently practical, it makes sense for us to explain action research processes through the way we conduct our own action enquiries. Besides, the whole idea of action research is that the kind of theory that is most appropriate for explaining its processes is already within the practice, and emerges from the practice as the research develops. This is what we have tried to do. We have set out our own action research account, and, at the same time, commented on the process of what we are doing as we conduct our research and generate our own living educational theories. These theories are living in the sense that they are our theories of practice, generated from within our living practices, our present best thinking that incorporates yesterday into today, and which holds tomorrow already within itself.

Because this is a pedagogical text, we mix and match different voices. The main text is spoken in our shared voice as researchers, and throughout we engage you, as our reader. In some instances, specifically in Part 2, which deals with some of the more practical issues of data gathering and generating evidence, we change to a more pedagogical voice, where we specifically offer ideas about how you can do these things for yourself. We do not tell you what to do, but offer ideas that you may wish to try out for yourself. We explain how and why they work for us, and for many others. Throughout we adopt a critical voice, where we comment on what we are doing and invite you also critically to engage with us as we tell our research story and make judgements on our own processes of communication. It is for you to decide if we manage to realize our identified standards of judgement, mainly by producing a text that is authentic and helpful. In many ways, this is an experimental text for us, yet, in our view, this is what we are about as action researchers, finding innovative ways of conducting our lives and telling our stories in a way that other people can learn.

We are always glad of feedback that helps us to modify, refine and strengthen our work. We therefore depend on you, our critical audience, to provide that feedback. Please let us know what you think. You can contact us at our e-mail addresses below. If you write, we will respond.

Jack Whitehead can be contacted at A.J.Whitehead@bath.ac.uk
Jean McNiff can be contacted at jeanmcniff@mac.com

Working with the text

This book contains an account of our current action research. We have written the book as our research report, and we have organized it into parts and chapters. Each chapter addresses a specific question in our action plan.

Each part introduction contains a brief overview of its content.

To provide an overview of the issues addressed in the book, here are variants of the chapter summaries. While the summaries appear at the end of each chapter, placing them here like this as a whole constitutes a summary of the book, and, we hope, will provide a guide to your reading and indicate what may be seen as the overall significance of the work.

Chapter 1   Background to our research: reasons and purposes

What are our concerns?

In this chapter we set out our research concerns and questions. These are about the future of educational research, and action research in particular. We explain that the social sciences are currently the dominant form in educational research, with their own tried and trusted methods for assessing quality. These methods position practitioners as capable of generating quality policy-informed practices but not so capable of generating quality theory. Practitioners need to remedy this situation if they are to participate in public debates about the future of evidence-based educational practices, by showing that their claims to be generating quality theory should be taken seriously. They can do this by demonstrating their competence in making scholarly judgements about their work, and by making the standards of judgement they use in assessing the quality of their own accounts available to peer action researchers and the wider educational research community. These matters need urgent attention, especially since the introduction of recent influential performance management orientations in some action research literatures that share the same epistemological values of domination and control as many of the social sciences. Our current research questions are therefore to do with how we can disrupt the epistemological hegemonies of the social sciences, accompanied as they are by performance-management-style action research literatures, by encouraging practitioners to show that they are focusing on matters of assessing the quality of their work, and making their findings available to their peer action researchers and the wider academic educational research community.

Chapter 2   Contexts of our research

Why are we concerned?

We outline some of our research contexts in this chapter. These contexts are to do with the nature and uses of theory. We explain the reasons for our concerns in relation to how theory is used to maintain the current epistemological hegemony of the social sciences. We make the case that, while we value the social sciences for their immense contributions to educational research, and draw on those contributions in our own research, we also see great value in the contributions of practitioners who are conducting their action research in their own educational settings. To make this case we explain some of the ontological, epistemological and methodological assumptions of different kinds of research and theory, in terms of their underpinning values and logics. We explain that practitioner action researchers should be seen as capable of making significant contributions to quality theory, but to achieve this perception, they need to show how they engage with issues of theory and knowledge in explaining why their research should be assessed in its own terms and from within its own now established scholarly traditions.

Chapter 3   Looking for data

What experiences can we describe to show why we are concerned?

We offer as the starting point of our action research the idea that many of our values, including those of justice and democracy, could be more fully realized by the participation of practitioner action researchers in debates to do with the future of educational research. We present three case stories that describe the experiences of three practitioners whose values of justice and entitlement have similarly been denied because of the exclusion of themselves and the children they teach from public recognition as worthwhile knowledge creators and citizens. This, we suggest, is because their contributions to practice-based theories are not acceptable within normative understandings of how contributions to educational theory should be judged. We therefore introduce ideas about what new kinds of standards of judgement should be introduced and developed. We explain what these may look like in relation to our own research, and how we are articulating them in this book.

Chapter 4   Monitoring practice and gathering data

What kind of data will we gather to show the situation as it unfolds?

In this chapter we adopt a pedagogical voice alongside our scholarly voice. We explain what kind of data to look for to support claims to improved learning for improved practices. In processes of data gathering, we say, the aim is to gather data primarily in terms of the study of oneself, in order to show progress in the growth of one's own learning and how that learning can influence future learning and action. While data also need to be gathered in relation to research participants' improved learning for improved action, those data need to be understood in relation to testing the practitioner action researcher's own claim to improved learning. We show this process in action by setting out some of the ways we gather data to test our claims that we are improving our learning in order better to encourage practitioner action researchers to raise their capacity in gathering the kinds of data that are going to help them also make quality judgements on their work. By gathering appropriate data, they will be able to generate the kind of evidence that will enable them to withstand robust critique in testing their claims to knowledge.

Chapter 5   Interpreting the data and generating evidence in relation to living critical standards of judgement

How do we explain our educational influences in learning?

In this chapter we speak about the need to generate quality evidence in support of a claim to knowledge. We outline some of the practicalities of generating evidence, explaining that evidence can be distinguished from data by showing how it stands in relation to identified criteria and standards of judgement. We then go on to set out the kinds of standards of judgement we consider appropriate for producing evidence in action research, and we suggest this in terms of the transformation of ontological values into living critical standards of judgement. Focusing on our own ontological, epistemological, methodological and pedagogical values, we explain how we transform these into living critical ontological, epistemological, methodological and pedagogical standards of judgement. By doing this, we explain how we are observing the epistemological and methodological rigour of showing how we are attending to matters of identifying appropriate criteria and standards of judgement in making evidence-based claims to knowledge.

Chapter 6   Validity, legitimacy and moral authority

How do we show that any conclusions we come to are reasonably fair and accurate?

In this chapter we show how we take care in supporting our conclusions by submitting our research findings to the critical scrutiny of others. This, we say, is an epistemologically and methodologically rigorous research process, as well as one that shows our own epistemological, methodological and moral accountability. We explain how we take Habermas's (1987) criteria of social validity as the core criteria we use in judging the quality of evidence of the educational nature of our relationships with others. We explain how the criteria contain linguistic descriptions of our embodied values, and we go on to explain how we transform them into our living critical standards of judgement. This process, we claim, helps us to achieve necessary ethical and moral validity in the production of our research account, which we believe is a core standard of judgement by which to demonstrate the ethical and moral nature of validation and legitimation processes.

Chapter 7   The potential significance of our research

How do we show the potential significance of our research?

In this chapter we outline what we consider to be the potential significance of our research for education and educational research. We explain how we have influenced our own and each other's learning, and also the learning of others, specifically as they are members of social formations in education. The kind of influences we aim to exercise, we say, are those that encourage others to exercise their capacity for freedom and creativity. We explain that the examples we produce as evidence for these claims show how people are contributing both to new educational practices in their own settings, and also to new forms of educational theory, by showing how the practice itself can contribute to a form of practical theorizing in action. We choose specific examples of work in the UK, South Africa and China, to show how the work has implications at a global level, and how this supports our own stance as making our evidence-based claims to personal knowledge with universal intent.

Chapter 8   Case studies

How do we show the implications of our research?

The two case stories in this chapter contain ideas about how practitioner educational researchers can contribute to new social practices through undertaking their action enquiries. Working with limited financial and practical resources, both men show how, through their struggles to realize their educational-values-based visions, they have managed to inspire others in turn to achieve their own educational values. They have both managed to encourage a culture of enquiry within the social contexts of their countries' educational and cultural transformation. These stories also show the deep implications for new practices at global level. Because the stories are about managing cultural renewal through educational action research, they also demonstrate the potential contributions of action research for the creation of sustainable social orders.

Chapter 9   Evaluating the account of our research

How do we evaluate the evidence-based account of our learning?

Here we return to the theme of demonstrating the validity of our work, where we focus on issues of social validity, and we now introduce the theme of demonstrating the validity of the account of our work, where we focus on issues of textual validity. Again we draw on Habermas's (1987) social criteria of comprehensibility, truthfulness, sincerity and appropriateness in judging the validity of the evidence-based account of our own learning. As before, we explain how we transform these criteria into our living critical standards of judgement to assess the quality of our text. We go on to explore the idea that by demonstrating our capacity to make these processes transparent we are aiming to develop trust between ourselves and our audience, so that our scholarly and moral credibility can be validated and acted upon. At this point we appeal to you, our reader, to be aware of how you are exercising your own originality of mind and critical engagement as you make judgements on the validity of our account.

Chapter 10   Into new research

How do we modify our concerns, ideas and practices in the light of our evaluations?

In this final chapter we explain how we are modifying our concerns, ideas and practices in the light of our evaluation of our research so far. We explain how we are moving into new research areas of encouraging others to show how they judge the quality of their work in relation to their identified standards of judgement. We also explain how the ideas we are exploring here are already having some influence among the practitioner action research community and in the community of academic educational researchers. While we do not ask all completely to embrace our ideas, we do ask all to give attention to the crucial issue of how they meet the standards of originality, significance and rigour as they offer their accounts of practice. Without such attention, we believe, practitioner action researchers will continue to be relegated to the ranks of good practitioners but not good theorists. With such attention, we are convinced that practitioner action researchers will demonstrate their capacity to contribute, through educational theory, to the formation of the kind of societies that are the manifestation of the values that honour and sustain humanity. With collaborative attention by both communities of practitioner and academic educational researchers, we believe that all can show the transformative potentials of the communicative action of the social formations of educational researchers who are committed to social renaissance.

PART 1

Backgrounds and Contexts

In this part we make clear that we are writing an account of our own action research, and we set out the background and contexts. We explain our reasons for the research, and we outline our purposes. We identify specific research questions, and say how we intend to address those questions. Throughout we adopt a critically reflective stance to what we are saying. *This part contains the following chapters:*

1 Background to our research: reasons and purposes
   What are our concerns?

2 Contexts of our research
   Why are we concerned?

3 Looking for data
   What experiences can we describe to show why we are concerned?

1 Background to our research: reasons and purposes

What are our concerns?

This chapter sets out the main issues in the current phase of our ongoing research programme. These issues are deep concerns about what is happening in educational research and educational theory, and how this is influencing thinking and practices in education and the professional education of teachers. We also set out our concerns about what is happening in action research, specifically in relation to how it is used in education. In setting out our concerns, we are giving the reasons for our research, and saying why we are doing it. We are also stating the purposes of our research, that is, what we hope to achieve.

The chapter is organized as two sections:

1 The current status and future of educational research
2 The current status and future of action research

1 The current status and future of educational research

Here is a story that sets out our concerns.

In May 2005 a seminar was organized by the British Educational Research Association (BERA) on 'The Future of Educational Research'. The seminar took place in Oxford, and was attended by delegates from around the world. Two strong themes emerged. The first was that educational research should continue to be approached via a traditional social sciences perspective. The second was about the status of practitioner action research. Delegates agreed that practitioner research was having a considerable influence in debates about the nature of pedagogy and the professional status of the teaching profession, and could indeed provide a credible alternative direction for the future of educational research. However, the issue of identifying appropriate standards for judging quality was a sticking point. The social sciences had well-established procedures for identifying what counts as quality and validity, and its very credibility as a tried and trusted research methodology made it attractive to policy makers. While practitioner research seemed to present exciting new departures, its procedures were not yet well developed, especially in terms of making judgements about quality. There was little doubt that practitioner research was a valuable form of professional development, and, since the 1990s, governments and other bodies had shown a keen interest in practice-based research in education. Two examples of initiatives that promoted practice-based research were first, the Best Practice Research Scholarship Scheme, whereby teachers in schools are funded to explore identified aspects of practice, and second, the networked learning communities supported by the National College of School Leadership, whereby groups of teachers are brought together to share ideas about good practice and learn from one another within a context of shared collegiality. Yet while the promise of practitioner research is generally widely acknowledged, it is still bedevilled by the particular issue of what counts as quality and what kinds of standards of judgement can be used in assessing quality (see Furlong and Oancea 2005).

This situation represents our concerns too. While we value contributions from social science approaches to educational research, for reasons which we set out in the next section, we are resistant to its hegemony; and while we promote the development of practitioner research, for reasons we articulate in Section 2, we are aware of the need to develop coherent standards of judgement for assessing the quality of practitioner research. For us, showing how and why we make judgements on our work, and justifying our reasons, is at the heart of quality scholarship. Agreement needs to be reached about standards of judgement, both by practitioners as they produce their research accounts, and also by the higher education research community as they assess the quality of practitioners' accounts. These concerns about the need for quality scholarship in action research, which include articulating its processes of demonstrating judgement, give us the reasons for our current research focus, and are the main themes of this book. We are interested in what kind of standards of judgement are appropriate in action research, how they can be agreed by the practitioner action researcher community and the higher education community, and what kinds of validation and legitimation processes are necessary for such agreement to be reached.

First, however, we need to clarify why we promote practitioner action research in the first place, and this means saying what we find in action research that we do not find in the social sciences.

Social science research and action research

We understand research as more than activity. Non-research activity is when we do things unreflectively, such as laughing or waking up, or do things in a routine manner, such as shopping. Research however is purposeful investigation, which involves gathering data and generating evidence in relation to articulated standards of judgement, in order to test an emergent theory. While research and shopping are both purposeful activities, the purposes are different. The purpose of shopping is to buy bread or milk, whereas we see the purpose of research as generating and testing new knowledge.

The main feature of social science research that distinguishes it from a living theory approach to action research is that a researcher aims to generate new knowledge (theory) about what other people are doing. They observe what other people are doing, and describe and explain those people's actions. They tend to maintain a spectator, outsider perspective throughout (but see the section below on insider research). The theory generated is the researcher's theory about other people. The researcher also tells the research story, so it is the researcher's theory that goes into the public domain. This remains the state of affairs also in some action research contexts. Practitioners investigate their practice, observed by an external researcher. The researcher observes, describes and explains what they are doing, so the theory is generated and owned by the researcher, and is about other people.

In action research, the focus swings away from the spectator researcher and onto the practitioner researchers. Practitioners investigate their own practice, observe, describe and explain what they are doing in company with one another, and produce their own explanations for what they are doing and why they are doing it. Practitioner researchers already know what they are doing in their everyday lives in the sense that knowledge is embodied in what they do. Each person already has their own tacit theory within themselves about how they should live, and they work collaboratively to make sense of what they are doing by talking through their ideas, and monitoring the process. They monitor what they are learning, and how their learning influences their actions. Because they are doing research, they bear in mind that they need to explain how what they are doing counts as theory, so they produce their accounts of practice to show how their social activity can be seen as purposeful research activity. The theories they generate are their own theories, and they constantly test these theories against the critical responses of others to see if the theories can withstand criticism, in other words, have validity. To establish the validity of their theories, they articulate the standards of judgement they use, that is, the way they make judgements, in evaluating whether the theories they generate actually reflect the values that inform their practices.

We develop these ideas throughout. An important starting point is to establish what a social science perspective to educational research means, and to consider some of the possible implications for education.

The nature of the social sciences

The social sciences were originally modelled directly on the physical, or natural, sciences. The physical sciences were about studying the physical environment, at first to understand its nature, and later to understand how it works in order to control it. The objects of enquiry (what was being studied) were the phenomena of nature, and also the relationships of the phenomena to one another. Scientists studied nature; they described and explained it, in an empirical way, by maintaining an objective stance and studying what was 'out there'. For some, this empirical approach became an empiricist approach. This remains the dominant form of government-funded research in the United States. They studied nature in order to control it, often with the idea that, if they could control nature, they could also predict what would happen, and so control the future. This view of research is still very much alive today, as when, for example, an agriculturalist experiments with plant food on tomatoes in order to find the best way of increasing the yield.

This process may work well in relation to tomatoes, but the analogy breaks down when the assumptions and methods of the physical sciences are transferred to the social sciences, that is, when humans become the objects of inquiry and are regarded in the same way as tomatoes, and are also expected to behave in the same way. Humans of course have minds of their own, and do not always do what a scientist expects them to. They tend not to conform to the scientist's preconceived ideas about correct behaviour.

However, many scientists, and their social scientist counterparts, do not accept this situation, because they tend to see their mental models as more important than the people whom they expect to fit into those mental models, and they often assume that so-called non-conforming people are the problem, rather than their own entrenched assumptions about the reified nature of mental models.

The social sciences have developed over recent centuries, and different people have developed different attitudes and methodologies. Some have continued to adopt the largely positivist methodologies of the natural sciences, while others have not (see below). Those who adopt positivist attitudes believe as follows:

- An object can be objectively and dispassionately studied by a social scientist, who remains outside the situation they are studying. The responsibility of the social scientist is to maintain a value-free perspective. This will ensure non-contamination and purity of results. This purity is the factor that qualifies the research findings to be applied to other situations.
- The social scientist will be able to provide descriptions and explanations for human behaviour in the same way that descriptions and explanations can be offered by natural scientists for, say, the growth of vegetables. Descriptions and explanations make up theories, so, in the same way that a physical scientist offers their theories about the nature, origin and workings of the physical environment, the social scientist also offers theories about the nature, origins and workings of human behaviour from their spectator stance.
- On the basis of these theories, the future behaviours of people can be predicted and controlled. The best way to ensure a good society, in terms of the positivist social scientist's vision, is to apply the theory, which involves moving people around, in the same way as a natural scientist arranges appropriate conditions, in terms of what the scientist thinks is the right way to test their own theory.

Other social scientists however do not share these views. The disciplines of anthropology and ethnomethodology are premised on the idea that a researcher observes people in their natural settings and respectfully offers descriptions and explanations (theories) for what the people are doing. Mitroff and Kilman (1978) made the point that four distinct approaches to social science methodologies exist. These are the methodologies of the analytic scientists, the conceptual theorists, the conceptual humanists, and the particular humanists. Each methodology is distinguished by its preferred logic of mode of inquiry. Carr and Kemmis (1986) also seriously critiqued positivist assumptions as rooted in technical rationality. Whatever their internal differences, however, the social sciences maintain an overall position that takes human behaviour as an object that can be studied from a spectator point of view.

Different social scientists also hold different views about knowledge (to do with epistemology) and forms of thinking (to do with logic). Some – not all – believe the following:

- Knowledge can be discovered. Like the external physical environment that the scientist is studying, knowledge is also 'out there', so it can be studied from outside. Again, the scientist stays out of the field of enquiry, so as not to contaminate their findings. Sometimes however researchers do get involved in the situation they are studying. They then become insider researchers, working with the people they are investigating. However a difference in status in the relationship remains. The researcher is still in charge of the research process, and the researcher's account and theory, not the people's, go into the public domain. Occasionally, social scientist researchers get so drawn into participants' lives that they abandon their externalist perspective and begin to investigate their own practice and their relationships with their research participants, but then they transform themselves from social scientists into action researchers. For us, a distinguishing feature of our approach to action research is that practitioner researchers enquire into their own practice.

- Knowledge can be organized into laws, such as the laws of gravity or electricity. These laws apply universally, to humans as well as to physical phenomena such as tomatoes. Theories work in the same way as laws, so theories cannot be changed. They are established for all time.
- Knowledge can be applied in like-to-like situations. Physical objects should not break the laws. Apples should not fall upwards, and humans should not behave in aberrational ways (but of course they do).

The key point is that many social scientists, like physical scientists, believe that there is a correct view of knowledge, and that they know what it is. They also believe that theirs is a correct form of logic.

Some social scientists also use logics that are

- linear and one-dimensional, because they move towards a specific end point, to find the answer that is assumed to be there;
- mechanistic and functional, because they often force an answer even when no obvious answer is available;
- imperialistic, because they apply the answer to each and every situation, without regard for local contexts.

(Ideas about knowledge and logics are developed in Chapter 2.)

We said earlier that not all scientists assume this to be a view of knowledge or a form of logic that is appropriate for scientific enquiry. Scientists such as Sir Peter Medawar, Thomas Kuhn and Paul Feyerabend maintained that scientific inquiry involves disciplined episodes of empirical testing as well as creative episodes of imaginative thinking. Throughout his work, Popper (1959; 1963; 1972) also stressed the importance of being open to criticism. He advocated testing the validity of ideas through criticism rather than applying the answer to each and every situation. Most scientists would probably say they are testing the validity of their hypotheses rather than applying the answer to each and every situation. Many debates go on in the literatures of the social sciences about these different perspectives. Prasad has produced one of the most compelling accounts of different traditions in the social sciences with the unfortunate omission of action research:

> This book has outlined what I believe to be the major traditions influencing much of qualitative research on work and organizations in contemporary society. This is not meant to indicate, however, that the book is a completely comprehensive treatment of the field. Entire scholarly traditions have been excluded (e.g. action research, cultural

> studies, queer theory), and some traditions have only received partial treatment (e.g. institutional theory) under the rubric of structuration and praxeology. Obvious limitations of time, space and personal expertise have restricted the scope of the book in many ways. (2005: 283)

Our book may serve to remedy this exclusion to some extent.

Social science remains the grounding of dominant forms of educational research today. Furthermore, and to return to the concerns we are setting out, a clear recommendation from some researchers at the BERA conference mentioned above was that educational research should continue to pursue a social science perspective in the future. We believe that the ideological hegemony of social science researchers will find support in the 2005 BERA Presidential Address of Geoff Whitty on 'Education(al) research and education policy making: is conflict inevitable? (Whitty 2005). This kind of support is deeply alarming, because of the links that are assumed to exist between educational research and educational practices, and specifically the professional education of teachers. Here are some of those implications.

Some implications of social science approaches to educational research

In some accounts of the history of educational research, authors such as Ellen Condliffe Lagemann (2000) explain how the predominant social sciences assumption that things could be studied from an externalist perspective began to be applied to education, and the professional education of teachers. The assumption was that education and teacher professional education could be studied and analysed by external researchers. Lagemann explains how the persistent search of the social sciences for universal laws often came to grief because of its flawed underpinning epistemological assumptions. She cites as an example the first issue of *Educational Review* in 1891, whose first article was by Harvard philosopher Josiah Royce:

> Entitled 'Is There a Science of Education?' the essay suggested that teachers should have 'a scientific training for their calling', by which Royce meant opportunities to reflect on their craft. According to Royce, however, teachers should not be asked to master any formal pedagogical system, since none was or could be adequate. In Royce's opinion, there was 'no universally valid science of pedagogy ... capable of ... complete formulation and ... direct application to individual pupils and teachers'. (2000: ix)

In other words, while the professional education of teachers should be firmly grounded, this should be seen as a process that involved reflection, rather than be seen as an applied science. The professional education of teachers could not be systematized in terms of specific bodies of knowledge that would give direction to their work. Royce (1891) went on to describe his own 'unwillingness to apply so pretentious a name as "Science" to any exposition of the laborious and problematic art of the educator'. According to Lagemann, 'whether there is or can be a science of education remains controversial to this day. Despite [however] the persistence of the issue, education became a subject of university study at the end of the nineteenth century, and as that happened, a new domain of scholarship began to emerge' (2000: ix). This signifies an important development. Education was taken over by higher education, both the education of young people in schools and other educational settings, and also the professional education of their teachers. The professional education of teachers therefore now became a new domain of scholarship. This is where the debates in this book are centred, around whether the professional education of teachers and other practitioners should continue to be seen as guided by the methods of the social sciences, and the systematic incorporation of those methods into educational studies, or by practitioners' own understandings of practice, as in action enquiry. How do practitioners understand their work? How do they show that their practices influence their own learning, the learning of others, and the learning of the members of a social formation (see page 121)?

The entire field is now in flux. However, educational research is not alone in this. Major shifts have taken place recently in the epistemological base of human enquiry, and these shifts are evident across the disciplines, such as in linguistics, the earth sciences, physics and economics. In education, the effort to turn the study of education into an exact science has moved towards new perspectives that regard education itself as the grounds for thoughtful investigative practice. Here is an example of how these shifts manifested in education in a British context.

Shifts in the epistemological base of professional education

In 1950s Britain, the systematic study of education developed into the study of the so-called 'foundational' disciplines of education, such as the philosophy, sociology, psychology and history of education. This became known as 'the disciplines approach'. Each discipline was seen as a freestanding body of knowledge. This view strongly influenced a view of schools curricula as the collation of subject knowledges, and pedagogical practices as the delivery of those subject knowledges. By extension, and largely associated with the writings of Peters and Hirst at the London Institute (see Peters 1966; Hirst and Peters 1970), the professional education of teachers also came to be informed by the disciplines approach, so teachers were expected to learn about the different disciplines and apply their acquired knowledge to their practice. Consequently, a linear relationship was assumed between bodies of knowledge, to be assimilated by teachers, which were in turn to be applied to practice. Much of the system appeared to stay true to the conventional epistemological bases of scientific inquiry, which were about demonstrating a relationship of cause and effect, and to a conventional logic of domination (Marcuse 1964), which sought to create neat boxes of practice and thinking, and which excluded the contradictory elements of the imaginative creation of possible new futures and the values base of educational practitioners. Many philosophers of education and many social scientists however understood the importance of analysing human action in terms of intentional rather than mechanistic forms of causal relationship, and pressed for a shift in the epistemological base of educational theory. The kind of epistemological shift needed in educational theory was demonstrated in 1983, when Hirst acknowledged a mistake in his thinking. He now acknowledged that much understanding of educational theory would be developed

> in the context of immediate, practical experience and will be co-terminous with everyday understanding. In particular, many of its operational principles, both explicit and implicit, will be of their nature generalisations from practical experience and have as their justification the results of individual activities and practices.

> In many characterisations of educational theory, my own included, principles justified in this way have until recently been regarded as at best pragmatic maxims having a first crude and superficial justification in practice that in any rationally developed theory would be replaced by principles with more fundamental, theoretical justification. That now seems to me to be a mistake. Rationally defensible practical principles, I suggest, must of their nature stand up to such practical tests and without that are necessarily inadequate. (1983: 18)

However, in spite of generous acknowledgements such as Hirst's, traditional views remain, many still based on the methodologies of the social sciences, and, because there is as yet no alternative methodology that is strongly credible in terms of well-established methods for demonstrating validity and rigour, the methodologies of the social sciences are assumed to be the only correctly worked out ones and therefore the ones to be used.

Furthermore, the methodologies of the social sciences have influenced the nature of educational practices. A divisive kind of logic has remained dominant, and has led to the practical separation of policy makers, researchers and practitioners, as well as to a public perception of the discrete positioning of these people in debates and decisions about the real-life implementation of educational practices. Policy makers are assumed to make policy and arrange for its implementation by practitioners. These policies are based on the most important findings of educational research, which are created by identified educational researchers, usually in higher education settings. The responsibility of researchers therefore is to pursue research and generate evidence-based conclusions in the form of theories, which policy makers can use to inform their decisions. It is a truism to say that many higher education researchers complain about the fact that policy makers do not read their research findings, or, if and when they do, they take only those findings that support their own politically constituted interests. Whatever may be the case, a strong mutually beneficial relationship appears to exist between the communities of policy makers and higher education researchers (whose ranks are largely made up of social science researchers), which often manifests in ways that are beneficial to both parties, such as continued funding for specialist research centres and the increased prestige of policy makers.

Because many educational researchers continue to locate their work within the traditions of the social sciences, and because the methods of the social sciences are tried and trusted in terms of the established standards of judgement they use to assess the quality of research (unlike the emergent traditions of practitioner research, which, while promising much for improvements in teaching and learning, are still premised on standards of judgement that have not yet been fully endorsed by practitioners in the production of their research accounts or by the research community in the assessment of those accounts), the social sciences continue to be accepted as the dominant form. It seems to be a case of better the devil you know, rather than an angel who has not yet quite got their wings.

These then give us the reasons for the current phase of our research. Over the years we have contributed to the legitimation of practitioner research by supervising practitioners' higher degree studies and supporting their validation by the higher education research community. We have succeeded in this, as attested to by the considerable number of masters dissertations and doctoral theses now in the public domain that clearly communicate the capacity of practitioners to show how they are contributing to new practices and new theories (see for example www.actionresearch.net). Our research focus now changes. As well as continuing to support higher degree studies, and to intensify our activities in that regard, we also now turn our attention to how we can establish the kind of standards of judgement appropriate for assessing the quality of practitioners' research accounts, and how to get those kinds of standards accepted both by practitioners who produce their accounts of practice and by those who are responsible for assessing the quality of the accounts.

While setting out some of the reasons for our research (why we are doing it), we now also begin to clarify the purposes of the research (what we are doing it for).

2   The current status and future of action research

We begin by saying that we know what can be achieved through action research. We know from experience what can happen when practitioners intervene in and improve their own learning, in their attempts to influence the learning of others about how they in turn can improve their own learning and their own situations. We have first-hand experience of working with practitioners in practical contexts, and also of supporting them as they undertake their workplace and higher degree enquiries. These enquiries tend to take as their starting point the question, 'How do I improve my practice?' (Whitehead 1989), as practitioners systematically search for ways of influencing their own and others' learning. We know the kind of contributions that can be made to new practices and new theories through the production of practitioners' accounts as they create their living theories of practice.

Here are two examples to show what this looks like.

Beatriz Egus de Grandi

Beatriz Egus de Grandi works in Argentina. She writes in the abstract to her dissertation:

> This dissertation is a self-study in the growth of awareness in the practice of my personal values that provide me with standards of judgment against which I test the influence I try to exercise on the development of motivation and empathy, to generate creativity and critical thinking in my students. In this process, the development of my own creativity and critical thinking kept pace with that of my students and co-researchers in an equal participation in the task of an action research project that carries throughout the aim of 'How can I improve my practice?'
>
> I describe the birth of my pedagogical concern in child centred education that transformed me from source of knowledge to facilitator of resources to construct skills that allow the practice of discernment in learning. A central theme in my dissertation is the deconstruction of my pedagogy to highlight my manner in teaching, which is the vehicle of choice to transmit my values of honesty, integrity, freedom and justice.
>
> The voices of my students guided this journey through my practice, presenting evidence of conflicts when I failed to live up to my values. These living

contradictions impelled me to engage in the soundless dialogue of myself with myself to generate a living educational theory. This theory emerges from my manner in teaching that fostered in my students dispositions to reflect and open their minds and hearts to honesty through trust and compassion through acceptance of differences. These mature dispositions reflect the values that give purpose to my life and my practice, and allow me to claim them as standards of judgment to test the validity of my living educational theory. (Grandi 2004)

You can download Beatriz's entire dissertation from http://www.bath.ac.uk/~edsajw/grandi.shtml.

Daisy Walsh

Daisy Walsh works in the UK. She writes in the abstract to her dissertation:

This dissertation is concerned with showing how I, as a Programme Area Team Leader, for Vocational 'A' level, GNVQ and GCSE ICT, at a Further Education College in the United Kingdom, have focused on my commitment as an educator and team leader in an action enquiry research. Using a reflective journal I recorded my thoughts on significant events throughout my practice. Using narratives I constructed representations from the data gathered. I traced and explored my journey as a team leader in Further Education. My concern was to improve my understanding of my leadership practice for the benefit of my team and my students. In examining my self-development, I have extended my own professional knowledge. I aim to be a better team leader for the formation of a more effective team. This dissertation makes an important contribution to my personal, educational and professional development as a team leader. Vocational education, its leadership and management, is uncharted territory for many school and further education teachers who hold leadership positions. By putting the work of my dissertation in the public domain, I hope that other team leaders in a similar vocational education context can relate in part to some of my experiences. (Walsh 2004)

You can download Daisy's entire dissertation from http://www.bath.ac.uk/~edsajw/walsh.shtml.

However, while we vigorously support the development of communities of practitioners in pursuing their action enquiries, both for the improvement of workplace practices and also for their contributions to new theory, we also know that we are working within a global context where, in some quarters, action research is construed somewhat differently. This new construction is embraced by policy makers who also want to control education, especially in terms of eliminating public participation in policy debates and reduced access to education provision, within a broader policy of privatizing education.

Two things are going on in action research, which give us reasons for concern. One is perhaps more alarming than the other. A brief account of the history of action research, and how thinking has developed, provides a context for our first concern.

A brief history of action research

Throughout its development, different people have come to understand action research in different ways. From its beginnings in the 1930s, it was seen as an applied social science. Kurt Lewin, one of its acknowledged founding fathers, was himself a social scientist, who saw action research as a procedure that would allow workers to have a greater say in their work contexts. He promoted action research on the basis that workers' greater involvement would probably improve their productivity.

The idea of action research was taken up vigorously in education in 1950s America (see Corey 1953), but later went into decline (see McNiff and Whitehead 2005b: Chapter 4). In the 1970s it received a new impetus in the UK through the work of researchers such as John Elliott, Jack Whitehead, Wilf Carr and Stephen Kemmis.

John Elliott at the University of East Anglia, building on the legacy of Lawrence Stenhouse's Humanities Curriculum Project, developed action research as a form of professional development for teachers. Throughout, this took an interpretive approach, that is, an approach which allows for participation by practitioners, but which nevertheless remains grounded in the social sciences, because an external researcher is still seen as the one doing research into other people's practices. Elliott's views have been highly influential in establishing action research, but, from our perspective, the approach is still problematic in the assumption that, although practitioners do the research and gather data in order to generate new theory, the theory itself is generated by the spectator researcher. In other words, the power to interpret the data, establish the validity of the work, and disseminate it for legitimation within critical public forums still rests with the external researcher. Power has never been entirely devolved to practitioners.

At the same time as John Elliott was developing his work, Jack Whitehead at the University of Bath was also developing a new approach to action research. Unlike interpretive researchers making claims about the theories of other practitioners, he took the view that teachers were perfectly capable of generating their personal theories by systematically studying their practice. Their theories would contain the descriptions and explanations they offered for their practices as they asked, 'How do I improve what I am doing?' (Whitehead 1989). He maintained that the work of teachers should be supported (but not directed) by higher education personnel, who would in turn provide intellectual and emotional support to the teachers, as well as advice about further resources and pathways to accreditation. The relationship here was a democratic partnership, in which all participated in a dialogue of equals. The work of higher education personnel also was to study their practice, in collaboration with the teachers who were studying theirs, so that all could learn and grow together.

The work of Elliott and Whitehead has been profoundly influential over the years in presenting action research as a legitimate educational research methodology.

Back to our concerns

Our first concern therefore is about the continuing dominance of the social sciences and consequently the continuing dominance of interpretive approaches. Now a second concern has emerged, which in our opinion constitutes a threat to the democratic impulses of action research, and threatens to turn action research into a form of performance management. While maintaining a social science perspective, this new form also introduces a note of driving control, by insisting on the implementation of prescribed action plans, seasoned with an unspoken threat that unless you do action research in this particular way, you will fail as a teacher.

Certain epistemological and logical assumptions underpin this performance management form of action research. As noted in Section 1, the dominant forms of social science tend to assume that people will access knowledge in order to use it, and knowledge itself is assumed to exist as packages of information and theory that can somehow be downloaded from one person's mind (in this case, the researcher's) onto the blank slate of the other person's mind (in this case, the practitioner). It is precisely this technical rational approach that Carr and Kemmis critiqued in their text *Becoming Critical: Education, Knowledge and Action Research* (1986). In this text they did groundbreaking work, heightening awareness of the significance of Habermas's theory of a critical social science, in which 'one of Habermas's principal targets is the positivist belief in the logical and methodological unity of the natural and social sciences' and in which he shows that 'the symbolically structured domain of "communicative action" is not reducible to scientific knowledge' (1986: 134, 135). They also emphasize the importance of the economic and political relations that influence the lives of practitioners. We have drawn consistently on the work of Carr and Kemmis to strengthen our own insights as we exercise our creativity and critical judgements in generating and testing our own living educational theories. It is therefore out of this deepened awareness that we now express alarm at how action research is being turned into a process that aims for technical expertise through the implementation of prescribed action plans and defines itself in terms of targets and outcomes.

We continue to develop these themes shortly, but at this point it is important to consider some of the underpinning assumptions of the issues at stake, and this means engaging with some key terms, so that the arguments make sense. The terms are *ontology, epistemology, methodology* and *social purposes*.

Ontology, epistemology, methodology and social purposes

Ontology refers to a theory of being, which influences how we perceive ourselves in relation to our environment, including other people. Ontology is not the same as cosmology, which refers more to one's worldview.

Your ontological perspective tends to influence how you see other people, and also the kind of approach you adopt in research. If you see yourself as separate from other people, you may assume an outsider approach to research. This is the

(Continued)

(Continued)

common spectator form in the social sciences. Your task would be to observe other people and offer descriptions and explanations for what they are doing. If however you see yourself as part of other people's lives, and they of yours, you may adopt an insider, participative approach, which would involve you offering descriptions and explanations for how you and they were involved in mutual relationships of influence.

Epistemology refers to a theory of knowledge, which involves two parts:

- a theory of knowledge (what is known);
- a theory of knowledge acquisition (how it comes to be known).

Your epistemological stance is inevitably influenced by your ontological stance. If you believe that the world and its inhabitants are 'out there', separate from you, you may regard knowledge in the same way. You may even reify knowledge (turn it into a thing), which you could study and analyse. If however you believed that you were part of the world and not a fly on the wall, you would probably see knowledge as something you create, in company with other people who are also creating their own knowledge. Because you would see yourself as interacting with others, you could see your own process of interaction as a process of testing and critiquing what you already know and transforming it into something better. Epistemologies usually contain (1) an understanding of the unit of appraisal, in the sense of what is being judged; (2) the standards of judgement in the sense of how valid judgements can be made; and (3) a logic in the sense of the form that the reasoning takes in understanding the real as rational (Marcuse 1964).

Methodology refers to a theory of how we do things. It should not be confused with 'methods', which are the specific techniques we develop for finding something out.

Your methodology will in turn be influenced by your ontological and epistemological assumptions. If you believe that the world and its inhabitants are 'out there', you would set about studying and analysing them, and also study artefacts such as books that contain explanations (theories) about what they do. You would aim for definitive answers, or closure. On the other hand, if you perceive yourself as a participant in the world, interacting with others, you may see your interactions as a process of creating new knowledge individually and collectively. You would test any provisional understandings against the critiques of your companions. This living process would require an openness to new possibilities, and a resistance to closure.

Social purposes refer to what we want to achieve in the social world, and why.

(Continued)

> *(Continued)*
>
> A strong relationship exists between what you hope to achieve in terms of your existence as a human being, and your ontological, epistemological and methodological assumptions, which can all influence each other and transform into the other. For example, if you perceive yourself as an island at the centre of your own universe, where people and knowledge are separate from you, you may come to see them as objects which you can use for your own purposes, from your position as centre. However, if you perceive yourself as in living interaction with the world, and also involved with others in processes of knowledge creation, you may come to see social purposes as finding ways of improving both your own processes of interaction and knowledge creation.

It is not difficult to see the differences in the underpinning assumptions of living action research and social science forms of action research, especially the technical forms of the new performance management kind of action research. In interpretive action research, the ontological assumptions of the researcher position the researcher as separate from their objects of inquiry, namely, the practitioners they are studying. This separation between researcher and researched is deepened in the new technical forms, where the researcher's responsibility is to create action plans for a practitioner to implement. The values base of control appears to give rise to a focus on passive consumerist learning, and the ignoring of the real-life vagaries of practice in the drive towards closure through the achievement of specific behaviours.

Compare these views with the underpinning assumptions of living action research approaches. Action researchers who work in a living theory tradition tend to espouse the humanitarian values of care and compassion, a concern with freedom and the right of all to make up their own minds about how to do their research and how to live their lives as they wish, in negotiation with others who wish to do the same. We, Jack and Jean, articulate our own values in these terms. For the purposes of this book, we identify those values to do with ontology, epistemology, methodology and social purpose.

- Our ontological values are that we value other people's capacity to come to know in their own way. We are thinking of ontological values as flows of life-affirming energy through which we give meaning and purpose to our lives. We do not believe that people have to be told what to think. We have faith in our own and in other people's intellectual capacities, so we avoid telling them what to do, confident in the grounding of our faith in the philosophies of Polanyi (1958), who says that all people possess a vast store of tacit knowledge already within themselves; of Plato (see de Botton 1999), who says that knowers are able to hold the one and the many together at the same time; and of Chomsky (1986), who speaks of the innate capacity of individuals to create language, an idea which we extend to the creation of their own knowledge in an infinitude of new forms. From the grounds of this faith, we value embodied knowledge, the nature of which practitioners come to understand as they work with their practice and create their own theories of education. We value enquiry learning, and we encourage all to engage with questions of the kind,

'How do I improve what I am doing?', which involves their imaginative responses to problematic questions.

- We value epistemology because of its connection with rationality and knowledge. We recognize knowledge as existing in different forms. We do not regard knowledge only as packages of information, although this may be one form of knowledge, nor do we see the creation of knowledge simply as the delivery of packages. We value the capacity of all people to create their own knowledge, to draw insights from the knowledge of others, and to show how they identify their unit of appraisal as the explanation they give for their educational influence in their learning and in the learning of others.
- Our methodological values are of the kind that lend discipline and systematization to our enquiries. We encourage others to engage in their systematic enquiries as they ask how they can improve their understanding of their work, and exercise that understanding as educational influence. Some of these enquiries extend over a period of five or six years, and practitioners' accounts show how they engaged with the processes of emergent understanding. Many exercise their methodological inventiveness (Dadds and Hart 2001) as they trace the growth of their own knowledge through the creative struggle of seeking to understand (see Glenn 2004; Moreland 2005).
- We are committed to our identified social purposes of promoting equality and democratic practices. We reject imperialism as a set of power relations that distorts the potentials of social formations for their own healthy evolution. Our aim is to promote the idea of postcolonial practices as dismantling the ideas and practices of the deliberate exclusion and alienation of persons through the application of categories such as colour, ethnicity, gender, or any other 'alterity' that may be drawn upon to justify colonization. These social values transform into pedagogical values, as we encourage others to interrogate their own assumptions, and the normative assumptions of their cultures, in their search for more inclusive and relational ways of living.

The values we are setting out here are, we believe, the kind of values that can contribute to the sustainability of humanity and the planet we live on. Values of domination and control are the kind that devalue the planet and rob children of their inheritance. They are the kind that lead to the alienation of people, while the values we are endorsing are, in our view, of a kind that encourage inclusion and caring relationships. These values are especially important for action research, with its acknowledged potentials for emancipatory practices.

In setting out the reasons for our concerns, and our aims and purposes, we show how our values come to inform our practices. In Chapter 6 we shall explain how we judge our practices in terms of these values, so the values themselves come to act as the living standards by which we make judgements about the quality of our practices. At this point however we have outlined our values, and we now explain how the denial of these values acts as the starting point of our research.

The starting point of our research

We take as the starting point of our research the idea that we experience ourselves as living contradictions when our values are denied in our practice (Whitehead 1989). This idea was first put into the literature by Jack in 1976, when he wrote about how he observed a videotape of himself in a science lesson (Whitehead 1976). Like Feyerabend

(1975) and Medawar (1996), he believed that science was not a fixed body of knowledge but a creative process of investigation. However, the video showed him actively denying the values underpinning his ontological commitments to creative independent investigation, because he saw himself imposing his own ideas on his students and telling them what to do and think, rather than encouraging them to find things out for themselves and explore their own ideas. (The videoclips of supervision sessions with Jackie Delong (in Whitehead, 2004c, at http://www.arexpeditions.montana.edu/articleviewer.php? AID=80), and Je Kan Adler-Collins (see http://www.bath.ac.uk/~edsajw/multimedia/ jwjac.mov) show how, over the last thirty years, Jack has systematically worked at improving his practice of enquiry learning by responding to people in a way that will encourage them to have faith in their own capacities to create their own knowledge.)

The practices of domination and control in all their forms actively deny our values of compassionate relationship. While we personally manage to realize our values in our practices for much of our working lives, we still sometimes find ourselves in contexts where we are not living our values as fully as we would like. However, while we are familiar through long experience with such situations, we are deeply concerned about how teachers and other practitioners are systematically bullied by dominant forms of research and theory, and are persuaded to think that they cannot think for themselves or participate in public debates about education and the future of professional endeavours. The fact that some people are actively prevented from participating, and actively discouraged to think of themselves as researchers and theorists, is for us a deep denial of our values. We develop these ideas in Chapter 2.

At this point therefore we are able to formulate specific research questions, including the following:

- How do we encourage educators to participate in public debates about the future of educational research?
- How do we enable practitioners to produce accounts that show the creative processes of their own living educational theories?
- What kind of resources do we produce to enable them to do so?
- What kind of practices do we personally need to engage in as we support their personal professional enquiries?
- How do we encourage practitioners to show that they understand the need to articulate the living critical standards by which they make judgements about their practices and their theories?
- How do we hold ourselves accountable as we do these things?

Addressing these and similar questions gives direction to our research and provides the reasons and purposes for writing our research account in the form of this book.

S U M M A R Y
In this chapter we have set out our research concerns and questions. These have been about the future of educational research, and action research in particular. We have explained that the social sciences are currently the dominant form in educational research, with their own tried and trusted methods

for assessing quality. These methods, which are often modelled on those of the physical and natural sciences, especially in the United States' government funding policy for research in education, position practitioners as capable of generating quality policy-informed practices but not so capable of generating quality theory. Practitioners need to remedy this situation if they are to participate in public debates about the future of evidence-based educational practices, by showing that their claims to be generating quality theory should be taken seriously. They can do this by demonstrating their competence in making scholarly judgements about their work, and by making the standards of judgement they use in assessing the quality of their own accounts available to peer action researchers and the wider educational research community. These matters need urgent attention, especially since the introduction of recent influential performance management orientations in some action research literatures that share the same epistemological values of domination and control as many of the social sciences. Our current research questions are therefore to do with how we can disrupt the epistemological hegemonies of the social sciences, accompanied as they are by performance-management-oriented action research literatures, by encouraging practitioners to show that they are focusing on matters of assessing the quality of their work, and making their findings available to their peer action researchers and the wider academic educational research community.

2 Contexts of our research

Why are we concerned?

Having set out our concerns and research questions in Chapter 1, we now explain why we are concerned. Saying what concerns us, why we are concerned, and what we intend to do gives us our explanatory frameworks. We also begin to address our research questions, about how we can support professional learning, by explicating some of the underpinning assumptions of educational research and making them accessible to you, our readers.

Our concerns revolve around which forms of research are likely to influence the future of education. Research is always undertaken to create new knowledge or theory, so asking questions about forms of research means that we are also asking questions about forms of theory. As we said in Chapter 1, research activity is not in the same category as unintentional activities such as blinking or tripping over, or even intentional activities such as shopping. Blinking, tripping over and shopping are not usually undertaken to generate evidence, though they could be. While research is also activity, it is undertaken to generate and test new theory, and involves the disciplined practices of gathering data and generating evidence as the basis for testing a claim to knowledge (a new theory). Also, because there are different kinds of research, which are informed by different intents and social purposes, so also there are different kinds of theory. In asking which kind of research is going to be influential for future directions in the field, we are therefore also asking which forms of theory are going to have greatest influence in how the field develops and how it will influence educational practices.

In this chapter we focus on theory. We outline the characteristics of different kinds of theory, and explain how, just as different forms of research are grounded in people's ontological perspectives and preferred epistemologies, so too are different forms of theory. Theory generation is far from neutral, but is a deeply politicized practice. In terms of our concerns, we explain that practitioners tend not to participate in the discourses of theory generation in mainstream educational research, and so participate infrequently in policy formation. Therefore we now begin to address the key issues of what kind of theory is most appropriate for practitioners' explanations of practice, and what kind of standards of judgement need to become a core unit of appraisal in theory generation. Practitioners must address these issues if they wish to participate in the discourses on their own terms.

This chapter is organized to address these issues, and contains the following sections:

1   What is the nature of theory?
2   How is theory generated?
3   How is theory used?

1   What is the nature of theory?

In broad terms it is possible to say that when you claim that you have a theory, you are making a claim to knowledge. When you say, 'This is the way things are', you are expressing a knowledge claim. You are saying, '(I know that) this is the way things are.' In this sense, all theories can be understood as knowledge claims. Knowledge claims by definition contain explanations, because when you say, 'This is the way things are', you are also implying that you can explain why things are the way they are. If ever you get stuck on the word 'theory', try replacing it with 'claim to knowledge' or 'explanation'.

There are however different kinds of knowledge claim, because there are different kinds of knowledge, and people organize their thinking in different ways (use different kinds of logic) as they make sense of their experience. They also represent their knowledge claims in different ways. Hence theory generation becomes political, because people tend to want their own ideas to be accepted, so they claim that theirs is the only correct form of theory, or logic, or way of representing their knowledge claim. The idea that there is only one form is however not the case. There are diverse kinds of theory and theorists.

You need to decide which kind of research you wish to do, and which kind of theory you wish to generate. In order to do so, you need first to get to grips with the key factors that will influence your choice. We set out some of these issues here.

Please bear in mind, as you read, that issues of theory, knowledge, logics and values are inextricably linked and interwoven. We are setting out the ideas separately, for purposes of analysis, but, inevitably, terms from one area are used in another. All the issues in this chapter overlap, and you should engage with the complexity in your own writing.

Four sections follow:

• Ideas about theory
• Ideas about knowledge
• Ideas about logic
• Ideas about forms of representation

Ideas about theory

There seems to be a common understanding – better, misunderstanding – that 'theory' is a self-contained body of knowledge, usually scientific knowledge, which can explain and be applied to practice. This view of theory, which is itself a theory, and stems from the natural sciences, has been around for so long that it has become entrenched in the public psyche, so it often goes unquestioned. Many theories about the world are assumed to be the truth, rather than provisional ideas, and the main form of representation is assumed to be the printed word. This is often a false premise. In the process of theory generation, all claims, or theories, have to be tested. You cannot say, 'Here is my theory', and expect other people to accept what you say without justification. Theories need to be tested against their evidence base, and people other than the researcher need to scrutinize the evidence base and say that it is a reasonable ground for the validity of the theory. The idea of research as a systematic enquiry made public (Stenhouse 1975) implies that there are comprehensible grounds for testing the validity of the theory. Living educational action researchers believe that their theories constantly need revisiting and reforming as the circumstances of their lives change, so their theories are always in a state of live modification. However, many people in the educational research community continue to believe that there is one 'correct' way of thinking, and one 'correct' form of theory. This idea is anything but correct.

To avoid falling into this trap yourself, bear in mind that any field, left to its own devices, contains a range of varieties, whether it is a field of wild flowers or a field of concepts. When a field is cultivated by someone with a particular ideal kind in mind, they will inevitably organize the field according to their own preferences. They may weed out all the buttercups and leave only the daisies. It is the same in the field of theory. There are different kinds of theory, and no one kind is 'the' correct kind (in the same way that there is no such thing as 'the' scientific method; while there is scientific method, it does not come in only one form). However, many writers of textbooks prioritize one kind (their own), so they claim that their kind of research and theory is 'the' right one. Skinner and Thorndike held theories about stimulus and response relationships, and promoted the idea that these were the correct ones for explaining most human practices. Piaget wrote about assimilation and accommodation as correct explanations for some forms of learning. This situation should not surprise anyone, because books are written by people with particular political interests. This includes us. We are interested in developing emancipatory and inclusional attitudes and practices in educational research. Because we are committed to inclusion and diversity, we promote inclusion and diversity and speak in inclusional terms. Not everyone holds this view however.

It is important also to remember that each type of theory can be understood in terms of its content and form (which ideas it contains and how they are presented), and each is informed by particular logics and values. These points are often overlooked in the mainstream literatures of educational research.

So here is an outline of different kinds of theory and their research methodologies. We distinguish three kinds of theory: propositional, dialectical, and living. Propositional and dialectical theories have a 2,500 year history. In contrast, living theories were first articulated in the 1970s, although the idea had been around tacitly for a long time before that.

Propositional theories

Propositional theories contain propositions, or statements, about the way things are. They tend to be grounded in a quest for certainty, and are communicated in the form of general statements in response to particular answers. These statements tend to be definitive and prescriptive, taking the form, 'This is the way things are.' People who believe that 'this is the way things are' tend to hold clear positions about what is correct and incorrect. The logics they use (page 34) tend to take an 'either–or' form. Consequently, many public debates take the form of arguments that block further discussion, and often communicate an entrenched mindset through closed statements such as, 'You are either with us or against us.' Many people are categorized as 'this' and 'that', and people frequently suffer when they are placed in a minority category. To experience this for yourself, go to the Apartheid Museum in Johannesburg where, regardless of your colour, you have to walk through one of two gates, one labelled 'white' and the other 'non-white'. Perhaps you simply need to go to your workplace. A body of literature exists that challenges this form of 'grand theory' (for example Lyotard 1984), on the grounds that human living cannot be understood solely in terms of sets of propositions, nor can it be improved just by the application of abstract theories.

Dialectical theories

Dialectical forms are fluid and open, because they are grounded in contradiction. A statement is assumed to be the answer to a previous question, and it is acceptable to respond to a question with another question. In dialectics everything is open to modification, and all events and experiences contain contradictory elements. According to Comey (1972) the three laws of dialectical thought were derived by Engels from Hegel. The laws are (1) the identity and conflict of opposites; (2) the transition of quantitative into qualitative changes; (3) the negation of the negation.

As noted, debates about propositional and dialectical forms have raged for over 2,500 years. Propositional and dialectical forms are acknowledged as having their roots in the ideas of Aristotle and Plato respectively. Plato celebrated multiple ways of thinking, holding the one and the many together at the same time, whereas his student Aristotle thought in terms of 'either-or'. According to Aristotle, contradiction had to be eliminated from correct thought. His law of contradiction said that something could not be both one thing and another at the same time. Therefore a plant could not be both a leaf and a flower at the same time, nor could people be both male and female. Real life however shows that plants can be both leaf and flower. Goethe built his botanical philosophy on the idea of the *Urpflanze*, the 'original' leaf that transformed into a flower. Similarly, many contemporary psychologists explain how all humans contain elements of maleness and femaleness, and many people identify themselves as both female and male. However, Aristotle was talking not about real-life experience, but about the life of the mind, and which form correct thinking should take, so he promoted the idea of 'pure' theories that eliminated contradiction. The formalization of this idea is in the law of contradiction, which holds that two mutually exclusive statements cannot both be true simultaneously.

The debate about propositional and dialectical forms of theory has recently been further developed by analytical philosophers, working in a propositional tradition, who maintain that it is important to eliminate contradiction not only from thought, but also from forms of expression. On this view, the use of metaphor is suspect in the generation and testing of theory, and theory cannot be expressed in metaphorical forms such as poetry. At the same time, and from a different perspective, dialectical philosophers, such as Ilyenkov and Marcuse, challenged the assumptions of propositional philosophers by explaining that theory needs to be related to real-life experience. Drawing on the thought of philosophers such as Hegel, Ilyenkov (1977) suggested that living experience was full of contradictions, and this awareness should be factored into the generation of theory. Marcuse (1964) also said that philosophers who pretended that contradiction did not exist by focusing only on linguistic analysis were using a propositional form to mask their own contradictory life experiences.

However, so far no one had yet found a way of showing the idea of the contradictory nature of life as a form of theory. Ilyenkov had asked (but never answered), 'If an object exists as a living contradiction, what must the thought (statement about the object) be that expresses it?' (1977: 320). In other words, what kind of logic needs to be used, and what kind of theory generated, to find an appropriate way of communicating the contradictions of living and especially of oneself as a living contradiction? This is crucial within a context where the dominant propositional form eliminates contradiction from its discourses. The irony was that dialectical philosophers had spoken about dialectical theory in a propositional way, which in itself was a contradictory situation.

Living theories

The response of Jack Whitehead in 1976 was to develop the idea of living theories. He said that practice was a form of real-life theorizing. As we practise, we observe what we do and reflect on it. We make sense of what we are doing through researching it. We gather data and generate evidence to support our claims that we know what we are doing and why we are doing it (our theories of practice), and we test these knowledge claims for their validity through the critical feedback of others. These theories are our living theories. Jack is in education, so he works with living educational theories. These contain the descriptions and explanations that people offer for their practices. They show how people can position themselves as living contradictions, because they hold certain values while also experiencing the denial of these values. Some practitioner researchers continue to present their theories in a words-only propositional form, but others are now finding new creative ways of presenting their theories using multi-sensory forms of communication, such as pictures and graphics, and video and other electronic technology. Newer forms of technology are often able to communicate living experience more effectively than only linguistic forms.

The idea of living theory has come to be enormously influential over recent decades. Jack has also developed the idea of living logics (see below page 39).

So far we have talked about forms of theory. We now move to forms of knowledge.

Ideas about knowledge

Knowledge is to do with epistemology, which involves both a theory of knowledge and a theory of knowledge acquisition. This section deals with epistemological issues, about what is known, and about how it comes to be known.

The western intellectual tradition has been strongly influenced by Aristotle's ideas about knowledge and thought. At the same time many eastern intellectual traditions have embraced Plato's ideas. Aristotle wanted to remove from thought all ambiguities and contradictions, whereas Plato embraced and delighted in them (see his Phaedrus).

The Aristotelian view was promoted by analytic traditions, and is well summed up in Gilbert Ryle's *The Concept of Mind* (1949). Ryle explains that some people understand knowledge as an empirical object of rational enquiry, that is, it can be understood by adopting a spectator approach, as a spectator analyses a play from a distance. A person could look at knowledge as they would look at a table, and analyse it into its component parts. A table could be defined as an object made of a hard substance such as metal or wood, with a flat surface, and with one or several legs. Similarly, knowledge could be analysed into its separate components. Following others, Ryle explained these components as *know that* and *know how*.

Know that refers to knowledge of facts and figures, and is often also called propositional knowledge or technical rational knowledge. Knowledge is seen as a thing (it is reified). In postindustrialized 'knowledge-creating' societies, knowledge is often seen as a saleable commodity. The person with the most knowledge has the greatest power. *Know how*, or procedural knowledge, refers to skills and competencies, such as knowing how to speak a foreign language or fulfil a task. Like *know that*, *know how* is greatly prized for its commercial value. Many professional development programmes, including programmes in education, aim to provide access to increased participation or influence in work contexts, so they focus on knowledge of what works and how to make it work. The kinds of knowledge claims communicated by *know that* and *know how* are claims to objective knowledge. Objective knowledge is generally held as the dominant form by the scientific community. These different views of knowledge inform many contemporary curricula. *Know that* and *know how* are the most prized forms of knowledge in our technological societies, and public examinations test people's capacity in using these kinds of knowledge.

Louis Arnaud Reid (1980) and others challenged this view. Reid said that *know this*, the idea of knowledge with a direct object, was valid and legitimate, as in the claims, 'I know this song' or 'I know John.' Also, *know*, without a direct object, was valid and legitimate, as in the claim, 'I know', in response to utterances of the form, 'You need to hurry up.' These are subjective claims to knowledge.

The problem here was in validation, or verification, procedures. It is relatively straightforward to produce empirical and testable evidence to support objective *know that* kinds of claims, such as 'I know that today is Friday', or *know how* kinds of claims, such as 'I know how to ride a bike', by producing empirical evidence that can be pointed to, such as a calendar or riding a bike. It is however more problematic to produce empirical and testable evidence to support subjective claims of the kind, 'I know what I am doing', or 'I have toothache.' Yet the lack of empirical evidence to support the claim that you have toothache would not invalidate the experience of having toothache, and your claim to know what you are doing would involve the production of authenticated evidence to show that your claim had validity. This would in turn need to be tested out against the responses of critical others, in order to achieve intersubjective agreement about the validity of the claims. Different kinds of evidence and different kinds of validation processes are used in claims to objective knowledge and claims to subjective knowledge. This has political implications, because the methods for testing objective claims to knowledge are held by most research communities as the only legitimate forms, so until recently these forms have been applied to subjective claims to knowledge. However, subjective claims require a different form of validation, and these new forms are only now being worked out systematically, as in this book.

The idea of making subjective claims to knowledge has wide credibility, although it still tends to be scorned in some of the mainstream scientific literatures, and many influential texts communicate the power of subjective knowledge for debates about which forms of living contribute to the public good. In his *Personal Knowledge* (1958), Polanyi pointed out that people have a vast repertoire of experiential knowledge that they draw on for making any one of the split second decisions that are a feature of everyday practice. He spoke about the tacit dimension of personal knowledge, pointing out that we know more than we can say. We cannot always articulate or explicate the processes we go through that lead us to say, 'I just know.' This view has influenced large bodies of literature across a range of disciplines. In 1983, Donald Schön wrote *The Reflective Practitioner*, which developed the idea of practice as a form of reflection in action on action. This has become a seminal text. Further influential texts have followed, such as Sternberg and Horvath (1999). More recently, in *Blink* (2005), Gladwell sets out the idea that seemingly snap decisions are grounded in complex developmental processes of knowing from experience. It is ironic that books in this genre of popular writing sell in significant quantities, while much of the scientific community still struggles with the idea.

The different kinds of knowledge are well represented in contemporary educational research communities. Broadly speaking, propositional forms prioritize objective *know that* and *know how*. Living theory however is grounded in the personal knowledge of *know this* and *know*, because practitioners systematically relate their work to their values, and draw on those values as the standards of judgement by which they evaluate their work. The values they hold at an ontological level emerge at an epistemological level as articulated epistemological standards. These transform again into the living moral standards by which practitioners make judgements about the educational nature of their influence.

We now turn to a discussion of forms of logic.

Ideas about logic

Marcuse speaks of logic as 'the mode of thought appropriate for comprehending the real as rational' (1964: 123). 'Mode of thought' refers to how we organize and shape our thinking.

Although Marcuse speaks about 'the real as rational', it is of course possible to comprehend the real as non-rational, as when we believe in superstitions and premonitions, and divine the future by casting runes or reading teacups. These can be powerful ways of thinking, and it would be a foolish person indeed who did not place at least some value on the power of faith in unseen forces, whether these are internal or external to the person. Such forms of thinking comprehend the real as irrational, and irrationality is formless, not grounded in reasons or evidence, but grounded in blind faith. At best, faith can move mountains, physical and mental. At worst, it descends into chaos, no less real, but the real is irrational.

Comprehending the real as rational means looking for reasons, purposes and empirical evidence. In this case, the form that thinking takes can be of different kinds, and these different kinds inform different kinds of knowledge and different kinds of theory.

In the same way as we have distinguished three different kinds of theory, so we can distinguish at least three different kinds of logic. Propositional theories use a propositional form of logic, and value propositional ways of knowing; dialectical theories use a dialectical form of logic and value dialectical ways of knowing; and living theories use a living form of inclusional logic and value living and inclusional ways of knowing. Because living theories are inclusional, they value and include propositional and dialectical forms.

Here are some ways of making sense of the idea of different kinds of logic. To support our explanations of different forms of logic, we draw on Gaston Bachelard's *The Poetics of Space* (1969), which is one of the loveliest texts available to set out the different kinds of logic, using a poetic form. This book uses the thematic metaphors of the house as a space to live and as a living space.

Propositional forms of logic as closed spaces

Propositional logics assume many faces. They are all logics of unambiguous lines and geometrical forms. In walking to your house, you walk along pathways, which all lead to somewhere. It is easy to find your way along these pathways, because there are frequent signposts pointing in the right direction – 'Turn right here, go straight ahead there' – until you come to your planned destination.

When you think of your house, you see it as it emerged from the blueprint. Here is the living room, there the kitchen. Each room is seen in a structural relationship with the other, and each room has a definite purpose. From your architect's plans you can see the topographical structures of your house. You can see a top and a bottom, a vertical up–down and a horizontal left–right. These structural relations can also be seen in the relations of the people who inhabit the house. They are brother and sister, or husband and wife, and the above–below relations of the structures of the house can manifest as the above–below relations of its occupants. This was also the view of Bourdieu (1990), who studied with Bachelard. Hence, historically in some societies, brother tends to be seen as superior to sister, and husband to wife, and this kind of up–down structural thinking can give rise to a logic of domination, where one is seen as superior to another, and up is seen as superior to below. Bachelard says that whenever we imagine a flight of stairs leading to the attic, the stairs tend to go up, whereas the stairs leading to the cellar go down. This for Bachelard is symptomatic of what goes on in our imaginations:

> We come aware of this dual vertical polarity of a house if we are sufficiently aware of the function of inhabiting to consider it as an imaginary response to the function of constructing. The dreamer constructs and reconstructs the upper stories and the attic until they are well constructed ... when we dream of the heights we are in the rational zone of intellectualized projects. But the cellar, the impassioned inhabitant digs and re-digs, making its very depth active. (1969: 18)

The attic, which can be understood as representing the rational, is seen as a more desirable place to be than the cellar, which can be identified with the irrational and the unknown. We would rather go into the attic, where we are separated only by a roof from the light, whereas the cellar is bounded only by a single wall with the entire earth behind:

> In the attic, fears are easily 'rationalized'. Whereas in the cellar ... 'rationalization' is less rapid and less clear; also it is less definitive. In the attic, the day's experiences can always efface the fears of night. In the cellar, darkness prevails both day and night, and even when we are carrying a lighted candle, we see shadows dancing on the dark walls. (1969: 19)

The propositional logics of up–down and either–or are an essential part of the western intellectual tradition, formalized by Aristotle, and communicated through the discourses and thought patterns of western cultures. These propositional logics of binary divides often emerge as imperialistic logics, which in turn often manifest as practices of imperialism and domination (see Chapter 6). In some African cultures, the logics of binary divides are often meaningless, because those cultures do not perceive relationships as exclusive. My mother's sister can also be my kin-mother, so I cannot be an orphan because I have other mothers and fathers in my extended family. Yet the western intellectual tradition, when presented as a system of education, emerges as a logic of domination through the imposition of a curriculum of self-contained packages of knowledge. These packages of knowledge, and the people who produce them, are delivered via the straight and narrow pathways that lead to the vertical schoolhouse, their final destination. It is easy to get to the schoolhouse because route maps are always provided for travellers, and the schoolhouse is clearly indicated. These maps, which are represented in symbolic form, can easily map onto the field of human enquiry, to represent the symbolic power of the all-knowing colonizer.

Propositional logics tend to work in terms of closed modes of thinking, with everything in its designated place. When you think about your house propositionally, you would probably think of a room with four walls, which act as boundaries, fixed demarcations. The mental models involved in understanding living spaces as organized into boundaried rooms are symptomatic of a mode of thinking that understands physical reality as organized as closed spaces, social reality as organized as specific modes of conduct, and underlying modes of thought as closed. Propositional logics tend to make statements about the way things are, with no room for argument. Propositional logics are grounded in the Aristotelian idea of binary divides, where things must be either–or, and cannot be both–and. Because they are bounded within fixed delimitations, you are not allowed to step outside the 'either–or' boundary by asking, 'What if ... ?' or 'I wonder ... ', which are the kinds of questions that work through stretches of the imagination.

Many social science researchers work according to geometrical blueprints, both mental and physical. They organize their thinking to stay within the fixed boundaries of generating general theories that respond to specific questions. Popper (1963) spoke about theorizing as a process of solving problems and testing the answers with a view to refuting them. His idea of theory was that it could be tested stringently, yet would not break under pressure. He did not accept the idea of contradiction in theory generation. For him, the idea of dialectics was based on a 'loose and woolly way of thinking' and any theory that involved a contradiction was 'useless as a theory' (1963: 316, 317).

Look at how boundaries are understood. In propositional modes of thought, boundaries tend to be seen as keeping some things in and other things out. Many people think of them as enclosing empty spaces. The enclosing metaphors in our modes of thinking can lead us to close down on any possibility that there may be another way. The divisive metaphors of our social modes of being can lead us to exclude others and position them as unwelcome strangers who are intruding into our spaces.

This view of logic remains the dominant form today in the western postindustrialized intellectual tradition, possibly because we feel secure within a given system. Fromm (1941) says that the greatest fear is the fear of freedom, and Rayner says it is the fear of uncertainty:

> For thousands of years, faced with the variability of our surroundings and needing to secure our own survival, we human beings have made an enemy out of uncertainty. The principal combative tactic ... has been to try to exclude or confine it by imposing closure upon it. That is, we have tried mentally and/or physically to box uncertainty inside or outside absolutely fixed and sealed boundaries. In this way we have consciously or unconsciously sought the security system by means of which we can wield control over the wildness that we perceive both in nature and, if we allow it free access and expression, within ourselves. (2005: 2)

Locating oneself within a secure and given structure can be comforting, because we are not required to move out of the box or exercise our own creativity or acknowledge responsibility (although this can also be constraining for some). It is also easy to see how this form of thinking, and the metaphors of closed spaces and bounded and regulated forms of thinking, transfer to how we make sense of the experiences of our lives. In most postindustrialized cultures, many schools actively teach people to think in limited and limiting ways, according to the metaphors of empty, bounded spaces that are assumed to be there, waiting to be filled.

Dialectical forms of logic as open spaces

Dialectical logics work on the assumption that every statement is a response to a question. The question may be unspoken, but it is there, in a tacit form. The statement, or proposition, 'Today is Friday' exists in relation to the unarticulated question, 'What day is it?' Collingwood (1939) says that it is important to ask the right kinds of questions that will keep a conversation open. He emphasizes the idea of rightness, rather than truthfulness, because a focus on searching for truth, which is about finding answers, can often close down conversations, which are about posing questions. To illustrate this, here is an account by Gladwell (2005) of what he calls 'the structures of spontaneity'.

Gladwell tells of a drama group who stage improvised performances. They perform a play according to an idea put forward by the audience, and the plays are usually highly successful. They are successful, however, only when they abide by specific rules. When the rules are broken, the performance fails. The primary rule is to keep the conversation open. This is done by acting in response to tacit questions about what is the next 'right' response. Any responses that block action lead to premature closure.

As an example of a premature closure, Gladwell cites the following conversation:

A: I'm having trouble with my leg.
B: I'm afraid I'll have to amputate.
A: You can't do that, Doctor.
B: Why not?
A: Because I'm rather attached to it.
B: [losing heart] Come on, man.
A: I've got this growth on my arm too, Doctor.

By not agreeing to pursue the game according to the rule of speaking in response to the right kind of question, speaker A, according to Gladwell's thinking, blocks the creative conversation.

Here is an example of a successful conversation that works on the principle of inviting responses by asking the right kind of question, that is, the kind of question that will keep the conversation open:

> A: Augh!
> B: Whatever is it, man?
> A: It's my leg, Doctor.
> B: This looks nasty. I shall have to amputate.
> A: It's the one you amputated last time, Doctor.
> B: You mean you've got a pain in your wooden leg?
> A: Yes, Doctor.
> B: You know what this means?
> A: Not woodworm, Doctor!
> B: Yes. We'll have to remove it before it spreads to the rest of you.
>   [A's chair collapses.]
> B: My God! It's spreading to the furniture! (2005: 115–16)

Look at the conceptualization of the spaces of thinking here. They are open and supportive. The questions and answers stand in a dynamic relation to one another, which is informed by a commitment to growth. Although each of the actors, A and B, has their own distinct identity, they are willing to merge the boundaries of their identities in their commitment to keeping the conversation open.

In Bachelard's metaphors of the house, the blueprint rises off the page and becomes a house for living in. The house and its occupants are seen in a dialectical relationship, the one forming the other. A study of a house, says Bachelard (1969: 8), is inevitably also a study of the persons who live in it, a kind of topoanalysis, the systematic psychological study of the sites of our intimate lives. The house is not simply an object of study, a geometrical block, but a place in which we live. It is part of us. 'The house we were born in is an inhabited house. In it the values of intimacy are scattered, they are not easily stabilized, they are subjected to dialectics.' The diagrammatic blueprint of propositional forms is embodied in the life of the person who lives there: 'We are the diagram of the functions of inhabiting that particular house.' The house takes on the form of its occupants and their life hopes: 'it is also an embodiment of dreams'. The house and its occupiers live in a dialectical relationship: 'We are the unity of image and memory, in the function composite of imagination and memory' (1969: 14–16).

When you think of your house, using a dialectical mode of thinking, you would probably draw a picture of open-plan living, where the walls perhaps took the form of movable screens, or disappeared altogether. The literary houses of great poets, says Bachelard, 'are immense dwellings the walls of which are on vacation'. Your living room could as easily become a bedroom, and the inside of one wall would be seen as the outside of another. We are freed from our 'utilitarian geometrical notions', because 'Inhabited space transcends geometrical space' (1969: 52, 53, 47). You would perceive the person with you not in terms of structural relationships – 'This is my partner' – but in terms of your lived dialectical relationships – 'We share our lives.' The idea of open space technology (Owen 1996) is grounded in dialectical forms of thinking.

However, although many people think in dialectical ways, conventional scientific enquiry continues to be based on propositional forms, because propositional forms have traditionally been seen as superior to dialectical forms. Once again it is a question of what is legitimated rather than what is most appropriate.

Living logics as generative transformational spaces

Living logics are logics of the imagination. They are the kinds of logics that see the potentials in everything, and that see everything as in relation with everything else. The idea of living logics has been a consistent theme throughout the history of ideas, but has only recently been named by Jack Whitehead (2004d).

Living logics are living in the sense that they have emergent property, the capacity for self-recreation in infinite innovative ways. They are inclusional, in that they include propositional and dialectical forms of thinking, including all people and their practices within the field of enquiry, and they are relational in that they see the unfolding nature of relationships in everything. They are logics of the imagination because they see future potentials within present forms. They celebrate visions, the realization of values, and the redemptive qualities of transforming pain into joy. Bachelard sees the need for such logics:

> But it would seem that this element of unreality in the dreams of memory affects the dreamer when he [sic] is faced with the most concrete things, as with the stone house to which he returns at night, his thoughts on mundane things. William Goyen [n.d.] understands this unreality of reality: 'So this is why when often as you came home to it, down the road in a mist of rain, it seemed as if the house were founded on the most fragile web of breath and you had blown it. Then you thought it might not exist at all as built by carpenter's hands, nor had ever; and that it was only an idea of breath that had blown it, could blow it all away.' In a passage like this, imagination, memory and perception exchange functions. The image is created through co-operation between real and unreal, with the help of the functions of the real and the unreal. To use the implements of dialectical logic for studying, not this alternative, but this fusion, of opposites, would be quite useless, for they would produce the anatomy of a living thing. But if a house is a living value, it must integrate an element of unreality. All values must remain vulnerable, and those that do not are dead. (1969: 59)

We, Jack and Jean, began to formalize our understandings of the processes involved in living logics in the 1980s (see McNiff 1984). The idea of the inherent capacity of all living things to generate and transform themselves into an infinitude of new forms is a theme in the work of Goethe, Husserl, and Chomsky, among others. Bachelard (1969: 55) cites the poetry of Jean Bourdeillette, who speaks of a peony as an empty house in which each of us recaptures night. The peony encloses a sleeping insect in its red night, and every chalice is a dwelling place. We authors tried to express similar ideas in 1992, in the passage given on page 56, now rather outdated, but still valuable for communicating the original ideas, and for showing, through our research focus, our use of mental images to communicate an expression of social practices, and how underpinning logics can transform into social practices.

A dreamer of houses, says Bachelard (1969: 55), sees them everywhere, and anything can act as a germ to set him dreaming about them. Think of your house. See how, in realizing your dialectical potential, the blueprint rises off the page and transforms into a real three-dimensional house. See how your original vision of your house has become a reality. See how, in realizing your transformative potential, you have transformed the metaphors of your inner mental life into the personal and social realities of lived experience. Nor is your vision of your house bounded by a physical reality. 'In such images we have the impression that the stars in heaven come to live on earth, that the houses of men form earthly constellations', says Bachelard (1969: 35). Your potentials are in the stars, and the stars are in you.

The kind of relationships in living logics are free-flow. The relationships are inclusive in the sense that they include and synthesize propositional and dialectical logics, which exist in our minds, within the reality of lived experience; and they are dynamic, because they are always transforming themselves into more developed forms of their original form. Whitehead describes the perceptual shift involved in his own learning, drawing on the work of Alan Rayner (2004), as he moved into living logics:

> The shift in perception into inclusionality focused on the development of a relationally dynamic awareness of space and boundaries with other people. An inclusional awareness involves experiencing boundaries as relationally dynamic connections. The boundaries are also co-creative and flow with space. Inclusionality also involves a sense of oneself as complex. For Rayner (2004), a complex self is a fully contextualised understanding of self-identity that is formed through the reciprocal coupling of inner and outer spatial domains through an intermediary self-boundary. (2005b: 16)

Moving into living logics can however be risky. You are always on the brink, never knowing what the next step will be. This is a commitment to learning, embracing the unknown future and accepting that the present is all we have. What we do with the present creates all our futures. This is an open-ended, acceptant form of life, a commitment to risk, but which also has untold rewards. 'It is better to live in a state of impermanence than in one of finality', says Bachelard (1969: 61). We authors agree. We commit ourselves to life, to the creative impulses of our own learning, to the vision quest of generating new theories that communicate the lived experience of the present moment, and that hold the potential of new forms already within themselves. The aim of action research is to help practitioners realize those potentials in and through their practices, and to show that the impermanent and imperfect state of their theorizing is better than resting in a place of propositional finality.

Ideas about forms of representation

This section deals with the forms of representation appropriate to propositional, dialectical and living forms of theory.

Propositional forms of theory are represented as written text on a page. The statements within the text are non-contradictory and obey a logic of inference. Here is what two eminent educational theorists have to say. Stephen Gorard says:

> theory is a set of statements or principles devised to explain a group of facts or phenomena, especially one that has been repeatedly tested or is widely accepted and can be used to make predictions about natural phenomena. (2004: 8)

Richard Pring says:

> 'Theory' would seem to have the following features. It refers to a set of propositions which are stated with sufficient generality yet precision that they explain the 'behaviour' of a range of phenomena and predict what would happen in the future. An understanding of those propositions includes an understanding of what would refute them – or at least what would count as evidence against their being true. (2000: 124–5)

The validity of a theory resides in how accurately the theory is expressed in words, and whether statements stand in a logical relationship with one another. Propositional theorists are concerned primarily with theories as interconnected sets of statements.

Dialectical forms of theory have until recently been represented as case studies. People have told their stories in narrative form, and new genres such as narrative inquiry (Clandinin and Connelly 2000) have been developed. These forms have also been legitimized through their acceptance as valid forms of representation by prestigious universities such as the University of Alberta. A large literature on narrative inquiry is now available and the legitimacy of narrative accounts goes largely unquestioned (see Clandinin in production), as long as validity can be established. Clandinin has campaigned vigorously for decades for the recognition that narrative accounts require different kinds of criteria from normative propositional accounts, and this view has been taken up by other prestigious researchers such as Bassey (1999), who also calls for new forms of criteria such as authenticity and relatability as appropriate for judging the quality of case studies.

Living forms of theory can be represented linguistically, as in the story on page 106 of this book, but are perhaps most adequately represented through multiple media, including written texts that tell narratives in written form, and also visual media such as video that tell visual narratives (Whitehead, 2004c, at http://www.arexpeditions.montana.edu/articleviewer.php?AID=80; Tian and Laidlaw, 2005, at http://www.arexpeditions.montana.edu/articleviewer.php?AID=87). The narratives thus communicated represent the real lives of people as they interact with one another and share their learning. Whatever form of representation is used, the work needs to show its own generative transformational potential, in that new learning emerges from previous learning, and any new learning already holds within itself its own potentials for improved learning. The idea of the generative capacity of narrative forms is further developed on page 117.

The idea of living theories as communicated through multimedia forms of representation has now entered the academy. In 2004, a landmark decision was made by the University of Bath to make changes in the university regulations to allow multimedia accounts using e-media. This has opened opportunities for communicating the meanings of living epistemological standards of judgement using visual narratives. Here is what two practitioner researchers have to say.

Mary Hartog

Mary Hartog's thesis, 'A self-study of a higher education tutor: how can I improve my practice?' (2004), was the first thesis, under the new regulations, to submit a visual narrative and analysis of educational relationships. The explanation of learning connects ostensive definitions of loving and life-affirming educational relationships with word-only definitions. Mary says in her abstract:

> Evidence is drawn from life-story work, narrative accounting, student assignments, audio and video taped sessions of teaching and learning situations, the latter of which include edited CD-R files. These clips offer a glimpse of my embodied claims to know what the creation of loving and life-affirming educative relations involves.

You can download Mary's entire thesis from http://www.bath.ac.uk/~edsajw/hartog.shtml.

Eleanor Lohr

In the draft prologue to her doctoral enquiry 'Love at Work' (2004), Eleanor Lohr writes:

> In this thesis I represent the meanings of love as I experience love at work in my life. By writing, I learn how to craft the words that express that knowledge. By seeing the visual images, I begin to understand the power of loving presence. By listening to the reverberations of my body, I bring critical judgement into my action and articulate this judgement as living epistemological standards of love. These loving standards enable me to judge the value of my practice, and to be better accountable for what I do.

You can download the draft prologue to Eleanor's enquiry from http://www.jackwhitehead.com/elFront%202.htm.

We now turn from the nature of theory to how theory is generated.

2   How is theory generated?

Some theories are generated through research, and some are not. Some are generated through the experiences of living. If you put your hand on a hot stove you will rapidly develop a theory of what hot stoves are about. Most people hold tacit theories about the world and their own relation with the world. These are their embodied theories. However, most public theories of education in the literature are generated through research, and most tend to be grounded in the methodologies of the philosophy, sociology, history, economics, politics, psychology, and management of education. Some theories tend to be generated through a research process that uses a hypothetico-deductive method, which works as a two-step process, like this.

The hypothetico-deductive method

First, a researcher observes certain regular events 'out there' in the natural or social world. They systematically note what is happening, and come to a general conclusion about it. They test their idea of what will happen in a particular case through an initial experiment, by forming it as a hypothesis of the kind, 'If I do this then that will happen.' The process of moving from the particular to the general is called induction.

The second step is to test the hypothesis through further experiments and randomly controlled trials, from which the researcher gathers data and generates evidence, usually of a statistical nature. Once the hypothesis has been tested, and evidenced generated, it is then assumed to be robust and is generalized to the wider population. This process is called deduction. Together, the two steps form the hypothetico-deductive method.

Richard Pring says of this process:

> A theory or set of interconnected and explanatory propositions would be suggestive of hypotheses which need to be tested out. Hence, a theoretical position is always open to further development through reflection, testing against experience and criticism. (2000: 125)

Core assumptions in this process are that research has a standard format, which is replicable to all like circumstances. The results can be generalized to other like situations. Once tested, the knowledge is considered quality knowledge and may now inform future policies and practices.

This method has wide credibility because it has been tried and tested over decades of work. Although it is primarily a method of the natural sciences, it has been taken up and used extensively in social science, and in educational research. Slavin (2002) takes it as the basic model for educational research. In a presentation to the American Educational Research Association annual meeting he said:

> The most important reason for the extraordinary advances in medicine, agriculture, and other fields is the acceptance by practitioners of evidence as the basis for practice. In particular, it is the randomized clinical trial – more than any single medical breakthrough – that has transformed medicine … the experiment of choice is the design of choices for studies that seek to make causal connections, and particularly for evaluations of educational innovations. (2002: 16, 18)

Although this view has been critiqued (Goldstein 2002), it remains powerful, and the messages that such technical rational forms should be accepted as the norm are reinforced and perpetuated. It does however raise questions about the relationship between theory and practice, which is a core issue in educational research.

The relationship between theory and practice

Debates rage all the time about the relationship between theory and practice. One of the most entrenched assumptions in the orthodox literatures, as seen in the preceding section, is that abstract theory should be generated in order to inform practice. Theories can appear as models, and the theory, or model, is superior to the people who are expected to conform to it. If people do not fit into the model, they are at fault.

This view has been critiqued. One such critique has come from the seminal work of Pierre Bourdieu (1990), who originally held a view of theory-into-practice, and shifted to a view of practice as the grounds of theory.

While working as an ethnographer in Algiers in the 1960s, Bourdieu had concerns about the form of research he was doing and the form of theory it was generating. The aim of Bourdieu's research was to observe people in their natural settings, and explain their behaviours by describing and classifying what they did in terms of patterns and structures. Bourdieu's work fitted into the broad area of structuralism, an approach that recognized all phenomena as in some kind of structural relation with other phenomena. 'Brother' could be understood as in relation to 'sister'. What one person did could be explained in terms of what others were doing in their social context, and had done before in their historical context. The focus was on the structures, not the people, because structure itself was the key to understanding and explaining human behaviour. Bourdieu wanted to see the extent to which people's actions fitted into the structure.

He began to reflect on some of his own mental assumptions as he researched. He began to critique the idea of a given structure as an explanatory framework for human practices. He also critiqued the idea that theorists should stipulate theories about how human practices work. Much of his *The Logic of Practice* (1990) is about how he came to see people as free agents, who did not fit neatly into given structures, but made their own decisions about how they should live. This led Bourdieu to consider the idea that perhaps practice could be the grounds for the generation of new theory.

The idea that practice can be the grounds for the generation of new theory, which in turn feeds back into new practices, is at the heart of the living educational theories that practitioners generate as they study their practice and engage with questions of the kind, 'How do I improve what I am doing?' They identify the values that inform their work, and find ways of realizing them. The values they espouse are of the kind we outlined in Chapter 1. Their ontological and epistemological values are to do with the freedom of all to come to know in their own ways, and exercise their choices responsibly; their metho-dological values are to discipline their enquiries to show the systematic and rigorous research processes involved in making their claims that they have realized their values; and their social purposes are to do with developing ethical educational cultures that are free of colonialist impulses.

The idea of eliminating colonialist impulses is core to what has always been under-stood as the emancipatory project of action research (see Carr and Kemmis 1986). Practitioners understand their ontological, epistemological and methodological values as the grounds for the exercise of their educational influence. They judge the quality of their influence in terms of the extent that they encourage others to think independently, and to make informed choices about whether or not to be influenced. They understand that all people are capable of thinking for themselves and will mediate any influence through their own originality and independence of thought. This capacity for mediat-ing influence is also understood as a key factor in the education of social formations (page 120).

The generation of living educational theories is not a solitary exercise. Because critique is a core assumption of action research, practitioners produce their progress reports as their first attempts at theorizing, and make them available to a wider critical audience, in the form of critical friends and validation groups, in order to receive the kind of critical feedback that will help strengthen their claims and their evidential base. The accumulation of an evidence base is essential to support their claims that they have improved their practice.

Creating this evidence base is the theme of Chapter 3, but before that, it is also impor-tant to consider how theory is used.

3   How is theory used?

Research is always undertaken with social intent. The intent can be to generate theories of control as well as theories of liberation. Some writers take as their key theme the idea of dismantling the hegemony of propositional forms. Michael Polanyi, for example, took as his life's work the task of encouraging people to think in ways 'which centuries of critical thought [technical rational thinking] have taught them to distrust', and stripping away 'the crippling mutilations imposed by an objectivist framework' (1958: 381). Polanyi's own commitment was to a decision 'that I must understand the world from my point of view, as a person claiming originality and exercising his judgement responsibly with universal intent' (1958: 327). Feyerabend also took emancipation as his aim. In his contribution to the influential *Criticism and the Growth of Knowledge* (Lakatos and Musgrave 1970), he showed how objectivist ways of thinking entered formal education, when children were taught to think in certain ways, which closed down their opportunities for critical thinking: 'What is excluded is the attempt to "educate" children in a manner that makes them lose their manifold talents so that they become restricted to a narrow domain of thought, action, emotion' (Feyerabend 1970: 210). The task of research, he believed, and its relevance to education, was to create 'a methodology and a set of institutions which enable us to lose as little as possible of what we are capable of doing and which force us as little as possible to deviate from our natural inclinations' (1970: 210). Marcuse, one of the foremost critics of propositional thinking as the grounds for a social technology of control, says:

> This immediate, automatic identification [of the individual with their society] ... reappears in high industrial civilization; its new 'immediacy', however, is the product of a sophisticated, scientific management and organization. In this process, the 'inner' dimension of the mind in which opposition to the status quo can take root is whittled down. The loss of this dimension, in which the power of negative thinking – the critical power of Reason – is at home, is the ideological counterpart to the very material process in which advanced industrial society silences and reconciles the opposition. The impact of progress turns Reason into submission to the facts of life, and to the dynamic capability of producing more and bigger facts of the same sort of life. The efficiency of the system blunts the individuals' recognition that it contains no facts which do not communicate the repressive power of the whole. (1964: 10–11)

For us, Jack and Jean, our work is committed to revealing the hidden assumptions of different forms of theory-generation processes, and to show how orthodox ways of thinking, including thinking about action research, are influenced solely by propositional logics and forms of expression. As such, they constitute a repressive canon that in turn transforms into a technology of control. We see its power in our daily lives, how people are actively prevented from thinking for themselves through the body of official knowledge, and then how that knowledge is pedagogized into specific ways of teaching and learning, and institutionalized into specific technicist epistemologies. We know what happens when people are prevented from exercising their capacity to question, the gradual loss of excitement, and the quietude of acceptance.

We also know what happens when people engage in lively dialogue, where they generate their own living theories of education, and test those theories against the critical responses of others. This is why we choose to work in a living theory approach to action research, why we encourage people to engage in debates and to exercise their capacity for original contributions to knowledge. We have first-hand experience of the power of this approach at work. To give a sense of what the work looks like, as we aim to encourage people to find ways of transforming their own situations through learning, we move into the next chapter, which addresses the question, 'What experiences can we describe to show why we are concerned?'

S U M M A R Y

We have outlined some of our research contexts in this chapter. These contexts are to do with the nature and uses of theory. We have explained the reasons for our concerns in relation to how theory is used to maintain the current epistemological hegemony of the social sciences. We make the case that, while we value the social sciences for their immense contributions to educational research, and draw on those contributions in our own research, we also see great value in the contributions of practitioners who are conducting their action research in their own educational settings. To make this case we explain some of the ontological, epistemological and methodological assumptions of different kinds of research and theory, in terms of their underpinning values and logics. We explain that practitioner action researchers should be seen as capable of making significant contributions to quality theory, but to achieve this perception, they need to show how they engage with issues of theory and knowledge in explaining why their research should be assessed in its own terms and from within its own now established scholarly traditions.

3 Looking for data

What experiences can we describe to show why we are concerned?

In this chapter we ask, 'What experiences can we describe to show why we are concerned?' By addressing the question, we outline some of the contexts of our concerns.

As professional educators, our contexts are to do with both theory and practice. As theorists, we work with ideas, so in Chapter 2 we explained why we are concerned in terms of the underpinning assumptions of the contexts of theory. As practitioners we work with people, so in this chapter we explain why we are concerned in terms of how the underpinning theoretical assumptions manifest in the contexts of real-life practices.

We have explained how some of our values were being denied in relation to theory. Now we explain how they are being denied in relation to practice. We explain why the experiences we describe here give us grounds for concern by explaining how they represent a denial of our values, and what we therefore need to do to ensure that we come to live in the direction of our values.

In saying that these contexts represent a denial of our values, we begin to make judgements. These judgements are about what is happening in the contexts we are describing, whether or not they are a fulfilment or a denial of our values, and what kind of action we need to take. However, we believe in justice and equality, holding that it is a basic moral principle that one person should not expect another to do something without first doing it themselves. Therefore, making judgements and taking action on the strength of those judgements as professional educators mean that we also have to make judgements on ourselves, as we act. How do we ensure that our actions contribute to learning? How do we ensure that we exercise our educational influence, and do not contribute to deepened prejudice? This means identifying the standards by which we make judgements on our own practice, so that we can say, 'We know what we are doing and we can explain why we are doing it.'

This chapter addresses the two issues outlined:

1   What experiences can we describe to show why we are concerned?
2   Which standards do we use to make judgements on our practices?

1   What experiences can we describe to show why we are concerned?

As noted above, we work as professional educators. This means that we support the scholarly enquiries of educators as they undertake their action enquiries in their practice contexts. We work with educators in a range of settings. Jack, a lecturer in education at the University of Bath, works with teachers, educational managers, police, and health service personnel. His main focus is to support their doctoral enquiries, and he has been successful in supervising masters and doctoral degree studies for accreditation by the university. He also works with other academics around the world, working intensively to develop the theoretical base of action research. You can find many practitioners' accounts and many of Jack's writings on www.actionresearch.net, as well as links to other groups of action researchers nationally and internationally. Jean is a professor of educational research at St Mary's University College, London, a position that also affords her considerable professional independence to work with teachers, educational managers, and academic staffs, in Ireland, London and South Africa, in a range of institutional settings. Her aim is to support practitioners in their action enquiries, both for non-accredited workplace learning and also for higher degree accreditation. The masters and doctoral studies she supports have been accredited by the various higher education institutions with whom she works. Much of her writing focuses on providing practical resources that will help practitioners undertake their action enquiries, and produce research accounts, which will stand as the highest form of scholarship. You can find some of these on her website, www.jeanmcniff.com.

We can cite many stories from practitioners whose studies we have supported, which show how they have managed to overcome some of the difficulties of their own situations. We reproduce three of them in this chapter. We are doing this to show that many practitioners live and work in situations that represent a denial of their and our values. We encourage those practitioners to find ways of overcoming the contradictions, and to find ways of living and working that are more fulfilling for themselves and those for whom they may be responsible. In doing this, practitioners are transforming their stories of potential ruin into victory stories (Lather 1994, cited in MacLure 1996), as they demonstrate their educational influences in their own learning. This does not mean that the victory came easily, but it does mean that practitioners can achieve a considerable sense of wellbeing when they learn how to work through the difficulties and find ways of living that are more in harmony with what they believe in.

The stories you are about to read are stories of learning from experience (Winter 1989). They are the stories of three individual educators: Caitríona McDonagh, Bernie Sullivan, and Margaret Cahill. All are involved in their doctoral studies with Jean, and all live and work in Ireland. Each of these individuals has a high level of personal and professional integrity, so, when they found themselves dealing with situations of deep injustice, they decided to do something about it.

Caitríona McDonagh's story

I work as a teacher of children with specific learning disability (dyslexia). Some have difficulty in distinguishing the shapes and sequences of letters as words and sentences. These are otherwise 'normal' children with an average IQ. Some have no difficulty in mathematics and are perfectly capable in art and geography. Some have good memory span, and some excel in physical education. Their difficulty is that they cannot read. Consequently they are labelled 'disabled' and are designated as in need of special support (from me).

The fact that they are designated 'deficient' is, for me, the demonstration of considerable injustice. It also presents a fundamental conceptual and practical contradiction. Children who also have average IQ, yet who experience significant difficulties in music, art, mathematics or sport, are not designated as learning disabled, nor do they qualify for remedial support. The children I teach, many of whom have average IQ, yet experience significant difficulties in reading, are however so designated, and suffer the external stigmatisations of failure, such as receiving remedial support, which sets them apart from those who are seen as 'normal'.

Furthermore, the contradictions for me are that the labelling is an outcome of professional practices that are grounded in a commitment to linguistic definitions and which work from within a logic of alienation (Marcuse 1964). 'Disability' is understood in terms of the numerical measurement of human capability. Children are valued in terms of how well they achieve on standardised tests. Their scores become a measure of their worth as human beings. Furthermore, these technical standards of judgement are the kinds of standards that inform the teaching profession. Teachers also collude in the injustice, on the general belief that there is a commonly agreed professional language by which we all make judgements about terms such as 'disability'. Derrida (1976) has demonstrated that it is erroneous to assume that something outside a text bestows a single fixed meaning, and has explained how multiple meanings can often clash in everyday discourses. He also suggests that discourses that hold to a fixed 'language of reason' exclude all that is different.

I undertook my research initially into how I could learn to teach my children more effectively. As I began to delve deeper into my conceptual frameworks, I developed a heightened awareness of contradictions everywhere – in the conceptual underpinnings of normative standards of judgement, and in my own perception of myself as a living contradiction when my values were denied in my practice. The focus of my research therefore expanded from a main focus on practice, during the masters phase of my research (C. McDonagh 2000), about how I could learn to teach in ways in which my pupils could learn more effectively, to a focus in my doctoral studies on how I could theorise my practice as learning to work through the contradictions and celebrate difference, while avoiding the temptation to present my own claims to knowledge as binding.

I have come to understand how difference is presented in the dominant literatures of educational research and practice as alien Otherness, which I have also come to understand as a core element in divided societies. The perception on the part of colleagues of my children as 'different' because they were outside normative standards of reference was a source of moral outrage for me (Purpel 1999). For me, social norms and normative standards are socially constructed and politically constituted, and therefore need to be scrutinised and challenged. In my educational philosophy, the very act of positing a norm that acts as a universal standard by which everyone is judged is an act of injustice, because of the resultant expectation that everyone will fit into the parameters that the norm defines, and so distort their own potentials for creativity and originality. I therefore take justice as the core value that inspires my research, and throughout I explain how this value comes to act as the standard of judgement by which I am eventually able to claim my practice as a form of justice in action.

I am currently writing up my thesis. I will claim that I have created my own living theory of practice. My thesis contains episodes that describe how I have made significant contributions to new practices. I also claim that I am making significant contributions to new theory in that I offer explanations for my new practices and show their validity in terms of the improved quality of learning experience for both my children and myself. During the period of my research I have investigated new forms of pedagogy, which have greatly facilitated the learning of my children. Those same pedagogies however are grounded in my capacity to understand the contradiction of how normative forms of theory act as constraining devices that inhibit the capacity of my children's learning, and to find ways of enabling my children to come to know in ways that are right for them. Drawing on the work of Bernstein (2000), I have developed new theories about learning difference, which for me are about the development of symbolic emancipation, and are different from traditional theories of learning, which are about symbolic control. I have also learnt about the pedagogisation of knowledge (Bernstein 2000), and in my thesis I explain how my own pedagogies have become forms of emancipatory agency, grounded as they are in my commitment to nurturing the unique preciousness of each and every individual, regardless of whether they are good at art, music or reading. Whatever their strengths and limitations, all children are precious to me, and, regardless of my own strengths and limitations, I also have a valuable contribution to make, both to my children and to my profession.

Bernie Sullivan's story

A deep sense of dissatisfaction with existing educational provision for Traveller children in my place of work, as well as a strong conviction that it was possible to influence the development of the situation, were the factors that inspired me to undertake my research. In agreement with, among others, Connell (1993), Kenny (1997) and Lynch (1999), I value the rights of all children to equal entitlement in the area of educational provision. However, because, over the years, this right has been consistently denied in my workplace, I decided to undertake my studies to see whether I could change existing situations into opportunities for children who had previously experienced marginalisation in schooling. As my studies progressed, I became aware that those same values of justice and entitlement were emerging as the living standards of judgement I used (Whitehead 2004a) to establish the validity of my research. Here I would like to outline some of the issues that raised my awareness around the need for emancipatory action, and my subsequent attempts at improvement.

A particular incident that raised my awareness of how my values were being denied in my practice (Whitehead 1993) occurred when I was a mainstream class teacher, prior to taking up my current position as Resource Teacher for Traveller children. In my class was a new Traveller child who had major learning difficulties, yet who was not receiving any learning support or resource teaching. When I enquired from the school authorities why this was the case, I was informed that the child's mother had not signed the consent form that was required in order to obtain a psychological assessment, and without parental consent, the child could not be assessed for a placement in a special class. I arranged a meeting with the Traveller child's mother shortly afterwards, and, after I had explained the situation to her, she readily agreed to sign the consent form.

The Traveller mother's willingness to sign the form at my request led me to question how she had been approached initially for her permission, and how it was assumed that she had refused this permission. The likely explanation was that the form was simply sent home, which was the normal practice for communicating with parents, ignoring the widely acknowledged fact that most Traveller parents have problems in the area of literacy, as it had not been common practice for their generation to attend primary school for any significant length of time. MacAongusa (1993) refers to the lack of formal education among Traveller parents, and she further states that those parents are now anxious that their children should have a better opportunity of participating in the educational system. W. McDonagh (2000) mentions that some Traveller parents are reluctant to send their children to school because of the negativity and discrimination that they themselves suffered while at school, and this also suggests that the parents' attendance at primary school was for a relatively brief period of time, as a result of the sense of alienation that they experienced while in school.

I have come across many other similar situations since the incident that I have described here, where Traveller parents have been kept unaware of events in school through the school's inappropriate form of communicating the relevant information to them. It would appear to be necessary, therefore, that schools should factor into their policies and practices the need to recognise these aspects of Traveller culture through endeavouring to make personal contact with Traveller parents, instead of engaging in the manifestly futile exercise of sending home letters that cannot be read or acted upon. This latter practice can appear to be demoralising and demeaning from the point of view of the Traveller community, since it reinforces their positioning, by the dominant group in the educational community (which are also the discourses of the settled community), as inferior because of their lack of literacy skills. It can also lead, on the part of the school authorities, to the mistaken assumption of a lack of interest, or a refusal of permission, or even cooperation, by Traveller parents, when letters sent home remain unanswered.

The incident I have outlined here also compels me to question the claims of some educational institutions that they treat all their pupils equally, since their practice of communication with parents appears to discriminate against a minority group within the school population. This situation has wider implications in the fact that Irish society is becoming increasingly multicultural, with many non-Irish-national children appearing in the educational system. Tormey and Haran (2003), drawing on research conducted by the National Consultative Committee on Racism and Interculturalism, explain that the number of individuals seeking asylum in Ireland rose from 39 in 1992 to 10,929 in 2000. Such increases can have significant implications for schooling. Frequently the parents of these pupils do not speak English, which raises the question of how schools can best communicate with the parents. The time seems opportune, therefore, for educational institutions to review their policies and practices for interaction with parents, to ensure that the methods of communication are respectful of the differing circumstances of the Irish indigenous minority group, as well as of the other newly arrived ethnic minority groups.

My research has focused on combating the negative and demoralising effects of discriminatory practices, such as the ones I have described above, on the educational opportunities and life chances of Traveller children. I have suggested instead a view of education as a positive and inclusive experience that can encourage Traveller children to develop a sense of belonging and ownership of the process of their own education, while celebrating a pride in their own culture, its history, and its language. I have systematically studied my own practice, in order to create safe and caring spaces in my classrooms where Traveller children may give voice to their concerns around their experiences of schooling. My research reports include these voices of Traveller children. My research has significant implications for both school practices and policies, in terms of accommodating minority cultures within existing dominant cultures, recognising difference without jeopardising their individual integrity. In this I am reminded of the words of Julia Kristeva (2002):

> Each person has the right to become as singular as possible and to develop the maximum creativity for him or herself. And at the same time, without stopping this creativity, we should try to build bridges and interfaces – that is to say, foster sharing … This is the great challenge in the modern world. It is not a question of creating a community in the image of the past; it is a question of creating a new community on the basis of sharing singularity. (cited in Lechte and Margaroni 2004: 162)

My aim in undertaking my research is to find ways in which I can create new communities on the basis of sharing singularity. In presenting my theories of practice I hope both to influence my own institution's policies, and also to contribute to the education of wider social formations in Ireland and elsewhere. As I write my thesis I focus on establishing its validity by articulating my values of justice and entitlement as the ontological and epistemological standards by which its validity may be judged.

Margaret Cahill's story

I work as a learning support teacher in Irish schools. This means that I work with young people who are designated intellectually disadvantaged, such as children with difficulties in literacy and numeracy. It also means that I work with those who are marginalised because of their minority status as an ethnic group, such as the children from Traveller families and newly-arrived immigrants who cannot yet speak standard English. My research focuses on how I can break down barriers of discrimination and marginalisation through contributing through my work practices and scholarly writings to the development of new institutional epistemologies (Schön 1995) which are grounded in a celebration of human capabilities (Sen 1999).

In this paper I want to tell of some of the background experiences that have led to my deep commitments to justice and equal entitlement to access of opportunity for all children. I explain how these early experiences taught me about processes of discrimination and prejudice first-hand, and how they have influenced my decisions to become a teacher, specifically a teacher of marginalised and underprivileged children.

I was born in a rural setting in the south-east, the youngest of three children. My parents had great educational aspirations for us children, and insisted that we all finish second level education and consider third level. Following my own leaving certificate examinations, I decided to go on to college and become a teacher.

School experience had always been problematic and often far from easy. On hearing that I wanted to go to college, one of my then teachers asked, 'Why don't you join the civil service? Still, I'm glad you have chosen teaching instead of law or medicine. You should leave those jobs to the people who can afford them.'

For me, this comment was indicative of my school experience, where opportunity, praise, encouragement or recognition was directly relational to the pupils' social class and family finances. Those from disadvantaged backgrounds or homes without wealth were not considered worthy of teachers' time and effort. It was accepted that such children would never amount to anything. If they did, it was a freak event.

While my early years in a mixed rural school were enjoyable, transfer to an urban convent school at the age of eight heralded the beginning of a frustrating experience that remains vivid to this day. The class teacher introduced me as 'the new girl from the country school'. She went on to express her disdain for the country school which in her opinion was inferior to the convent school. She proceeded in the following weeks to make me the butt of classroom jokes. My efforts at oral participation were ignored. I was sent to sit with other 'time wasters' in the class, namely children from minority groups and low socio-economic backgrounds. This experience was new for me. My previous experience was that all children had been treated with respect by the teacher, and pupils from a range of backgrounds mixed freely together. Now class distinction was rampant. Ability did not count for anything. Social standing was the only measure. I soon learned that I was inferior, rather stupid, and that my opinions were unwelcome on any topic. The class was divided into groups, who were singled out for certain treatments. Corporal punishment was discharged only to a certain section of the class. Competitions were always won by the same group. Blame was always assigned to the same individuals, while praise was given solely to the privileged. I learned to become reticent and lost interest in my childhood dream of becoming a teacher. Reading Russell many years later I came to understand that such practices are widespread and that it is indeed 'the social position of the fathers that determines that of the children' (2002: 94). Class distinction exists in many education systems where 'the children of the rich acquire a belief that they are superior to the children of the poor and an attempt is made to cause the children of the poor to think themselves inferior to the children of the rich' (2002: 94). This was definitely my experience. I was told what to think and how to think, and I learned to internalise the values that relegated me to inferiority and ultimately invisibility.

On reflection in my more mature years, and now as a professional teacher, I can understand what was going on. Children like me learned a pattern of failure, and teachers came to believe that such children would fail. Furthermore, teachers themselves promoted forms of professional discourse, which they presumably acquired from normative cultural discourses, and which themselves perpetuated the logics and values that underpin regimes of failure. I remember a former teacher of mine, frustrated by the apparent inability of some children to learn, saying, 'All the children in this room got the same teaching. What is wrong with you lot?' This victim blaming, as it is called by Ryan (1971: 8), is an excellent ideology for justifying a perverse form of social action designed to change, not society as one might expect, but rather society's victim.

Issues of equality, poverty, disadvantage, parental involvement, cultural factors and curriculum adaptation remain as major concerns for me in my current practice as a teacher. My own experience as a student led me to believe that education and schooling for most students involves learning obedience and the repression of independence. It is a period of regimentation and control, where 'children are schooled in deference to the status quo, whether or not it nurtures their burgeoning minds' (Namulundah 1998: 1).

I became a teacher because I believe that as well as being agents of repression, schools also have the potential to nurture equality and diversity. This is the basis of my research. I believe that as educators we need to find ways of interrupting the relations of domination and subordination, and challenge received wisdom on epistemology and methodology. Schools can be transformative provided teachers choose to develop pedagogies that encourage change without imposing the authoritarian power of the teacher onto the learners. Rather than treating students as passive recipients of knowledge, which serves to reproduce social, political and economic inequality, I have developed pedagogical practices that are rooted in my own vision of education, where students are freed from domination through the development of their own critical awareness. In my thesis I produce evidence to support my claims to knowledge that I have encouraged students to become full participants in my own classroom research, and to undertake their own personal enquiries into how they have learned to improve the quality of learning experience for themselves. By doing this, I believe I am contributing to some degree of social transformation.

My beliefs and values are central to my work and have shaped the teacher I have become. So has my personal history. I agree with Alexander that 'the most basic test of the rightness of one's teaching is the degree to which it is true to the educational values which the teaching claims to manifest' (1995: 304). Following Whitehead (2004a) I take this belief as the standard by which I judge my practice, and this is what I examine in my thesis.

2   Which standards do we use to make judgements on our practices?

We have reproduced these stories for two main reasons, which, we believe, show how we are contributing to both practice and theory.

First, the stories constitute the personal theories of the teachers who tell them. They contain the descriptions and explanations the teachers offer as they account for their own practices. They are stories of learning that set out how the teachers learned to transform contradictory experiences into more life-enhancing experiences.

Second, reproducing the stories enables us to theorize our own practices as professional educators, whose job is to contribute to new theory and new practice, with a focus on influencing the learning of professionals. We are showing how we have contributed to new practices by encouraging our colleagues to find imaginative ways of dealing with their own unsatisfactory situations. Now, by reproducing those stories in our report, we are potentially contributing to new practices (yours) by encouraging readers (you) to learn from the teachers' stories. We are also contributing to new theory, because now we want to explain how the telling of stories of learning (the teachers') are embedded within the telling of another story (our own). We visualize the patterns of our relationships as a kind of elegant fractal, where certain shapes re-create themselves in a constant process of unfolding. Each relationship is enfolded within the other, and unfolds in its own unique way, with its own potentials for creating new relationships. We theorize our relationships with the teachers we support as a dynamic process of unfolding relationships. In doing this, we explain how this commitment to new creation is an ontological value that manifests as the kind of inclusional and transformational logic we use to understand our life practices, and it is also a feature of our practical lives. Our ontological values have transformed into real-life practices, and this process of transformation is itself a manifestation of generative transformation.

In setting out the stories like this, and explaining how the telling of one story within another story is symptomatic of generative transformational processes, we are also addressing the idea raised by Todorov (1990) that stories themselves can show transformational potential. For us, it is not only necessary to show how stories contain generative transformational potential, but is also a core condition if the stories are to be seen as stories of learning.

This idea of generative transformational capacity needs closer examination because we need to ensure that we are communicating the ideas clearly, and also, remembering that we are writing a research account, which means producing evidence to test and support our claims to knowledge, we wish to gather data and generate the kind of evidence that will show the generative transformational and inclusional processes of our own learning.

The idea of generative transformational evolutionary processes

We believe our learning partnership has been strengthened through our shared commitments in relation to theory and practice. Both of us have worked with similar ideas for most of our professional lives and, over the past twenty-five years, those ideas have begun to merge and produce more refined and powerful ideas.

In the 1980s, Jean took as one of the core themes for her doctoral studies the ideas she had already begun to develop in previous work. She was especially fascinated by the idea of how a finite number of components have the capacity to transform into an infinite number of new creations. Each face has just so many physical components, yet each and every face ever created is unique. The languages of the world have just so many lexical and structural components, yet each and every person who speaks any language is able to create an infinitude of novel and unique utterances, none of which has ever been said before and never again will be. At the same time, Jack was developing some of his core ideas, including the idea of educational influence. We discuss this idea below, when we begin to link the themes that permeate our work, and show how they have become our core standards of judgement.

First we explain what we understand as generative transformational processes. To communicate our understanding of the processes involved, and to show the realization of those processes within our own process of learning, we reproduce here a piece of writing from 1992.

The generative transformational order of social change

Imagine you are a magician of infinite power. Imagine that, at a word, you could put into effect a process whereby every thing in the world started changing of its own accord into a different kind of thing, that was recognisably the same original thing, but that became more mature with each step in the process of change. Seeds started turning into plants, raindrops formed oceans, students became professors, one-man bands metamorphosed into orchestras.

The power you have unleashed is called generative power. The processes that it begins are called transformational processes. Imagine that each thing in the world contains its own blueprint of what it could be – a sunflower turns into a sunflower, left to its own devices – but no thing will actually fulfil its potential unless the generative power is available. The transformational processes at work in the world are grounded in the power of generativity. The number systems of the world are really meaningless unless they are used to calculate, and it is possible to perform an infinite number of calculations. The rules of language are meaningless unless they are used to create new language.

Now imagine that you want to teach other magicians how to use their power of generative creativity. Your own generative power has to work actively within you, otherwise you deny your own potential as a magician of infinite power. You show them the secret of setting the power in motion, and, by inevitable implication, they return the compliment, showing you the secret of their power. This is truly a magic circle whereby the power within you itself transforms your own community into a better, more fully-realised version of itself.

Now, transfer the analogy to the real you, in relationship with others. Consider how your individual life is transformed into a better version of itself, provided you are part of a community, each of whom acts in the others' best interest. This sort of community may be encouraged by each of you because you want to improve your own community, and spread the word into the wider world to show that it can be done and that you have done it by working together. You know how you have done it by working together, and you share the knowledge.

This idea of generative power acts as the basic unit of energy whereby each thing may transform itself endlessly in the process of its own realisation of potential. In terms of education and educational research, the development of educational knowledge can be seen as the process of an individual's ever-increasing consciousness, which is encouraged by the parallel processes of other expanding consciousnesses with whom we are in conversation. The development of our individual and collective understanding helps us to promote the evolution of our own society, each acting in the other's best interest. The generative power at work in any one person has the potential to transform the world, but only through the will of others who are equally aware of their own potential. (McNiff et al. 1992: 34–5)

As noted, we have included this excerpt to explain the idea of generative transformational processes. We have included it also to show how, although a fairly crude explication of an important idea, the excerpt acts as data of our early research. Over the years we have worked at refining the idea throughout our research, and you can see more refined explications in, for example, McNiff and Whitehead (2000). By comparing the two texts, you may see how our own learning has developed. In this early work, we were capturing the initial essence of an important idea that was to become a lodestar for both of us.

The idea of educational influence

Also in the 1980s, Jack began developing a key idea, to do with understanding the nature, origin and use of educational influence. To explain this, again in a simplistic form, here is another story.

The BBC recently broadcast a series of six documentaries on the rehabilitation of orphaned baby elephants in Africa. The films followed the process of how keepers worked with the elephants to encourage them to regain their confidence, and learn how to fend for themselves and live as a herd, with a view eventually of returning to the wild. Each group of orphans was mentored by a matriarch elephant, who had herself been orphaned as a baby. The films recorded the progress of one such herd, whose matriarch, Wendi, developed a strong bond of attachment with each orphan, so helping them to learn how to cope with the loss of their parents and also to find their own way within the herd and, hopefully, later in the wild. However, in light of her own maturing, Wendi was faced with a heartbreaking decision, whether to stay with the herd, whom she cared for and had grown so attached to, or whether to strike out on her own and begin to lead an independent life as a wild elephant. She decided to go her own way. The final documentary records the story of the head keeper, who had missed the day of Wendi's final departure, and wanted to see her once again, in the wild. He set out in his jeep to find Wendi. However, when he eventually found her, Wendi entirely ignored him because she was preoccupied with a new group of elephants, all of whom were clearly at ease in their own company. Although she was doubtless aware of his presence, she made no attempt to connect. Resisting the temptation to make contact, the keeper explained to the camera, with tears in his eyes, that this is what his work was about. It was his work, and his responsibility, to ensure that the orphaned elephants developed a sufficient sense of their own identity, and the capacity to make their own choices, that they would take responsibility for themselves in their own life world.

Although this story is about elephants, we believe that the same principles inform the work of some educators. The work of educators is to encourage people to become independent, even of the educator, to think for themselves, and to make their own life choices. This can be difficult for educators, because they may wish to remain in a position of influence with those whose learning they have supported. It can be difficult also when those people choose to make decisions that are contrary to what the educator may wish for them. It simply has to be recognized, however, that no one person has the right to tell another what to do, or to assume responsibility for the choices that others make. The most any person can do, or should do, is take responsibility for themselves.

This idea has even deeper implications when the matter is to do with exercising one's educational influence.

Drawing on the work of Said (1994: 14–15), who quotes a letter from Mallarmé to Valéry, Jack speaks about the idea that the influence that one person tries to exercise on another is always mediated by the other's own originality of mind and capacity for creative critique. When one person communicates something to someone else, it is not a straightforward process of putting the contents of one mind into another. Each person has their own creative capacity for choice. We can choose whether or not to listen to what is being said, and we choose whether to accept what another says. Therefore, when an educator aims to influence, they do so in the clear understanding that what they are trying to communicate will inevitably be filtered through the creative imagination of the other. Certainly it is not always the case that people can exercise their capacity for choice. All too often people are physically and mentally abused, so they have to obey what other people say, and can even come to believe it (see Orwell 1990; Foucault 1980). Frequently people are persuaded to accept uncritically the messages of the culture, and so do not even see the need to question. It is the job of educators to encourage people to see that they do need to question, in order to realize the full potentials of their humanity, as creative, free-thinking people, so that they can live together with others who, while sometimes radically different in outlook and appearance, are the same in their own inherent precious uniqueness. It is especially important to question when things seem satisfactory.

Identifying our standards of judgement

The values underpinning these ideas are those to do with freedom and love. We try to communicate these values through our writing by drawing on the metaphors of unfoldingness, free-flow creativity, and inclusion. These metaphors are themselves metaphors of relation and life-affirming connectedness. We try to communicate the values through our life practices by creating our lives, as a form of artistry, as free and loving human beings. The concepts of freedom and love need a real-life context to have meaning. You have to be free from something or free to do something (Berlin 1969), and you have to have someone or something to love, and be loved in return. We create our identities in terms of our attachments, says Raz (2001). Therefore our lives as free and loving human beings have to have a context of other people if our values of freedom and love are to make any sense. Our values need to be seen as in lived relation with others. For them to make sense, the values themselves need to be understood as real-life practices, not as abstract concepts.

It is out of this understanding, of values as needing to be lived if they are to make sense, that we now begin to articulate those values as the core standards by which we judge the value of our lives, in relation to families, friends, and colleagues. In our personal relationships, we make judgements about our practices in terms of whether our families and friends thrive on our own contributions to their lives. Because living, and lived values, are always a two-way street, we also judge the value of our lives in terms of how we respond to those people, and to our living planet. In our professional relationships we make judgements about our practices in terms of whether other people's lives are influenced by our contributions, and we by theirs. To what extent do we influence others, so that they come to think for themselves and make life choices that are life-affirming for themselves, and to what extent are we influenced by them, as we learn from their words and examples? To what extent do we influence others, so that they come to develop the same values of love and freedom, which they in turn can realize as living practices in order to set others free, and to what extent do we free ourselves by making ourselves vulnerable in relation to them? In other words, to what extent do we exercise our educational influence so that others will come to exercise theirs, and, in the process, develop understandings of their own need and capacity for holding themselves accountable for what they do, and to what extent do we do the same?

We want to emphasize that we are not claiming that we have educated anyone, except ourselves. We are not claiming that we have had any influence in the lives of teachers such as Caitríona, Bernie and Margaret, in relation to the development of their own values. We are however claiming that we have encouraged them to develop insights about the need to theorize their practices, and, as part of the process, to articulate clearly the standards of judgement they use to make sense of their work in terms of how they judge their own practices. The three case studies in this chapter are, we believe, evidence to show that our claims may be accepted as justified. We also want to emphasize that we judge our practices in terms of the extent to which we also hold ourselves open to new possibilities of life, learning and love. We do not know all the answers, about ourselves, let alone about anyone else. We are learning. We do however rejoice in the sheer excitement of being alive, which is for us an opportunity to engage in an ever-ready openness to learning.

At this point, then, we need to see how all these ideas transform into the real-life practices of generating quality evidence, and in order to generate evidence, we need first to talk about gathering data, which becomes the focus of the next chapter.

SUMMARY

We have offered as the starting point of our action research the idea that many of our values, including those of justice and democracy, are denied in the practices of the exclusion of practitioner action researchers from participation in debates to do with the future of educational research. We have presented three case stories that describe the experiences of three practitioners whose values of justice and entitlement have similarly been denied because of the exclusion of themselves and the children they teach from public recognition as worthwhile knowledge creators and citizens. This, we suggest, is because their contributions to practice-based theories are not acceptable within normative understandings of how contributions to educational theory should be judged. We therefore introduce ideas about what new kinds of standards of judgement should be introduced and developed. We explain what these may look like in relation to our own research, and how we are articulating them in this book.

PART 2

Gathering Data and Generating Evidence

This part deals with issues of monitoring practice, gathering data and generating evidence. *It contains the following chapters:*

4 Monitoring practice and gathering data
   What kind of data will we gather to show the situation as it unfolds?

5 Interpreting the data and generating evidence in relation to living critical standards of judgement
   How do we explain our educational influences in learning?

At this point we adopt a more pedagogical style and offer advice to you, the reader, on how to monitor practice, gather data and generate evidence. We also give examples of how we do this in our own research.

4 Monitoring practice and gathering data

What kind of data will we gather to show the situation as it unfolds?

In this chapter we set out our understanding of what monitoring practice and gathering data involve, and how we practise in this regard.

We understand data as referring to the actions and phenomena that are recorded, gathered and stored in artefacts such as computer files, notes and video tape recordings. They are gathered throughout the research on a systematic basis, to show the action as it unfolds. The purpose of gathering data is to generate evidence to support and test a claim to knowledge (theory). Data and evidence are different things (see Chapter 5), so, from the start, it is important to gather data that will give good quality evidence, to identify what is being looked for and plan how it can be obtained.

A lot of practical information about data gathering is available in our *Action Research for Teachers* (McNiff and Whitehead 2005a) and *All You Need to Know about Action Research* (McNiff and Whitehead 2005b). Here we summarize that information, and begin to focus on key issues in terms of showing how data and evidence stand in relation to standards of judgement and claims to knowledge; in other words, how the issue of judging the quality of an account has been addressed prior to submitting it in the public domain. Showing the relationship between data and standards of judgement involves asking questions about monitoring practice, in terms of which data are to be gathered, by whom and about whom, and how this is to be done. It is also vital to address the issue of the kind of ethical frameworks appropriate to gathering data.

The chapter is organized as three sections to address these questions:

1 Which data? Who gathers them?
2 How are the data gathered?
3 Ethical frameworks

In Chapter 5 we address the question, 'How are the data used?', which is about generating evidence to support and test a claim to knowledge.

At this point we adopt a more pedagogical style, offering advice to you, our reader, on the practicalities of monitoring practice and gathering data, as well as showing how we do that in our research.

1   Which data? Who gathers them?

Data gathering is like journalism. As a journalist your aim is to find out about a topic and present the facts as well as your own analysis. Journalists restrict the field to what they are looking for and keep the rest for later.

A good journalist always has the tools of the trade immediately available; notebooks for field notes and jottings, tape recorder and camera, and sometimes a back-up video camera operator. They systematically document what they see happening in the field as well as their reactions as they watch. Prior to going into the field, or afterwards, they do their desk research, accessing documentary sources and archived material such as letters and despatches, and talking with other people about their investigation. They ask people about their experiences, filter those testimonies through their own reflective process, and regularly maintain written and video accounts and diaries. Newsreaders and presenters of topical programmes spend hours in the newsroom prior to a broadcast, making sure they have sufficient and accurate information about the issue, preparing their own analyses, and checking these against the opinions of others such as their producers. Inaccurate reporting can have serious consequences. The credibility of the reporter can be compromised, and the watching public may lose interest in the field they are investigating.

Journalism is a kind of narrative inquiry (Clandinin and Connelly 2000), the building up of stories of people going about their daily business. It involves the capacity to sense what will make a good story, be alert to breaking news, and offer the kind of critical analysis that will keep listeners' attention and engage their imagination. These are essential elements for you, too. You have to capture breaking news, explain how the story is unfolding, and offer a critical commentary on the process.

Like a journalist, you will look for promising data, and use whichever data gathering methods seem right at the time. Unlike archived data, where you can take your time reading documents, live data do not wait for you to catch up. People have quick conversations and move on, so you need to capture what they are saying on the spot.

Your aim is to gather data in order to generate evidence. Your first question is therefore, 'Evidence of what?' Your 'what' is what you are studying, namely whether or not you are developing your own learning in order to influence the learning of others in an educational way. What you are looking for therefore is episodes of practice to show how you have developed your own learning (which means focusing on yourself), and episodes where you think your new learning has influenced the learning of others (which means focusing on them). These are distinct but interrelated issues. Keeping the right focus is essential in order to maintain your research as action research and not let it slip into social science research.

The rest of this section addresses these issues, and is organized as follows:

Focusing on you

- Monitoring your learning
- Monitoring your actions

Focusing on others

- Monitoring others' learning
- Monitoring others' actions

Focusing on you

When you study you, you study two things:

- your learning, what you do 'in here';
- how your learning influences your actions, what you do 'out there'.

Each of these involves different forms of monitoring and data gathering.

Monitoring your learning

Monitoring your learning involves self-reflection, as well as gathering data over time to show how your learning has been enhanced. This will involve maintaining a reflective journal or diary, in which you can record what you did, reflect on what you learned from what you did, and comment on its possible significance. A useful way to do this is to organize your diary into sections when you record the action, your reflections, and the possible significance of the learning, something like this:

Action

I tried a new seating arrangement in class today, grouping the children into threes rather than pairs.

Reflection

This seemed to work well. Perhaps introducing a third person into the activity provides a different kind of dynamic.

Possible significance of the learning

I think this idea of different kinds of dynamic could be important. When do I need to use pair work and when threes in my lessons?

Some people maintain their journals using this form of running commentary. Another way to present the same kind of information is to divide a page into three columns headed 'Action', 'Reflection' and 'Significance'. You could also add another column headed 'New action' to show how your learning from one episode of action–reflection fed back into new practice. You could regard the new action as the beginning of a new cycle, and organize your diary accordingly. This process emphasizes the cyclical nature of action – reflection, which is a core aspect of action research. One cycle transforms into the next, as learning informs action, and action informs new learning (in other words, practice generates new theory, and new theory feeds back into practice and generates new practices). It also emphasizes the element of duration in action research. Action research is not a one-off piece of practice, but has the potential to transform into never-ending new episodes of learning and practice.

How do we authors monitor our learning? We keep our own reflective journals, which enable us to keep a record both of what has happened, and also of our reflections on what has happened. We also work out our ideas in conversations and through our communications such as e-mail correspondence. Here is an example of how our learning develops. The example is taken from some e-mail correspondence as we were working on this book.

E-mail correspondence 10 July 2005

Jean: Hi Jack, In this chapter I am talking about legitimation processes, drawing on Habermas's ideas to do with social validity. I'm also thinking that it is important to establish ethical validity in the legitimation process itself, i.e. are all parties in the conversation demonstrating their own ethical awareness of their conduct by e.g. recognising the validity of rival standards of judgement?

Jack: Hi Jean, I've tended to use MacIntyre's 1990 text on three rival versions of moral enquiry and that quote at the end of his 1988 book Whose Justice? Which Rationality? 'The rival claims to truth of contending traditions of enquiry depend for their vindication upon the adequacy and explanatory power of the histories which the resources of each of those traditions in conflict enable their adherents to write' (MacIntyre 1988, p. 403) …

Jean: I don't know any major theorist who has done work on criteria for demonstrating ethical validity, i.e. supporting the claims by participants that they are acting morally. Do you? I am thinking they would be something like:
  • Recognise the other – drawing on work by e.g. Kristeva, Levinas.
  • Include the other – drawing on work by Habermas.

Jack: I like this. My own references would include Buber and I'd now draw on some African thinking on Ubuntu …

Jean: There's also something about recognising the need for uncertainty in knowing – drawing on the work of e.g. Berlin.

Jack: Crucial to recognise the importance of uncertainty.

Jean: And understanding that rival traditions have their own histories and canons – drawing on the work of e.g. MacIntyre.

Jack: Definitely.

Jean: I also came across some nice work by Joseph Raz but never read it in detail. I will maybe look it up later.

Jack: Don't know this.

Jean: Do you think this is a useful way to go?

Jack: I really do. In extending the engagement with the ideas of others, it might also be useful to embrace the words socio-cultural and socio-historical – for example, a socio-cultural theorist like Edward Said in 'Culture and

Imperialism' demonstrated how the ethical norms in certain literatures could serve to reproduce an existing colonial/imperialist culture. An appreciation of socio-historical analysis, like Habermas's awesome two volumes of the 'The Theory of Communicative Action', can help us to appreciate the evolving nature of the normative judgements that are embedded in what counts as moral action in particular cultures and can serve to reproduce/transform the social order. The reason why I think that what you are proposing to focus on is so significant is because I see what we value as moral/ethical as most important in motivating and guiding what we do. I also like the emphasis on engaging with the most significant thinkers of the day and drawing insights from their work in developing one's own form of life and contributing to a good social order.

When you come to Chapter 6, you will see that these ideas were developed throughout the chapter. This is just one example of how we monitor our learning, and how that learning then comes to influence our new learning and actions.

Monitoring your action

In order to establish whether you are enhancing your learning 'in here', and how this may be influencing your action, you need to observe and monitor what you are doing 'out there'. You can do this using a variety of data gathering techniques ranging from field notes to video. The key thing to focus on is what *you* are doing, not what other people are doing (but see next section). Where do you stand in the room? How do you speak? How do you respond to people?

You can also ask other people to observe and monitor you. These can be your research participants, such as the students in your class, and also outside observers. You would need to alert them to what you were looking for. In this case, you would clearly articulate your standards of judgement by saying, 'Could you please watch me to see whether I am acting in a way that is fair?', or 'Please note especially any instances where I respond in a respectful manner (or not, as the case may be).' By focusing your own and your observers' attention on what you are looking for in relation to how you understand the aim of your research as the realization of your values, you are also addressing the issue of how you are going to establish the validity of your own theory, in terms of your articulated standards of judgement, when you make your claim that you have improved your practice and have had an educational influence in someone's learning, whether the learning is your own or another person's.

How do we monitor our actions? We each have our preferred strategies. Jean enjoys working with written texts, so she tends to explain her actions through writing. You can see many examples of this in Chapter 6 of this book, as well as in other texts (see McNiff 2006; McNiff and Whitehead 2000; 2002). Jack enjoys working with video, and he tends to explain his actions visually. You can see examples of this at http://jackwhitehead.com/jwictr05key.htm in his keynote address to the 12th International Conference of Teacher Research on 'How can we improve the educational influences of our teacher-researcher quests?' (Whitehead 2005c). In the section on 'A loving flow-form of life affirming energy with Moira Laidlaw', Jack uses a visual narrative to establish the shared meaning, with Moira Laidlaw, of this ontological value and its communication as a living critical standard of judgement. In breaking the grip of print in educational research with the help of visual narratives, we believe that researchers like Mary Hartog, Marian Naidoo and Moira Laidlaw, all of whose work is referenced in this book, lead the way in the development of living critical standards of judgement.

Focusing on others

Your research is about evaluating the quality of your educational influence in learning, your own and others'. This means that the main focus is you, as already noted. However, you can evaluate the quality of your influence in the learning of others and in the learning of social formations only by checking how others respond to you, that is, whether or not they show in their accounts of learning that they have accepted or rejected your influence. Therefore you need to monitor their responses, as they reflect back to you how you enter their thinking and how they have begun to mediate your influence by incorporating your ideas into their own in their own original way and through the exercise of their critical judgement.

This aspect of data gathering is where you need to take extra care. We said above that to keep your research as action research you need to focus on you, and to resist the replacement of your own ontological values and practical principles by the conceptual frameworks of others. Social scientists offer their conceptual frameworks from studying other people, when they ask, 'What are those people doing? How can their behaviour be interpreted and explained?' They maintain a spectator view throughout, often ignoring that they are also part of the situation. Action researchers ask, 'What am I doing in relation to others? How do I interpret and explain my own behaviour?' They interpret and explain their behaviour in terms of how they learn, as they take heed of their own responses and the responses of others to their own learning and action.

Therefore, when you observe and monitor others, you do so in relation to how they are responding to you. In the same way that you monitored and gathered data about your own learning, you need to monitor and gather data about theirs, but this involves using different techniques. Like you, they are in the privileged position of commenting on their own learning. You may be able to comment on their actions, but only they can comment on the learning that enters into their actions through the exercise of their originality and critical judgement.

Monitoring others' learning

This means that you need to invite your research participants to maintain their reflective journals, or learning portfolios, recording instances where they learned something new, showing their reflections on their learning, and commenting on its possible significance. You also need to negotiate with them that they will allow you to use their data about themselves. You could turn data gathering into a lively exercise with young people, perhaps when you invite them to produce cartoon strips of their own learning and actions; or you could make video available to them to maintain their reflective diaries. You could turn it into an equally enjoyable exercise with workplace colleagues, where you invite them to post responses to your ideas via e-discussion boards or on a poster board in a staff room. Aim to make these processes public and transparent.

How do we do this? We use a range of strategies, which include written, oral and ostensive data. Here are two examples to show the processes.

Jean's story

In a recent evaluation of an academic staff development initiative, Jean asked colleagues to e-mail comments on what they had learned and the possible usefulness of their learning. They could identify themselves or remain anonymous. She negotiated with them that they would allow her to use their comments as part of her own public evaluation of her practice. Here are some of the comments she received.

> These sessions have given me the time to reflect and consider issues that are often discussed *ad hoc*, yet are of considerable importance to my professional practice. Questioning professional values and practice is a core element of this job.

> I have appreciated the fact that we are not being rushed into research, that time is needed for reflection and focus. I have learned to reflect on aspects of my own practice and, reassuringly, it has made me feel quite proud of some of my work.

> At the start of the year, I felt that the sessions only served to point out how little I knew, but during the last few months these meetings with the research group have helped me grow in confidence. I feel that the sessions have challenged me mentally and I have definitely become more reflective not only about what I do in my job but also about what I think about life in general and my own place in the world.

Jack's story

Here is an excerpt from an e-mailed response to Jack from Eleanor Lohr, whose doctoral studies Jack supports. Eleanor is responding to a draft of a paper Jack has written.

Eleanor Lohr: responding to Jack, 3 August 2005

Jack, this is how I place my thoughts alongside yours. I have been working with some of the ideas in your paper – I do recognize them! I particularly like your way of explaining the movement of life-affirming energy. When you wrote these words:

> I imagine that you are all familiar with the experience of the flows of energy in living critical standards of judgement. I mean this in the sense that in asking questions about the meaning and purpose of your lives you are aware of the flows of energy in making judgements of value in what you do, about what you have done, and about what you intend to do.

You wrote that. As I write the words you wrote, I notice my bodily responses, and make decisions with that in mind. It is this sensing that I mean, which is always what I mean when I refer to 'embodied knowledge'. This is how I link my (o)ntology with my (e)pistemology. These inner and outer movements need to have something in common for me to know that this is a good thing to do or write. You are writing about anticipation of and reflection on action. I am writing now about reflection-in-the-action-of-writing. Watching the movement, I sense the direction it is taking me in. I follow it, I enact it. If I am aware enough I can follow the inner sensing in the outer action ... This is how my actions tell me whether what I do is a good thing to do. This is also how my values are transformed in the action, because feedback from others involved in the action lets me know the social value of what I do.

Seeking this kind of feedback however can be risky, especially if you send out an open invitation to people. You never know if they are going to respond, and you also don't know what they are going to say if they do. You run the risk of receiving responses or seeing people's reactions that can be rather damaging to your own self-esteem, as well as uplifting. However, the risk is worthwhile. Action research is full of risk, and practitioner-researchers simply need to engage with it. We never know how we are doing until we check with other people, which is an essential aspect of monitoring practice if we are serious about improving it.

Monitoring others' actions

In the same way as you can monitor your own action and invite others to do so, and systematically gather data from these observations, you can also invite your participants to monitor what they are doing personally, and negotiate permission for individual participants to monitor others and make their data and their interpretations public. You can also negotiate with them for you and other observers to monitor and gather data about what they are doing, and to make their data and interpretations public.

For example, Mary Roche, whose studies Jean supports, negotiated with the children she was teaching (and the children's parents and her principal) to allow two visitors to observe a class on critical thinking. Mary gave the visitors a specific brief, in terms of her own standards of judgement, about how she was looking for data that showed the children's capacity to exercise their own originality and critical engagement, without a hint that they were doing so to please Mary. Here is what one of the visitors wrote.

Yvonne O'Flynn

On 6th February I sat in on Mary's class to do a second observation on cognitive development. The age group was mainly five year olds but there are a few six year olds too. Mary told the children a story called 'Dear Greenpeace'. It's a story about a little girl called Emily who wrote to Greenpeace to tell them she had a whale called Arthur in her garden pond. The children loved the story. Mary then asked would we like to talk about pets – ones the children have, or would like to have.

To be honest what happened was the most amazing conversation I had ever heard in a group of children in all my years caring for children. They started talking about their goldfish and their birds, their friends' pets and their grannies' pets and their cousins' pets. Then one child said that his dog made a plan to catch his cat because the cat tried to kill his goldfish. That led the children to talking about whether animals think and have their own language.

This then led on to a conversation about human thoughts and brains and if a brain was taken from one child and put into another child, would the second child that got the brain know all the memory and thoughts of the first child. They thought about it and discussed if their brain slept or not, did their skin stay awake while they were asleep, and they felt it had to, else how would they turn in bed at night.

I was enthralled at the whole conversation – it was the most thought-provoking morning. It was amazing that some children came back to talk about pets – it showed they were thinking their own thoughts. I always knew that children were amazing people and we, as adults, can learn so much from them, as well as them learning from us.

Alberto (who gave a comment in the circle) is in our school teaching Spanish to the children – he is on teacher training here for a year. He came into the class as we were starting the Thinking Time. He had never seen one before. He normally stays for a half an hour. He did not move out of the chair until the very end and he felt the same as I did – blown away by the whole thing and amazed that children of such a young age could have so much knowledge in their heads. His mum is a teacher in a primary school back in Spain and he wants to get her to do it with her class at home.

Mary could use excerpts from this conversation, or the whole conversation, as evidence to test her claim that she has learned how to influence the learning of her children in an educational way.

How do we monitor others' actions and produce data to support our claim that we are exercising our educational influence? We organize our data in relation to our claims to knowledge. We are claiming that we have improved our learning in order to influence someone else's learning. We therefore need to produce data that show these patterns of influence at work. In this section we have set out how we produce data about ourselves, from our recorded actions and recorded reflections on those actions, and about our research participants, and their recorded actions and reflections on their actions. We have given the specific example of Mary Roche. We have also established with Mary that her learning has been influenced by us, and we have this on record, as presented here in e-mail correspondence.

> *Mary:* Jean, my thesis is to do with teaching children to think critically and it is based on a philosophy of thinking for oneself. But first, in order to see that this was even necessary, I had to slough off years of training and indoctrination and start to become critical myself. As my writing shows, I'm now doing that. Your influence has been hugely significant in the development of my ability to think critically. (e-mail correspondence, 9 July 2005)

In a similar spirit, Eleanor Lohr wrote to an e-seminar about Jack's influence in her learning. She wrote:

> I may say that I am one of those PhD students that Jack has been supervising, and one that has been required to resubmit. I see my failure to reach the standard required by my examiners as an irritation, that the passion with which Jack

> supported me led me to my scholarship. If he had not expressed that belief (being on *my* side, and by my side) I would not have learned what I learned. And what I learned was what I needed to learn, not what the academy is now demanding. I think that I can give the academy what it requires because I am sure of my knowledge, because Jack supervised me in the way that he did. That is not to say that he could have encouraged me to be more careful. But being careful would not have allowed me to take risks, and without taking the risk of becoming utterly myself, I would not be so delighted in my scholarship. (e-mail correspondence, 14 July 2005)

When trying to show that we have influenced someone's learning, we bear in mind that we are not aiming to show a cause and effect relationship. No one caused Mary's or Eleanor's learning. They already knew these things. Conversations with Jean and Jack enabled them to surface their existing latent knowledge. All any of us can do is hope that we influence, and find ways of capturing written or visual testimonies to that effect.

2   How are the data gathered?

It is clear that data gathering is not random, but a disciplined and focused exercise. When you set out to gather data, always keep your wider research goals in mind, which you ultimately hope to present in the form of your claim to knowledge. If your research question is, 'How do I improve the quality of my educational influence by improving the quality of my interactions with others?', you will aim to gather data that show, first, an improved quality of your learning and influence and, second, an improved quality in your interactions.

This raises the question of gathering data over time, and how you can do this.

Your research will extend over some period of time, perhaps days or years. You will aim to show developments as they unfold during that time. A useful starting point is to identify a situation where you wanted to investigate something, perhaps when your values were not being realized in your practice, and you then monitored the learning and action over that period of time to when they were more fully realized. Remember you are not aiming for an end point where everything will come to neat and tidy closure. That end point probably does not exist. The time you feel you have achieved an end point is the time to start worrying and look at the thinking that leads you to think that you have arrived rather than are still on the journey. Rather than focus on an end point, you are more interested in what is happening here and now, primarily in the learning that is influencing what is happening. You need to record that action on a regular basis. This means building up the story of what is happening using a range of media.

The strategies you can use would probably take three main forms: written, graphic and multimedia.

Written forms

You can use a range of documentary forms, including those outlined above. These would include field notes, memos and letters. You should aim to gather data using these and other forms to show developments over time.

An example of the use of notes and letters is Eileen Brennan's story (adapted from McNiff and Collins 1994). Jean and Úna Collins supported Eileen's enquiries in Ireland.

Eileen Brennan

Eileen was trying to teach German to a poorly motivated first-year class. She wanted to find ways of developing more oral participation. Because the students were disruptive, however, she set them more writing than she wanted to, to keep them reasonably contained.

When she began her project, and to establish a baseline, she asked the class what they thought of their lessons. Responses that she gathered as field notes included:

> I think the class is much too long. Eighty minutes is just too much. It does your head in.

> I agree. We would learn a lot more in forty minutes. It's very boring.

> I can't enjoy it because I'm not sitting with my friend.

> I like it. It's a good buzz. I would prefer to talk it. I hate writing.

Eileen later asked them to write down why they thought she asked them to do so much writing. They wrote her notes, which she filed carefully:

> Because when we talk, we do your head in, Miss.

> Because you're punishing us because we're never quiet.

She tried a range of strategies, including pair work and role play. This was greeted with enthusiasm, and they wrote her further notes:

> I learned a lot by working with my partner. I can now tell somebody in German how to go straight ahead, left or right.

> Can we do this again next day, Miss?

> It was good having a break from listening to the teacher.

> I can't work with A. He just fools around all the time.

As well as inviting her students to write her notes and letters, Eileen kept other forms of documentary data, such as examination scores and responses from questionnaires.

She explored further strategies such as involving the students in writing to German penpals. At the end of the project she asked her students to write her brief letters about their experiences, to see whether she had influenced their learning in a positive way. The letters contained the following excerpts.

> In the future I would like to be a surgeon, but I need a language in school, and German won't do any harm. Even if I make it to be a surgeon, I might get a German patient or might go to Germany for a holiday and get a job somewhere.

> I would like to go on holiday and use German. I could order a meal in a restaurant or buy stamps for my postcards using German.

I would like to be able to ask for directions if I got lost somewhere.

I want to know how to say I'm sick or sunburnt so I don't have to suffer in silence. I heard it's very hot in Germany.

What is striking in Eileen's story is her focus on her own learning, as she developed new strategies in light of her students' evaluation of her teaching, and the quality of her educational influence that is evident in the increased involvement of the students in their own learning. You can download Eileen's full account from www.jeanmcniff.com.

Graphic forms

A useful way of capturing the action in a non-verbal form is to make representations using graphics. These come in a range of forms, such as charts and record sheets, diagrams such as spider diagrams and mind-maps, and cartoon strips.

Here is an example of a record sheet to show participants' interactions.

Record sheet to show participants' interactions

Number of interactions in 3-minute time slots	Minutes 1–3	Minutes 4–5	Minutes 6–9
Participants			
Charlie	JHT III	II	IIII
Rose	I	II	JHT
Mary	JHT	JHT JHT JHT	I
Joe	II	II	II

Uses of multimedia

Video and other multimedia are being used increasingly these days to generate evidence from the data. The use of multimedia carries with it special problematics, in that many authorities rightly stipulate that specific permission must be obtained from participants and, when appropriate, their parents or caregivers, to safeguard their personal rights and safety (see the next section on ethics). Some local education authorities have banned the use of multimedia because of current heightened awareness of their potential misuse.

However, when multimedia can be used, they can be especially powerful, because they capture the nature of reality in a way that verbal reports cannot. In her report on the second visit from the teachers, Mary, whose story appears above, noted the development in the thinking of a nine-year-old student, B. She wrote in her diary:

We discussed 'The Indian in the Cupboard', which is a novel about objectifying people, denying them their humanity and 'using' them. One child, B, a nine-year-old, said, 'Well, what's interesting for me is that Boone the cowboy is so stuck in his thoughts about Little Bull. He calls him a 'dirty stinking savage' even though Little Bull is always washing himself and Boone never wants to take a bath. Is that how wars happen, because people think other people's ways and habits are different and theirs are the right ones? They seem to think so. Why do wars happen anyway? Why can't people just get along and live with each other?'

Both teachers commented about the way that B's entire demeanour changed as he spoke. His voice went from being quiet into impassioned and his face expressed such seriousness as he struggled to articulate what he was thinking. (Roche 2005)

The use of video, had this been common practice in schools, would have enabled Mary to capture that change of expression from quietude into passion, and use it to test her claim that she had influenced B's thinking in an educational way. While the written word is adequate in this case, the use of video would have been far more powerful as a visual narrative.

Jack is especially interested in the use of multimedia and has succeeded with others in getting video and other multimedia accepted as evidence in higher degree studies. Mary Hartog, whose studies Jack supports, explains why her thesis contains CD-ROMs as an integral part of the work.

Evidence is drawn from life-story work, narrative accounting, student assignments, audio and video taped sessions of teaching and learning situations, the latter of which include edited CD-R files. These clips offer a glimpse of my embodied claims to know what the creation of loving and life-affirming educative relations involves. (Hartog 2004)

You can download Mary's thesis from http://www.bath.ac.uk/~edsajw/hartog.shtml.

It is also possible now to access and see for yourself the inclusion of visual narratives which have been submitted as evidence in support of, and to test, claims to knowledge. A seminal piece was Jack's contribution to *Action Research Expeditions*, which is an e-journal, hosted by the University of Montana, which has embraced multimedia forms of representation and is now at the forefront of the field of educational action research. From there you can access Part I of Jack's article, 'Do action researchers' expeditions carry hope for the future of humanity? How do we know? An enquiry into reconstructing educational theory and educating social formations' (Whitehead 2004c). From there you can also access the visual narratives of Part II on 'How valid are multi-media communications of my embodied values in living theories and standards of educational judgement and practice?' from http://www.actionresearch.net/multimedia/jimenomov/ JIME98.html (Whitehead 2004b). You can also access a presentation by Tian Fengjun and Moira Laidlaw on 'How can we enhance educational and English-language provision at our Action Research Centre and beyond?' at http://www.arexpeditions.montana.edu/articleviewer.php?AID=87 (Tian and Laidlaw 2005), which includes a section on educational standards of judgement. This connects a video clip of educational relationships to a claim that the values shown in the clip are not only in the public interest but are also contributing to the values of humanity that carry the writers' hopes for the future of humanity and our own. Works like these have set new precedents for what counts as data and evidence, the standards of judgement used in presenting personal theories in the public domain, and for presenting evidence in a way that is appropriate to showing the living nature of practitioners' educational enquiries.

Other practitioner researchers whose work is breaking new ground include Margaret Farren, who is a lecturer in e-learning at Dublin City University. She has shown how she is pedagogizing living theory theses – see http://www.webpages.dcu.ie/~farrenm/dissertations.html. She is developing her own living educational theory in her enquiry, 'How do I understand my pedagogy of the unique and web of betweenness?' with a focus on a pedagogy of the unique and a web of betweenness (Farren 2005, http://www.webpages.dcu.ie/~farren/research.html). Her website contains representations that show the multiple branching networks of relationships among her and her students as they enquire, individually and collaboratively, into their educational practices (http://www.webpages.dcu.ie/~farrenm/).

The most recent living theory thesis to be awarded a doctoral degree is that of Marian Naidoo. Marian presented a visual narrative of her thesis which expressed her meaning of her embodied value of a passion for compassion and, in the course of clarifying this meaning in the course of the enquiry, transformed the embodied value into a living, critical standard of judgement. Here is the abstract to her thesis.

I am because we are (a never-ending story): the emergence of a living theory of inclusional and responsive practice

I believe that this original account of my emerging practice demonstrates how I have been able to turn my ontological commitment to a passion for compassion into a living epistemological standard of judgement by which my inclusional and responsive practice may be held accountable.

I am a story teller and the focus of this narrative is on my learning and the development of my living educational theory as I have engaged with others in a creative and critical practice over a sustained period of time. This narrative self-study demonstrates how I have encouraged people to work creatively and critically in order to improve the way we relate and communicate in a multi-professional and multi-agency healthcare setting in order to improve both the quality of care provided and the wellbeing of the system.

In telling the story of the unique development of my inclusional and responsive practice I will show how I have been influenced by the work of theatre practitioners such as Augusto Boal and educational theorists such as Paulo Freire, and drawn on, incorporated and developed ideas from complexity theory and living theory action research. I will also describe how my engagement with the thinking of others has enabled my own practice to develop and from that to develop a living, inclusional and responsive theory of my practice. Through this research and the writing of this thesis, I now also understand that my ontological commitment to a passion for compassion has its roots in significant events in my past. (Naidoo 2005, retrieved 10 July 2005 from http://www.bath.ac.uk/~edsajw/arsup/mnabsok.htm)

How do we gather data? We have shown here how we gather data about our own and others' learning through the publicly recorded activities of producing our books, papers and websites. These however continue to act as data until we take the next step of turning them into evidence, by explaining how we show their significance in terms of testing our claims to knowledge by articulating our standards of judgement, and showing how we can find aspects in our data that can stand in relation to those standards of judgement. We develop these themes in Chapter 5.

3   Ethical frameworks

Demonstrating ethical behaviour is when people commit to respecting themselves and one another, and not to do harm. This is especially important in educational action research, where the aim is to generate and test new knowledge about educational practices and theory that will inform new developments in the field. It calls for a high moral awareness throughout, and an agreed framework of conduct.

You can find detailed advice and suggestions in our *All You Need to Know about Action Research* (McNiff and Whitehead 2005b), as well as exemplars of letters requesting permission, and ethics statements. We summarize these here, and then we move on to the equally serious issue of protecting intellectual freedom, which is at the heart of practices that call themselves educational. Protecting intellectual freedom means that pedagogies must proceed from an understanding of the individual's capacity for originality and critical engagement, and not present themselves as emancipatory when in fact they are a subtle form of imperialism through a sophisticated process of manipulation.

Advice about ethical frameworks

Ethical frameworks include three basic categories: access, safeguarding rights, and assuring good faith.

Access
If you are undertaking your own self-study as a reflective exercise that does not involve other people as participants, you do not need to negotiate permission. As soon as you are involved with others as participants in doing research together, however, you do need permission. You will need to negotiate and obtain oral and written permission from your manager or principal, and from participants themselves. If your participants are young or vulnerable people, you must get permission from parents or caregivers to include them. This is a potentially litigious area, so take great care and protect yourself against mishap. It is also an area fraught with tensions, because it is important to consider others' welfare within a context, such as in the UK, where academic freedom to express ideas and to test the ideas of others within the law is protected by law.

Safeguarding rights
Many people wish to be identified and have their contributions acknowledged, but if they demur in any way you must respect their wishes. It can be valuable to get written permission from participants who wish to have their identities revealed. You must also assure people that they always have the right to withdraw from the research you are doing together, at which point all data about them will be destroyed. Assure people of confidentiality at all times, and never discuss one person with another. Sometimes there are ethical issues concerning who counts as a participant in one's action research. For example, in 2005 a local authority employee was subjected to bullying, harassment and

racial discrimination by another employee. She complained and her claims were found to be justified. In a self-study of how she retained her life-affirming energy, in the face of the disabling pressure of bullying, harassment and racial discrimination, with the support of her loving family, the self-study researcher is within her rights and academic freedom to name without permission the individual whose actions she is responding to.

Maintain good faith

You need always to demonstrate and maintain your own good faith in all things. This means that you should draw up and distribute ethics statements to all participants, and write letters of permission. These must be kept carefully in your data archive, and placed into the appendices of your public accounts as appropriate. You must negotiate access in cases where a limited distribution is required, for example in contexts of a sensitive nature. If in doubt, turn the tables on yourself and check how you would feel if someone were to do to you what you intend to do to them. Be open and honest at all times.

How do we do this? In all our public writing and presentations, we ensure that we secure the permission of those whose stories we are reporting. Before this book went to print, we contacted all participants, and secured their permission in writing. While this has been relatively straightforward in terms of written documentation, it is more problematic in terms of the production of ostensive data, such as video. Again, in all instances, permission has been requested and obtained from all participants. Aspects of the book that refer to real people have been given to those people for editing and approval, prior to putting the text into the public domain. We maintain strict behaviours in these issues, as we hope that other people do in relation to us.

Maintaining intellectual freedom

This is a nebulous area, full of slippery concepts, and open to abuse.

The idea of intellectual freedom is rooted in an understanding that all are capable of thinking their own original thoughts and exercising their critical engagement in processes of discernment. This means that it is not only the intellectual freedom of researchers that needs to be protected, but also that of their research participants. It is easy to engage in the rhetoric of people's capacity for original thought, and promise to acknowledge this capacity through the protection of intellectual freedom, but difficult to carry the rhetoric through as consistent practice. Furthermore, if your research is about making a claim that you have done so, which is what you are speaking about when you say you are exercising your influence in a way that is educational, you also need to produce evidence that you have done so.

How do you produce data and generate evidence to show that you have honoured other people's intellectual capacity to think for themselves, and not to manipulate them or their meanings? It can be difficult to produce such evidence, which amounts to showing that you are being honest. We all know that it is possible to feign honesty, to get people on our side using a variety of strategies of persuasion. These can range from flattery to coercion. The hidden persuaders are so called precisely because they are hidden, and often hidden from the people who use them as much as the people they are used against. Advertisers deliberately use strategies to control the public mind, through the careful choice of words or colours, or the arrangements of images on a visual field. Yet while advertising firms have these techniques down to a fine art, the techniques are no less available to ordinary people, and no less skilfully employed. However, most of us develop sensitivities around these things. You know when someone is flattering you, through their tone of voice or general demeanour. You know when someone is not telling the truth. Yet sometimes people are good at not telling the truth, and sometimes they are not even aware of it. Self-deception is as common as the overt deception of others.

There are few safeguards. One way is to build up our own intellectual self-defences, so that we recognize deception when we are faced with it. Another is to challenge whatever appears to ring false, and to trust our basic instincts. This does not protect us from con-artists or skilled persuaders. Most of us fall foul of propaganda at some time, and end up doing something that we had not intended to do, and even thinking that it was our idea.

How to avoid this when you say that you are exercising your educational influence? The only way is to be ruthlessly honest with yourself. Do you actually value other people and their opinions, or do you pretend to do so? It is often impossible to produce evidence around these things, and well-meaning people will tend to take you at your word. So in this case, forget about gathering data, and look inwards, to check whether you make your claim in good faith and whether you are believable to yourself.

How do we do this? We have no hard data that we can turn into evidence. You will simply have to take us at our word, backed up by the body of our work, and the work of others whose studies we support. In cases like this, we follow Habermas (1979) in the idea that truth will emerge honestly and over time through a commitment to authenticity.

This brings us to the issue of how to generate the kind of evidence that will withstand stringent public critique, and this is the focus of the next chapter.

SUMMARY

In this chapter we have adopted a pedagogical voice alongside our scholarly voice. We have explained what kind of data to look for to support claims to improved learning for improved practices. In processes of data gathering, we have said, the aim is to gather data primarily in terms of the study of one-self, in order to show progress in the growth of one's own learning and how that learning can influence future learning and action. While data also need to be gathered in relation to research participants' improved learning for improved action, those data need to be understood in relation to testing the practitioner action researcher's own claim to improved learning. We have shown this process in action by setting out some of the ways we gather data to test our claims that we are improving our own learning in order better to encourage practitioner action researchers to raise their capacity in gathering the kinds of data that are going to help them also make quality judgements on their work. By gathering appropriate data, they will be able to generate the kind of evidence that will enable them to withstand robust critique in testing their claims to knowledge.

5 Interpreting the data and generating evidence in relation to living critical standards of judgement

How do we explain our educational influences in learning?

In this chapter we set out how we understand processes of generating evidence. Specifically we focus on the idea of identifying appropriate standards of judgement, whereby the data can be turned into evidence. We give some ideas about the kinds of standards that may be most appropriate for action research. We go on to outline our own standards of judgement, and we explain the processes we then engage in as we use those standards to generate evidence to test and hopefully support our claims to knowledge.

If, like us, you are doing your action research, at this stage you now have a strong data archive, which you need to analyse and interpret in order to generate evidence to test and hopefully to support your eventual claim to knowledge. The claim to knowledge you hope to make is to do with how you have influenced the quality of learning for yourself and others, perhaps those in the social formations of schools and other organizations, or even in governments. To test and support this claim to knowledge, you need to generate evidence from the data, which involves you articulating your criteria and standards of judgement.

This chapter gives advice on how to do this. It is organized to address these two issues:

1 Generating evidence and establishing standards of judgement
2 Deciding which kinds of standards are appropriate for judging the quality of practitioners' action research accounts

1 Generating evidence and establishing standards of judgement

Generating evidence involves several processes, which include the following:

- Sorting and categorizing the data
- Analysing the data for meanings

- Identifying criteria and standards of judgement
- Generating evidence

Sorting and categorizing the data

Chapter 4 explained how you can gather different kinds of data depending on what you are looking for and the kinds of questions you ask. If you are looking for information about a situation, you will look for data presented as analyses and stories, in documents and reports, and in charts and tables. If you are looking for data to show learning processes you will look for actions that appear to show learning taking place, and how the learning enters into actions. Note at this point that in searching for different pieces of data you are already thinking in terms of standards of judgement, in the same way as, when you search your wardrobe to find something appropriate to wear for a special event, you do so with specific standards in mind. Your judgements about what is appropriate for the beach are of the same kind as your judgements about what is appropriate for a wedding reception. The standards you use for both involve aesthetic standards (how you look), epistemological standards (knowing how you are going to be perceived and judged), ontological standards (how you feel about yourself), and social standards (what is appropriate for the situation). You will make practical decisions in light of how you use your aesthetic, epistemological, ontological and social standards of judgement. Similarly you make judgements about data in terms of the standards you use. You use those standards to decide whether to select as evidence a piece of data that shows actions that are influenced by learning, when, say, someone comments, 'I never thought of that!', or whether the data show action, but not necessarily learning, as when someone says, 'I'm going to the shops.'

The first stages of sorting and categorizing the data are fairly straightforward. You can sort your data in terms of categories such as 'conversations' or 'meetings'. These can be further subdivided as you go, into categories such as 'conversations with students' or 'conversations with parents', or 'meetings with critical friends' and 'meetings with research participants'.

Analysing the data for meanings

You now need to analyse the categorized data in terms of what they are saying to you. This means you will look for those things that you consider worthwhile. What is being communicated through the conversations with parents that is of value? Are you getting the message that these conversations show respectful relationships, which is a quality to be valued? Do your meetings with your research participants show that they are making their own decisions about what they want to learn, which is a practice to be valued? Can you say that the conversations demonstrate what you consider to be valuable understanding and caring relationships? You probably make judgements in terms of what is good or valuable about these situations. So what is being shown that leads you to make a judgement that a certain practice is good? What values can you see within the practices that you are looking at? Also, are you seeing data that are showing things as you would not want them to be? These data are real and will not go away. How do you take them into consideration for possible future action?

You are thinking in terms of standards of judgement, though you may not be articulating them at this stage. When you first sift through your data, looking for meanings, you already have in your mind what you will later articulate as your ontological standards, that is, the meaning and purpose you give to your existence in the sense of your theory of being. You will also be thinking about the validity of what people say about their learning, that is, your epistemological standards about how you judge the validity of claims to knowledge. We discuss these ideas more fully in a moment.

Identifying criteria and standards of judgement

Criteria and standards of judgement are different things. Criteria take the form of words and phrases that are used as markers of performance. For example, in a driving test, the criteria would be of the kind, 'Can execute a three-point turn' and 'Attends to traffic flows'. In a typing test the criteria would perhaps be, 'Can type x number of words per minute' or 'Knows how to set for single and double spacing'. The Teacher Training Agency has criteria in the form of checklists which enumerate competencies, and which can be ticked off when they are achieved by being demonstrated in practice.

Such criteria however say little about the quality of practice, that is, what is good about the practice. A driver could exercise a three-point turn, but mount the pavement on both sides in the process. A typist could type a required number of words per minute but incur twenty mistakes. Making judgements about the quality of practice means making value judgements, in terms of what you find valuable in the practices. Value judgements then become standards of judgement. You judge things in terms of what you think is good. The three-point turn can be said to have been achieved with care and due regard, and the typed sentence would show care for accuracy. Care and due regard, which are ontological values, about the way we are, would count as standards of judgement. They reflect our commitments in terms of who we are and how we understand ourselves in the world.

This idea is core to action research, which is itself premised on the idea of taking action in order to improve a situation, that is, move it in the direction of what we consider is good. Generating evidence involves identifying standards of judgement, which have their basis in what we consider is good. Standards of judgement enable us to make value judgements, from a reasoned position.

You can see these ideas demonstrated in Chapter 3, which contains the stories of three practitioners, who root their work in their values of justice. Each author aims to live their values in their practices. Each author uses those values as the standards by which they make judgements about their practices and about the claims they make. They articulate the values as their standards of judgement. Because they root their work in what they hold really important in life, which is to do with their ontological commitments, the values become ontological standards. Because they articulate the standards in terms of what they claim to know (their claims to knowledge, to do with epistemology), the values turn into epistemological standards. Because these standards are part of the lived realities of people's lives, they become living critical standards of judgement.

These are important new ideas in the field of action research, and could establish a new focus for how to assess quality. Until now, quality has been assessed using traditional criteria as standards of judgement. These criteria have usually taken an abstract form, often as performance indicators that indicate the execution of skills such as 'Can communicate ideas' or 'Explains concepts appropriately'. Introducing the idea of living standards of judgement as rooted in values gives a necessary dimension of values-based practice. Practice is seen as thoughtful educational engagement, and not simply the execution of skills. Practice is judged in terms of what is good about it, rather than only in terms of what activities have been performed.

The ideas are also central to showing how to establish the validity of action research, because, as we noted in Chapter 1, while practitioner action research is virtually universally accepted as a powerful form of professional development, it is not universally acknowledged as a valid form of educational research, especially not by social scientists and the politicians who draw on the social sciences, with their well-established criteria and standards of judgement, to inform policy formation and implementation. One of the reasons why this is the case is because practitioner action researchers themselves have not yet consistently articulated the kinds of standards of judgement appropriate for assessing the quality and validity of action research accounts, nor have they shown what those standards of judgement look like in practice. We authors are making our own start here, out of a belief that practitioners need themselves to say what they consider worthwhile in education, and make every effort to have their judgements accepted as valid. The practitioner community needs to pull together in this, because unless we articulate what we consider valuable in our work, and use those standards to make judgements about our work, we will continue to have inappropriate kinds of standards imposed on us and continue to lend ourselves to a corrupted view of what education and educational practice is about. We continue this theme in Section 2.

Generating evidence

You now have to select from your data those pieces that carry special meaning, in terms of showing the good in action, so that you can use them to justify and test your provisional claim that you are realizing your values – what you consider is good – in your practice. If, for example, you wanted to claim that your practice was grounded in the values of justice and entitlement, as the teachers in Chapter 3 do, you would take justice and entitlement as your living standards of judgement. You would make judgements about the quality of your practice in these terms. You would therefore pull out of your data archive those pieces of data that showed justice in action. Bernie Sullivan, who works with Traveller children, does this. She explains in her thesis (Sullivan 2005) that Traveller children are often marginalized because their own interests are not reflected in normative curricula. While there would probably be general agreement that children should learn to spell correctly, normative curricula emphasize the spelling of standard words within established vocabularies. Because Bernie saw the need to value Traveller culture as a basic requirement of a theory of justice for ethnic minority groups in schools, she focused on teaching reading through texts whose content would appeal to the life interests of Traveller children. Here is a small conversation that she uses to support her claim that she values Traveller cultures. The context is a conversation between Bernie and a Traveller child, N, in a language class. N has been assessed by the school psychologist and has been labelled as having a learning disability. Also assessed by a speech and language specialist, she has been found to have a very limited oral vocabulary. N is having difficulties spelling standard words.

Me: Why do you think we are having problems with these words?
N: I don't like the words.
Me: Why don't you like them?
N: Because they're too hard.
Me: What words would you like to learn?
N: 'Baby', and (after a few seconds thinking on the matter) 'new'.
Me: Why would you like to learn 'baby' and 'new'?
N: Because my mommy is getting a new baby. (Sullivan 2005)

Bernie shows throughout her writing how she helped Traveller children to build up quite extensive spelling vocabularies of words that were part of their everyday life experiences. When discussing her findings and putting forward her provisional claim to knowledge, she says:

> I examine the influence and relevance of the issues of justice and entitlement to my claim to have influenced in a positive way the educational opportunities for a marginalized group, namely Traveller children. I demonstrate how this improvement at the micro-political level has had repercussions at the macro level in terms of the achievement of social transformation. I draw on my embodied values of social justice and equality to provide the standards of judgement against which to test the validity of my claim to have improved my educational practice as well as the circumstances of my pupils. Finally, I show how, through engagement with more emancipatory pedagogies, I was able to promote a more equitable situation within the educational system for an ethnic minority group. (Sullivan 2005)

The issue now becomes which standards are appropriate for judging the quality of action research accounts, and how are they used in generating evidence. This brings us to the next section.

2   Deciding which kinds of standards are appropriate for judging the quality of practitioners' action research accounts

Because we are offering an account of our own research through this book, we will here set out the standards of judgement we use to judge the quality of the evidence base of our account. We are testing the validity of our own standards of judgement against your critical evaluation, as our reader, as a way of testing the validity of our evidence base. Throughout, and especially in Chapter 8, we set out our evidence base, in terms of how practitioners are contributing to new practices and new theory. Here we are articulating the standards of judgement we are using to test the validity of our claims and their supporting evidence. We are also articulating how we are observing issues of showing the rigorous nature of our research, in relation to criteria such as those outlined by Winter (1989).

We believe that the kinds of standards we are proposing are important. As noted above, we believe that practitioners need to say what is important in their work, and develop their sense of good practice into the kind of standards of judgement that will enable them and others to evaluate their practices in terms of educational good, rather than only excellent performance. While we do not expect the wider community of educational action researchers to accept our values or ideas uncritically, we hope that they will give attention to the business of articulating appropriate kinds of standards, and perhaps use similar standards of judgement in assessing the quality of their own evidence base. We also hope that the wider community of educational researchers will see, from the accounts that practitioners produce, that these kinds of standards are acceptable and provide a strong base for assessing quality and for establishing a living theory approach to action research as a form of research that can be widely accepted in terms of its established validation methods. What we are suggesting here, by proposing that values should act as the grounds for the kinds of standards appropriate for judging practices, is a move away from categories, such as those suggested by Furlong and Oancea (2005), which once again emphasize the need for the demonstration of skills which practitioners are supposed to apply to their practices.

In this section therefore we first set out how we articulate our values as our living critical standards of judgement, and how we analyse them. We then go on to explain how we understand what the significance of our work might be, in terms of developing these kinds of standards of judgement, and showing our understanding of the need to attend to such analyses as a demonstration of epistemological and methodological rigour.

Our values as our living standards of judgement

Our standards of judgement are rooted in a faith in a universal life-affirming energy. Jean understands this energy in theistic terms; Jack understands it in humanistic terms. We do not know the source of this energy, nor do we try to analyse it, but we accept it gladly. Like Bataille (1987: 11) we assent to life up to the point of death. Like Derrida (2003) we accept that faith is irrational. We also respect other people's faith commitments as often different from our own. We do not set out to influence the nature of people's faith commitments, although we do set out to influence the way in which faith is used, such as when it manifests as faith in selfishness and cruelty, but that is not so much a matter of having faith as a manifestation of human interests in using faith.

We analyse the kinds of values we hold, which are relevant to this book, as our ontological, epistemological, methodological and pedagogical values (we hold other kinds of values but do not discuss them here). These values come to act as the explanatory principles and living standards by which we judge our practice, and, because our theories are created from within our practice, they are also the standards by which we judge our theories.

We understand values in much the same way as Raz when he says:

> My use of the term [value] is uninhibitedly inflationary. Any property which (necessarily) makes anything which possesses it good (or bad) at least to a degree is an evaluative property, standing for some value. Somewhat more informatively, though less precisely, we could also say that every property whose presence in an item (action, person, institution, or anything else) can in itself make an action, a choice, or a positive or negative appreciation or preference, intelligible or justified, is an evaluative property. Comfort and convenience are values, and not only freedom and happiness. (2001: 43–4)

And so, we would add, are cruelty and unkindness. Abstract definitions themselves are words, and carry no value in themselves. Value is given to the abstract concept by what we do with it, when we make it come alive. What we do as rational beings is guided by our capacity to make choices. It is our choice whether to act in a way that is deemed life-affirming or destructive of life. There is no getting away from the idea that the meaning we give to our lives is in terms of which values we choose to espouse and make real through our living practices. We create our lives as the manifestation of our choices.

Here then is how we understand (and analyse, for purposes of this text) our values as our standards of judgement.

Our ontological values as our ontological standards of judgement

First we identify our ontological values. These are the foundation values that give direction to our other values. Ontology is a theory of being, and helps us to understand how and why we live our lives as we do. We agree with Bullough and Pinnegar that 'The consideration of one's ontology, of one's being in and toward the world, should be a central feature of any discussion of the value of self-study research' (2004: 319).

Our faith in life-affirming energy is the grounds for our ontological values and commitments to the universe and its inhabitants. Like Kauffman (1995), we understand ourselves as at home in the universe, and as having deep connections with the rest of creation (Ó Mhurchú 1997). Like Bateson (1972) we appreciate that we are connected to all things through invisible ties, with space and boundaries, and like Capra (2003) we understand that these ties are invisible and intangible, but they are no less real. We recognize ourselves as belonging to and as part of an inclusive and relational universe. We understand ourselves and other people as unique, because each one of us is an original creation who has never existed before and never will again (see Arendt's 1958 idea of natality). Each person is born with the capacity to make their original contribution and to engage critically with others, in relation to practices and ideas. We draw on Rayner's (2005) ideas about the nature of those relationships and how they come to be formed (see page 114). We understand our ontological values as the deeply spiritual connections between ourselves and others. These are embodied values, which we make external and explicit through our practices and theories.

We understand the universe, and ourselves and others as part of it, as involved in constantly unfolding processes of creation. We and the universe are not working toward closure, but are part of the growth that is always in a process of self-creation and new evolutionary forms. The nature of these processes is that they are free, self-transforming, relational and inclusive. Our belief in the nature of these processes travels to our belief in the nature of all growth processes, as free, self-transforming, relational and inclusive, and therefore co-creative. This means that we understand our life commitments, including our pedagogical commitments, as encouraging sustainable social and intellectual practices that are free, self-transforming, relational and inclusive. We formalize these understandings as our pedagogical commitments towards encouraging ourselves and others to develop free, self-transforming, relational and inclusive attitudes and practices.

Our ontological values transform into our educational commitments. We commit to the idea of embodied knowledge. Like Polanyi (1958) we understand that all people possess a vast store of tacit knowledge. Like Plato (de Botton 1999) we understand that people are able to hold the one and the many together at the same time, and, in the same way that Chomsky (1986) maintains that all people have infinite capacity for the creation of language, we also believe that people have infinite capacity for the creation of new ways of thinking and acting. Husserl writes about knowledge in the transcendental sphere: 'we have an infinitude of knowledge previous to all deduction, knowledge whose mediated connexions (those of intentional implication) have nothing to do with deduction, and being entirely intuitive prove refractory to every methodologically devised scheme of constructive symbolism' (1931: 12). We draw on this idea to communicate our understanding of people's capacity to turn their embodied knowledge into their living educational theories. This is the nature of our work in professional education. We encourage practitioner researchers to externalize their embodied tacit knowledge as explicit, clearly articulated theories of practice. We recognize that these theories are the intellectual property of their creators, and we insist on the academic freedom of practitioners to claim and retain ownership of their work, as we also do. We value enquiry learning, and we give expression to that value by encouraging others and ourselves constantly to adopt an attitude of enquiry as we ask, 'How do we improve what we are doing?'

Therefore, when we speak of understanding our values as our standards of judgement, we are asking, 'To what extent does the evidence base of our enquiry show that we are achieving those standards?' In other words, we ask, 'To what extent do we show that we are living in the direction of our espoused values?' We engage with these questions in Chapter 7.

We believe that the significance of our ontological values in educational relationships is that we encourage practitioners freely to create their living educational theories of practice. This leads us to articulate our epistemological values, which we transform into our epistemological standards of judgement. Our ontological values, as our embodied tacit knowledge, transform into ontological standards of judgement, and our ontological values transform into epistemological values and standards of judgement, because we now articulate them as having to do with the creation and testing of claims to knowledge. Furthermore, and commensurate with our own commitment to freedom and capacity for original thought and independent choice, we believe that all people can choose which choices to make. This is a deeply moral activity, which involves critical reflection and discernment.

Our epistemological values as our epistemological standards of judgement

The same faith commitments to freedom, co-self-creation, relationship and inclusiveness characterize our epistemological values and standards of judgement, which are to do with the creation and testing of educational theories. They also characterize the nature of the theories, and the processes involved in their creation and testing.

Our epistemological values, which are embedded within and emerge from our ontological values, are to do with the capacity of practitioner researchers (1) to identify and articulate clearly what they are studying; (2) to explain the intellectual and practical processes involved in its study; (3) to generate evidence via those intellectual and practical processes; and (4) to articulate their claims to knowledge in terms of the standards they use to judge the validity of the evidence. We explain these different elements in the following terms. When we speak about identifying and articulating clearly what is being studied, we are speaking about the object of enquiry and the unit of appraisal in our claims to knowledge.

From living theory perspectives, the unit of appraisal is the practitioner's own account of their educational influence in learning as they ask, research and answer questions of the kind, 'How do I improve my practice?' Explaining the intellectual and practical processes involved in enquiry learning means the articulation of what was learned and what was done during the process of the research. Generating evidence means gathering data, defining appropriate standards of judgement, and placing the evidence in the public domain to test its validity in terms of the specifically articulated standards of judgement. Articulating claims to knowledge in terms of the standards used to judge the validity of the evidence means making accounts of practice available to critical others, such as critical friends and validation groups, within a framework of the kind of standards articulated by Habermas (1987) as appropriate to judging the validity of knowledge claims in the attempt to reach intersubjective understandings, which may then be made public as agreed standards of validity (see Chapter 6 for further discussion).

We encourage the practitioner researchers we support to examine, clarify and articulate their own values as their living standards of judgement, which means that they also have to examine, clarify and articulate their logics. We identified in Chapter 2 how the kinds of logics appropriate for the co-creating of living educational theories are living, inclusive and relational in nature, which is a reflection of the ontological grounding of those living logics.

True to our commitments to people's freedom, and their capacity for original thought and critical engagement, we try not to impose these logics on others. True also to our commitments, which we articulated earlier, to exercise our moral capacity for making creative choices and for holding ourselves accountable for those choices, we also examine, clarify and articulate the nature of our own living logics of practice. Like those whose studies we support, we produce our accounts of practice. You are reading one right now. We hope you discern the living nature of the inclusional and relational logics we use in the creation and testing of the claims we make in this account. They are inclusional in the sense that we include both propositional and dialectical forms of theorizing in our accounts, and also in the sense that we include others as we account for our practice. Our logics are also co-creative, in that we include others in the creation and testing of our own theories. We are including you, our reader, in our process of testing our theories. If this book makes sense to you, and you see its relevance for your own practice, as a living practitioner action researcher, we can say that the validity of our claims to have exercised our educational influence in someone's learning is strengthened, through your acknowledgement of our influence. Of course, we will never know, unless you contact us to say this is the case, and you can do this easily through our websites. Nor do we actually need to know, because a claim can be pronounced valid in the author's absence (as, ultimately, was Galileo's). In that case, you will be the co-creators of our theories of practice, and form with us a community of enquiry as we all address the question, 'How do we improve what we are doing?', you through your research, and we through ours, as we enquire together.

Our methodological values as our methodological standards of judgement

We value methodology for the order and discipline that it brings to the processes of enquiry, and to the processes of communicating those enquiries as oral, written and visual narratives. We explain in this book how we have ordered our own enquiries in terms of questions about practice and theory. These take the form:

- What is my concern?
- Why am I concerned?
- What experiences can I describe to show why I am concerned?
- What can I do about it?
- What will I do about it?
- What kind of data will I gather to show the situation as it unfolds?
- How will I explain my educational influences in learning?
- How will I show that any conclusions I come to are reasonably fair and accurate?
- How do I evaluate the evidence-based account of my learning?
- How do I modify my concerns, ideas and practices in the light of my evaluations?

Many practitioner researchers have used these questions as guides to their own thinking as they produce their accounts. The accounts themselves can be seen as provisional answers to the questions. This book takes the same view. The questions are used as the contextualizations of the subject matters within each chapter, and each chapter shows the developmental nature of the enquiry as we engage with our own questions.

However, each of the practitioner researchers whose studies we have supported has gone their own way in deciding how they will adapt this series of questions for themselves. It could also be a matter of confidence. When practitioner researchers are just starting out, the security of a framework can help them organize their ideas in a way that provides reasonable yet flexible guidance and that is aimed at establishing the legitimacy of their claims to knowledge. As researchers progress in their studies, and gain confidence, they take a more adventurous stance and begin to experiment epistemologically and methodologically. We fully support and endorse this, because we believe that each practitioner's account should reflect their own creative capacity for new knowledge and an articulation of new forms of knowing. A glance at the accounts in www.actionresearch.net and www.jeanmcniff.com will reveal that some adhere fairly closely to the set of questions above, such as many of the accounts from the Chinese educators whose studies Moira Laidlaw supports (see http://www.actionresearch.net/moira.shtml), while others depart quite radically from the questions, such as Kathryn Yeaman (1995) in her research into creating educative dialogue in an infant classroom (see http://www.bath.ac.uk/~edsajw/module/kathy.htm). Here are some further examples, with their appropriate urls. All the accounts can be downloaded in full.

Patricia Kelly (2005) 'How do I understand my values of humanity in the classroom? An educational enquiry'. MA educational enquiry, http://www.jackwhitehead.com/monday/pkmaee1.htm.

Victoria Kennedy (2005) 'Why is inclusionality so important to me? Ticking the inclusionality box'. MA educational enquiry, http://www.jackwhitehead.com/monday/vkmaee1.pdf.

Mark Potts (2004) 'How can I improve my practice by communicating more effectively with others in my role as a professional educator?' Masters dissertation, http://www.jackwhitehead.com/monday/mpmadis.pdf.

Catriona Williamson (2005) 'How effective is Mere School at listening to "the pupil's voice"?' MA educational enquiry, http://www.bath.ac.uk/~edsajw/module/cwmaee.pdf.

It should be noted that each of the examples above shows the systematic nature of an educational enquiry. The studies of practitioner researchers usually last several years, from three to eight. One of the reasons for the time involved is that most practitioner researchers undertake their studies on a part-time basis, and finding time to fit in study along with a job can be extremely difficult, and calls for personal and professional discipline, parallel with the discipline required for the presentation of the account. The sustained, systematic nature of practitioners' enquiries is in itself a form of methodological value, which can transform into a living standard of judgement, as when the researcher is able to reveal the unfolding nature of the enquiry and the emergent nature of insights.

We can therefore show how our methodological values transform into our methodological standards of judgement. In asking you and other critical readers to attest to our awareness of the need for methodological rigour in the presentation of our accounts, and in the presentation of the accounts of those whose studies we support, we are claiming that we transform our values and love of discipline, coherence, order and systematic study into our methodological standards of judgement. When we write about rigour in practitioner research, we bear in mind that we are using the six principles defined by Richard Winter (1989), of reflexive critique, dialectical critique, risk, plural structure, multiple resource and theory–practice transformation.

The values we bring to our work, in the nature of our ontological, epistemological and methodological commitments, coalesce in the value we give to our pedagogies. This now brings us to a discussion of how our pedagogical values, which are grounded in our ontological, epistemological and methodological values, can emerge and transform into our pedagogical standards of judgement.

Our pedagogical values as our pedagogical standards of judgement

In our professional work, we place great value on our capacity to let our values inform our pedagogies. Bernstein (2000) uses the word 'pedagogization' to indicate the processes of organizing and communicating knowledge via specific and explicit pedagogies. He says of pedagogy:

> Pedagogy is a sustained process whereby somebody(s) acquires new forms or develops existing forms of conduct, knowledge, practice and criteria from somebody(s) or something deemed to be an appropriate provider and evaluator – appropriate either from the point of view of the acquirer or by some other body(s) or both. (2000: 78)

We have faith in the critical capacity of ourselves, and of those we support, to enact their own processes of discernment, in whether or not they deem our influence appropriate, in Bernstein's use of the word. By 'appropriate' we mean that they will find our influence educational, in the sense that we encourage them to become aware of their own sense of self, and build on that sense with confidence in order to create their own living educational theories.

To encourage this sense of self, we also need to have a deep sense of self, and how we are in relation to those whose studies we are supporting. We understand this sense of self not as a ring-fenced identity, but as in deep relation with those whose company we keep, similar to Raz's insights that we form our identities in relation to our attachments: 'Meaning is invested in the world by our attachments to it: meaning rests primarily in the objects of our attachments, and by association in other things' (2001: 16); and that we understand our practices in terms of our duties to those to whom we are attached, 'Duties and special responsibilities, not rights, are the key to a meaningful life, and are inseparable from it. In denying our duties we deny the meaning of our life. ... Duties are reasons for action' (2001: 21). We develop relationships of attachment with those whose studies we support, and we theorize the form of the attachment in terms of what Buber (1937) called an 'I–thou' relationship, a relationship which, he maintained, emerges through dialogue and attentive silence. We need to clarify how we draw on Buber's ideas.

In the original German, which was Buber's first language, and similar to French and other languages, 'you' can be expressed in two ways: in its polite form 'Sie' and in its familiar form 'Du'. The 'Our Father' prayer in German is spoken in terms of 'Du', and in many German-speaking countries, much is made of the event when two colleagues decide to adopt 'Du' forms rather than 'Sie'.

Buber understood that relationships can take different forms. They can take the form of 'Ich–es' (I–it), 'Ich–Sie' (I–you polite) and 'Ich–Du' (I–thou familiar). 'I–it' is when a person sees another as a thing, an 'it', a reified object. This is reminiscent of the positivist forms we spoke about in Chapter 2. 'I–you' (polite) is when we are in relation with another, but the relationship is polite, cordial, and at a formal distance. 'I–thou' (familiar) is when we develop a relationship that includes the other and sees the other as an extension of self. An encounter that takes the form of an 'I–Thou' relationship is not an absorption of one self by another, or the imposition of one identity on another, but a mutual sharing of identities, as each identity fuses with and merges with the other. This is similar to Bateson's (1979) idea when he explained how, through contemplation of an object, the viewer melds their identity with the identity of the object, in a process that, according to Rayner (2005), sees the dissolving of boundaries into permeable interfaces that constantly and dynamically co-create each other. We recognize the difficulty, however, that the meanings in original texts are often lost in translation, especially with terms like 'Sie' and 'Du' that carry far more than literal meanings. We therefore prefer to keep 'I–thou' for a relationship with a God (in Jean's case but not in Jack's), and 'I–you' for our relationships with others.

Buber also developed the idea of attentive silence. He said that in an encounter it is important to settle into the expectation of a dialogue, as a form of living contemplation, through an attitude of attentiveness, and this could often be accomplished through silence, not a hostile silence, but a silence full of anticipation, a pregnant silence, while we prepare to give the other our full and undivided attention. This contemplative attitude, he said, was the same attitude that we bring to prayer, to contemplation. For us, Jean and Jack, in our work as professional educators, the idea of purposeful contemplation of the other in developing living educational theories may be akin to James B. Macdonald's (1995) idea of theory as a prayerful act, for those with a theistic faith. Macdonald speaks of the need for the teacher to meet their students 'person-to-person, not status-to-person', and speaks of school settings as opportunities where 'the teacher may hold open the world for a child' (1995: 31, 25). We work with adults who work with children and with other adults. We aim to hold doors open for them, via the two-way doors they hold open for us. Our responsibility, as educators, is to understand the nature of our educational relationships such that we influence others also to develop relationships of 'I-you' and attentive silence. Do we succeed? Go back to the description of Mary Roche's lesson (page 70). The second observer, Alberto, commented in his report:

> The teacher had also a very important role, because she had to know how to direct the discussion by asking some questions, because if not, the topic might veer off in different directions and it could have been a disaster. The teacher had also to listen very carefully without speaking for a long time. This is a difficult skill for a teacher to learn because normally a teacher is one who does most of the talking in a classroom. In 'Thinking Time' the teacher must use her power wisely and discreetly so that the children have control of the discussion.

We are not suggesting that Mary did not already have these capacities. As a teacher of considerable experience, she knows the importance of making space for her students to learn, and exercises this knowledge with care. Her thesis work (Roche 2005) demonstrates this abundantly. Yet we also have on record how Mary acknowledges Jean's influence in helping her to articulate explicitly what she is doing on an intuitive level as her living epistemological standards of judgement: 'Your influence has been hugely significant in the development of my ability to think critically' (see above p. 71).

What we are claiming is that, during the process of their scholarly enquiries, we draw our research colleagues' attention to the fact that their understanding of practice can become their unit of appraisal, and also their understanding of the need to articulate their standards of judgement to test the validity of their claims to knowledge and their own living educational theories.

In more general terms we are claiming that we show how we transform pedagogical values of close relationship and attentive listening, while we encourage our own and the other's learning, into pedagogical standards of judgement. We judge our pedagogical practices in terms of the extent to which we fulfil our pedagogical values, and we articulate how our values emerge and transform over time into our living standards of judgement.

The significance of our learning

We believe that the significance of our learning has implications for possible future developments in educational action research and theory. We are pointing specifically to the need for clearly articulated standards of judgement. We understand those standards of judgement as grounded in and emerging from the values we hold at a tacit level. Because these values and standards are part of our lives as real living people, those same values and standards also are living, as they emerge through the processes of our living enquiries. Hence our emphasis on expressing and communicating the meanings of living critical standards of judgement in our educational theorizing (see http://jackwhitehead. com/monday/jwbera05pap.htm). We are saying that we judge our own lives in education in terms of the quality of relationship we enjoy with others, as manifestations of what we hold as valuable and good.

We also need to make the point that we are taking care to demonstrate the rigorous nature of our work, by attending to these issues of articulating and analysing the criteria and standards that we use to make judgements on our work. We believe that by doing this we are meeting the criteria for rigour as articulated by Richard Winter (1989), that is, the principles of reflexivity, dialectical critique, collaborative resource, risk, plural structure and theory–practice transformation in the conduct of action research. The demonstration of such epistemological and methodological rigour is recognized in the specification of the 2008 criteria (Research Assessment Exercise 2005) for the best quality scholarship that demonstrates originality, significance and rigour.

In Chapter 7 we explore further the idea of the nature of relationships between people's practices in relation to practice and to theory as dynamic, free-flow and co-creative. For now we conclude by saying that, having identified and articulated the living standards by which we judge our practice-based theories and the processes that generate them, we have a basis from which to test the validity of the evidence base of our own living educational theories, as expressed in this book and elsewhere, and we do that in Chapter 9.

Two further issues now arise. It is all very well to identify one's own standards of judgement, but it has to be remembered that accounts are also going to be judged by another audience who possibly hold their own, and different, standards. In the case of submitting your work for validation, especially in the form of university accreditation, how do you negotiate to have your standards of judgement taken seriously within a forum that already has its own established criteria and standards of judgement, some of which may be different from yours? These are issues not only of showing the validity of your work, but also of establishing its legitimacy.

Furthermore, in the process of reaching agreement about the validity of standards of judgement, it is essential also to address issues of the validity of the validation processes themselves, which brings us into the realm of establishing the ethical validity of decision-making processes. We address these issues now in Chapter 6.

SUMMARY

In this chapter we have spoken about the need to generate quality evidence in support of a claim to knowledge. We have outlined some of the practicalities of generating evidence, explaining that evidence can be distinguished from data by showing how it stands in relation to identified criteria and standards of judgement. We then went on to set out the kinds of standards of judgement we consider appropriate for producing evidence in action research, and we suggested this in terms of the transformation of ontological values into living critical standards of judgement. Focusing on our own ontological, epistemological, methodological and pedagogical values, we explained how we transform these into living critical ontological, epistemological, methodological and pedagogical standards of judgement. By doing this, we explained how we are observing the epistemological and methodological rigour of showing how we are attending to matters of identifying appropriate criteria and standards of judgement in making evidence-based claims to knowledge.

PART 3

Establishing Validity and Legitimacy

This part deals with issues of establishing the validity and legitimacy of the research. *It contains the following chapters*:

6 **Validity, legitimacy and moral authority**
   How do we show that any conclusions we come to are reasonably fair and accurate?

7 **The potential significance of our research**
   How do we show the potential significance of our research?

We explain throughout how we identify our values as the living critical standards that enable us to make judgements on the validity of our research.

6 Validity, legitimacy and moral authority

How do we show that any conclusions we come to are reasonably fair and accurate?

Because we authors are researchers, we constantly aim to develop new under-standings about ideas and practices. Because we are action researchers, our new ideas are frequently developed from within our practices, and tested against and incorporated into new practices. At this point in our research, we are asking questions about how, in the process of testing our evidence as the grounds for our provisional claims to knowledge, we can show that any conclusions we come to are reasonably fair and accurate. This chapter contains some of those new ideas, about social and ethical validity, which we have developed through studying our own involvement in validation and legitimation processes.

The chapter is about three things: (1) examining the concepts of validity and legitimacy; (2) issues of social validity, which involves ideas about what it takes to establish the validity and legitimacy of claims to knowledge, which is a social process; (3) issues of ethical validity, which involves ideas about what it takes to establish the validity and legitimacy of those very social processes that aim to make judgements about the validity and legitimacy of truth claims, which is a moral process.

The chapter is organized as three sections that address these issues:

1 Validity and legitimacy
2 Social validity: criteria and standards of judgement for establishing the validity and legitimacy of your research
3 Ethical validity: criteria and standards of judgement for transforming social criteria into moral standards of judgement

1 Validity and legitimacy

Validity and legitimacy are different but interrelated concepts. Validity is about establishing the truth value, or trustworthiness, of a claim to knowledge. Legitimacy is about establishing the authority of the person who is making the claim to knowledge, which also involves interrogating the authority of the regime of truth that can influence what is permitted to count as knowledge within a particular social context.

To show the difference between the concepts of validity and legitimacy, let's take the story of Galileo. Galileo claimed that the earth went round the sun. This was contrary to the established orthodoxy of the time, which was that the sun went round the earth. Galileo had tested his ideas rigorously, and had a substantial evidence base in which to ground his claim, so he was satisfied about the evidence-based validity of his claim. However, when he was called to account for his theories by the officers of the Church, and wanted to explain his position, which amounted to testing his theory against public critique, he was shown instruments of torture, and so forced to withdraw his claims. Similar stories can be found everywhere in the literature and in historical accounts. Bernard Shaw has his St Joan say that she will confess to anything to avoid torture, and the archives of Amnesty International are full of stories about how confessions are extracted under duress from political prisoners.

Two processes are going on here. The first is to do with establishing validity, which is about explaining why a claim to knowledge should be taken seriously. The second is about establishing legitimacy, by showing why the claim should be accepted in the public domain, and why a researcher should be listened to.

Establishing validity

Establishing validity is to do with showing the authenticity of the evidence base, explaining the standards of judgement used, and demonstrating the reasonableness of the claim. These issues were introduced in Chapter 5. Establishing validity is a rational exercise, that is, it is grounded in reason and not in opinion or prejudice and seeks to reduce bias and prejudice. Therefore, and pushing this a little further, establishing the validity of a claim is also about establishing the authority of the scholarship that leads to the claim. Because claims are always someone's claims, it becomes a case of establishing the authority of the researcher. Practitioners who make claims which are grounded in their practice are therefore automatically also making claims about the validity of their scholarship, and about their own authority as practitioner researchers. If you say, 'I know that my situation has improved', you are claiming two things. First you are implicitly saying, 'I am claiming that I am justified in saying that my situation has improved, because here is my authenticated evidence to show that this is the case.' Second you are implicitly saying, 'I am claiming that I am authorized to make the claim that my situation has improved, because I can show how I ground my case in the authority of my own scholarship.' In submitting your case, you are therefore appealing to others to agree that your claim is justified, and that your wish for your own authority to be approved is also justified.

This moves us into the second process, which is to do with establishing legitimacy.

Establishing legitimacy

Establishing legitimacy is about getting other people to accept the validity of your claim, but this is often to do more with power than rationality. Galileo was intimidated by those in power, and forced to recant his beliefs. Many people find themselves in similar situations. How to deal with them is often a matter of strategic or principled choice.

Some choose to confront the issues directly. Courageous individuals throughout history have refused to submit to the illegitimate use of power. Socrates drank the hemlock. Jesus went to the cross. Steve Biko went to the law, and then on to his death. The law itself approved the use of a specific kind of power. These individuals, and many others, refused to be silenced, and died for their convictions. Other people choose to use other strategies, such as what Barry MacDonald (1987) calls 'creative compliance', that is, recognizing the force of the prevailing wind and bending with it in order to work and transform a situation from within.

Dealing with power-constituted situations also involves establishing the validity of the standards of judgement that are deemed appropriate for the context. In Galileo's case, the standards that Galileo used to demonstrate the validity of his case were those of rational scientific enquiry. The standards used by his inquisitors to demolish his case and refuse it legitimacy were those of irrational prejudice, grounded in a desire for self-interested domination and dogmatic belief about the rightness of the power relations that upheld without question a particular interpretation of a religious faith.

The problematic of power-constituted contexts

Such practices are commonplace today. Power can be used to silence those who claim the authority of their own knowledge. This can be seen in many ways. Take racial or gender discrimination. Discourses are deliberately initiated and perpetuated to persuade people whose skin colour is other than white that whiteness is the norm, so they as non-white people are positioned as less than normal. Similarly, women in many cultures are persuaded to believe that male is the norm, so they as women should accept their positioning as second-class non-males.

Sometimes these discourses manifest in conversations like this:

A: This is a good film.
B: No it isn't.
A: Why not?
B: Don't ask. Just listen.

or

A: I want to be a dancer.
B: You can't.
A: Why not?
B: It's not a good profession for a boy. Besides, you can't dance.

If you are a practitioner researcher, you may even have been involved in a conversation like this:

A: My research qualifies for accreditation.
B: You must be joking.
A: No, I am serious. Have a look at my report.
B: Yes, but this isn't serious research. Practitioners can't do research. They tell good stories though.

Conversations like these are grounded in an asymmetrical relationship of power, where speaker B speaks from a dominating position of power and also from a position of seeming rationality. While speaker B may have good reasons for believing what they do, they are not articulating their reasons, or showing how their opinion is justified. Further, they are imposing their ideas in an autocratic manner, without justifying the process either for what they hold as valuable or not, or for why they feel they are authorized to make such statements.

Conversations like this take place all the time, and often manifest as bullying and oppression. They happen in contexts of scholarship too. Critics critique work, often without showing that they are competent to make appropriate judgements. The reasons for the incompetence can range from lack of knowledge, to favouring their own positioning, to poor quality scholarship on their own part. Whatever the reason, when a critic engages in statements of the kind, 'You are wrong because I say so', without giving justification for their own stance, they can be seen as violating the conditions of democratic evaluation.

This has serious implications for the legitimacy of practitioner action researchers. They are still positioned as a minority group, although they possibly outnumber higher education researchers, in the same way as, in recent South Africa, people from then officially designated black, Indian and coloured communities outnumbered those of the white community (this remains the case), yet were still positioned as minority groupings. Whites were deemed superior, and white forms of discourses and logics came to be internalized by non-white communities, and so became the accepted cultural norm. Indigenous knowledge was colonized and subjugated. The same principles underpin research discourses. The social sciences continue to inform the future of educational research, colonizing and subjugating the indigenous knowledge of practitioners. One of the best explications of this situation is in Schön (1995). Schön spoke of the academic high ground, occupied by higher education personnel, whose work was to generate theory, which could be passed on to and applied by practitioners, in workplaces and classrooms. The knowledge generated by those practitioners was accepted as practical knowledge, but was not worthy to be called theory. This situation continues in some contexts. When practitioners choose to challenge the situation by showing that their accounts should be treated as legitimate scholarship, they are told, 'No, it is not.' It is not a question of informed debate or scholarly enquiry. It is a case of the exercise of prejudicial power. Might is right.

What then does it take for you to establish the validity and legitimacy of your own research? How do you negotiate existing contexts, which prioritize their own standards, so that you are listened to and taken seriously? How do you negotiate legitimation processes, as well as validation processes? Do guidelines or frameworks exist which you can draw on in validation and legitimation processes, which are generally accepted by other practitioners as the kind of frameworks they can use as they produce their accounts of practice, and by the wider research community as the kinds of frameworks they also use to make judgements about the validity of the accounts? How do you show the validity and legitimacy of your research, and demonstrate the validity of your authority as a practitioner action researcher?

This is serious business, because it is not sufficient for you only to make your claim, which could be regarded as your opinion, or produce authenticated evidence, which could be construed as you rigging the data to suit your claim. You have to arrange also for your claims to knowledge, and your claims to the validity of your evidence base, to be scrutinized by external, sympathetic but reasonably impartial viewers, who you encourage to ask critical questions about the data, authentication procedures and evidence generating processes.

But this raises a new set of questions. The social processes of making judgements involve both claimants and judges. Raz (2003) rightly points out that judges are humans too, subject to their own biases. In democratic evaluation, which is the context of examining action research claims to knowledge, what kind of procedures need to be agreed so that practitioners present their work in a way that shows its methodological rigour and epistemological integrity, and so that judges are led to make judgements on the quality of the work in a way that does it justice on its own terms? In practical terms, what do judges expect of you as you make your case, and what do you expect of them, to ensure that you get a fair hearing? Is this process of presenting a case and making judgements a dialogue of equals or a power-constituted one-sided process?

The next section deals with these issues.

2 Social validity: criteria and standards of judgement for establishing the validity and legitimacy of your research

Any process of democratic evaluation has to be a two-way street, which may be used by practitioners and judges alike. To be an active participant means agreeing to the rules of the road and not blocking progress by driving on the wrong side or parking where you please. It means that you have a responsibility to others to act according to democratically negotiated rules, which themselves are grounded in a shared commitment to the transformative potentials of communicative action (Habermas 1987). The questions therefore arise, what kind of rules are appropriate, how do they come to be agreed, and how are they applied?

The scholar whose ideas have been especially influential in this regard is Jürgen Habermas.

Habermas's criteria of social validity

Throughout his work, and especially in his two volumes of *The Theory of Communicative Action* (1987), Habermas explains the evolving nature of normative judgements that are embedded in what counts as moral action in particular cultures that can serve to reproduce the existing social order. To appreciate these ideas fully means reflecting on the idea of normative judgements and how they can reproduce the existing social order.

The idea of 'normative' is that certain rules and practices come to be accepted as given. It is accepted without question in many cultures that women should take their husbands' names on marriage, and that straight couples should marry while homosexual couples should not. It is not considered necessary to stop and examine the underpinning assumptions that guide such practices, or to question where these rules came from or whether they are useful or outdated or even wrong; we are expected to accept things as the way they are and the way they should be. Normative values are held as the right, unquestioned values, and the cultural practices that the values inform are held as unequivocally correct. Hence racist cultures assume that one race is superior to another. Similarly there is a tendency in cultures with a dominant religious tradition to assume that members of the dominant affiliation get the best jobs and housing while members of the other affiliations get what is left. These attitudes are communicated through the discourses as basic truths and through social institutions as structurally integrated norms. In many parts of the world, fundamentalist churches preach a gospel of hatred against non-whites and non-Christians, while in other parts of the world, equally fundamentalist attitudes transform into bombings and racist discourses that require the death of all non-Muslims. Such attitudes do no service at all to the values of the religions whose interests the fundamentalist groups are allegedly supporting, and raise issues of how religion itself has become a secular mobilization of cultural institutions in the interests of those already in power. Many theorists, including Bourdieu and Passeron (1977) and Russell (1932), explain how, by unquestioningly accepting such attitudes and practices as normal, practitioners often contribute, albeit unwittingly, to reproducing the existing social order and so perpetuate the normative assumptions of the culture.

According to Habermas, the main way to transform entrenched normative social orders is to interrupt and transform public discourses. Doing this means establishing some basic principles for achieving intersubjective agreement. Here is what he has to say:

> I shall develop the thesis that anyone acting communicatively must, in performing any speech action, raise universal validity claims and suppose that they can be vindicated (or redeemed). Insofar as he [*sic*] wants to participate in a process of reaching understanding, he cannot avoid raising the following – and indeed precisely the following – validity claims ...
>
> The speaker must choose a comprehensible expression so that speaker and hearer can understand one another. The speaker must have the intention of communicating a true proposition (or a propositional content, the existential presuppositions of which are satisfied) so that the hearer can share the knowledge of the speaker. The speaker must want to express his intentions truthfully so that the hearer can believe the utterance of the speaker (can trust him). Finally, the speaker must choose an utterance that is right so that the hearer can accept the utterance and speaker and hearer can agree with one another in the utterance with respect to a recognized normative background. Moreover, communicative action can continue undisturbed only as long as participants suppose that the validity claims they reciprocally raise are justified. (1987: 2–3)

This has serious implications for processes of democratic evaluation, such as used in establishing the validity and legitimacy of claims to knowledge. It means that all participants, practitioners and judges alike, must speak in ways that are:

- comprehensible, in that a form of language is used that is commonly understood by all;
- truthful, in that all recognize these as true accounts and not fabrications;
- sincere, so that all parties can trust what the other says;
- appropriate for the context, while recognizing the unspoken cultural norms in which their discourses are embedded.

These criteria are criteria of social validity, that is, demonstrating how participants may act towards one another in terms of the norms which they wish to inform the evolution of their cultures.

So how do these criteria of social validity transform into standards of judgement that are appropriate for presenting and judging practitioner action researchers' claims to knowledge? What kinds of rules need to be accepted, especially in terms of the responsibilities of practitioner action researchers and their judges? The next sections set out what these might be.

The responsibility of practitioners in establishing the validity of knowledge claims

In practitioner action research, two processes are generally accepted as forums for evaluation and validation: personal validation, which usually takes the form of self-evaluation; and social validation, which usually takes the form of meetings with critical friends and meetings of validation groups. In institutional contexts, social validation can turn into institutional validation.

Personal validation

The point of departure in any process of public validation is your own personal conviction of the validity of your own interpretations and explanations. In this case, you probably rely on your own internal processes of critical reflection to validate your beliefs. Polanyi (1958) emphasizes the point that we can take a decision to understand the world from our own point of view as individuals claiming originality and exercising our judgement with universal intent. Developing confidence, without arrogance, about the validity of one's own perspective takes some courage and determination and a sense of professional identity, but it needs to be done if you are to persuade others that they should take you and your claims seriously.

Social validation

Social validation usually takes the form of meetings with critical friends and validation groups. The responsibility of a critical friend is to be both a friend and a critic. As a friend, you are supportive and available to listen to the practitioner's account of their research. As a critic, your work is to offer thoughtful responses to the account, raising points that perhaps the practitioner has not thought about. However, while your work is to offer responses, your work is not to be their counsellor, which means that you and the practitioner maintain a good professional working relationship for the duration of the research project.

The task of a validation group is to meet with the practitioner at regular agreed intervals, and review progress so far. At such meetings, the practitioner would tell the story of their research, produce evidence that they have generated in relation to their identified standards of judgement, and make what they see as their claim to knowledge so far. The responsibilities of members of a validation group are to listen carefully, to assess the quality of the claim to knowledge in relation to the evidence produced and the clarity and acceptability of the standards of judgement, and to agree or disagree that the work demonstrates sufficient merit to go forward to the next stages.

A key point here is whether what is claimed as evidence actually is evidence, and not data or illustration. Illustration is where we produce data to show an event or an idea. In the research account contained in this book, and to illustrate the claim 'Our values were being denied', we authors produced examples in Chapter 3 of those values being denied. Producing evidence however means articulating criteria and standards of judgement to show why the evidence should be regarded as evidence and not just illustration. We articulate our standards of judgement throughout, and especially in Chapter 5, so that we can show how the stories transform from illustration to evidence.

Institutional validation

We said that when processes of social validation are carried out from within an institutional context, they can turn into institutional validation, which is important for legitimation processes. It is especially important for the legitimation of practitioners' action research by the academy, because the academy is still seen as the highest legitimating body for what counts as scholarship. This is now happening. Practitioners are still required to show that they fulfil the criteria, as specified by the academy, but now enjoy a certain amount of liberty in setting their own criteria by which they wish their work to be judged. An important precedent was established by Mary Hartog, who submitted her doctoral thesis to the University of Bath in 2004.

The university gives the following criteria to examiners to guide them in the assessment process.

Requirements for the Degree of Doctor of Philosophy

Thesis

1 The thesis must address a clearly defined subject or field and must form a distinct contribution to the knowledge of that subject or field.
2 The thesis must consist of the candidate's own account of his/her own research and must show clearly the respects in which this work advances study of the subject.
3 The thesis must show evidence of originality and independent critical power, through the discovery of new facts or methods, or through the development and application of new critical insights.
4 The thesis in all or in part should contain material that, in the opinion of the examiners, is worthy of publication.
5 Work done in collaboration with fellow research workers (including the candidate's own supervisor) may be included as part of the thesis, provided that the candidate indicates clearly the extent of his/her personal contribution to the results reported.
6 Work already published, including that jointly published with others, may be included only if it forms an integral part of the evidence or arguments of the thesis and makes a necessary contribution to the main argument of the thesis.

(Guidelines for External Examiners for the Degrees of Master of Philosophy and Doctor of Philosophy, University of Bath, revised August 2003)

Mary opted also to put forward her own criteria, as follows:

If this PhD is differentiated or distinguished as a research process, it is because its methodology is underpinned by the values I as a researcher bring to my practice. It is with this in mind that I ask you to bring your eye as examiners to bear on the following questions, asking yourself as you read this thesis whether these questions are addressed sufficiently for you to say 'yes, these standards of judgment have been met'.

- Are the values of my practice clearly articulated and is there evidence of a commitment toward living them in my practice?
- Does my inquiry account lead you to recognise how my understanding and practice has changed over time?
- Is the evidence provided of life-affirming action in my teaching and learning relationships?
- Does this thesis evidence an ethic of care in the teaching and learning relationship?
- Are you satisfied that I as researcher have shown commitment to a continuous process of practice improvement?
- Does this thesis show originality of mind and critical thinking?

Your judgment may be supported by applying the social standards of Habermas's 'truth claims':

- Is this account comprehensible?
- Does it represent a truthful and sincere account?
- Is it appropriate – has it been crafted with due professional and ethical consideration? (Hartog 2004)

By taking this action, Mary shows how she respects the established authority of the university, while also exercising her own claim to authority in articulating the standards of judgement as the means by which she wishes her claims to educational scholarship to be assessed and acknowledged. Her thesis was in fact judged in terms of both sets of criteria, and she was awarded her doctoral degree without hesitation.

However, this process works only if judges themselves are prepared to abide by the agreed rules of the game. What can persuade them to agree in the first place, and to continue to act appropriately? How to arrive at a place where the criteria of social validity themselves come to be agreed as the living standards of judgement that judges, as well as practitioners, can use to judge the quality of action research accounts? For this, judges need to consider their own responsibilities as participants in the discourse.

The responsibility of judges in assessing the validity of knowledge claims

Meetings with critical friends and validation groups are conducted in the spirit of democratic evaluation. This means that those positioned as critics and judges, that is, those whose responsibility it is to say that the work is valid, or to offer critical feedback, have to agree to abide by the same rules as those who are presenting the work. If they do not agree to do so, then the evaluation becomes non-democratic, because then not everyone has equal status or an equal say. Therefore, when they make judgements on issues of validity, they also need to show that their judgements rest on the same kinds of agreed criteria such as comprehensibility, truthfulness and sincerity, and appropriateness. This is imperative, because it needs to be remembered that judges are human too, and they may have different opinions about the validity and the rightness of the claim because they may hold different views about what is valid and legitimate. At a simplistic level, one person could say, 'I agree that you have shown that you have managed to encourage a culture of enquiry because your video recording shows everyone is talking', while another may say, 'I don't see this as a culture of enquiry at all but as an unruly class.'

Achieving this agreement to agree to the rules of the game in a context of validating a practitioner action researcher's claim to knowledge means that all need to agree their standards of judgement, or at least hold themselves open to this agreement. These standards of judgement are grounded as values in the previously defined social criteria, and the transformation of those criteria into standards of judgement. The criterion of comprehensibility values clear articulation and explication; truthfulness values telling the truth and avoiding deceit; sincerity means telling things as they are, without falsehood or embellishment; and appropriateness means showing an awareness of the normative context of the encounter. Although the values exist in abstract form, such as 'comprehensibility', 'sincerity', 'truthfulness' and 'appropriateness', they manifest themselves in living, meaningful ways (Raz 2001: 8) when presenters and judges speak and act comprehensibly, sincerely, truthfully and appropriately. The values come to stand as the living standards of judgement, which both presenters and judges agree to abide by, and use to make judgements about their own conduct within the encounter.

When the criteria in question leave behind their abstract status and take on living form, they also transform themselves from social criteria into ethical criteria. By ethical criteria we mean the criteria by which the moral value of the encounter can be judged. When the encounter can be shown to have realized the social values agreed by all participants, participants can claim that they have acted morally in relation to one another, that is, they can claim moral authority for their practices.

This becomes the focus of the next section.

3   Ethical validity: criteria and standards of judgement for transforming social criteria into moral standards of judgement

This section is about how processes of making judgements themselves need to be subjected to critical reflection. Two steps are involved. First, participants need to show how they can come to realize in practice the kinds of criteria that Habermas spoke about. Second, they need to make it their active responsibility to identify the standards of judgement they use to check whether or not they are doing so. In this way, the criteria themselves begin to emerge as participants' living ontological and epistemological standards as they make judgements on the quality of their practices as democratically informed participants whose aim is to engage in communicative action in the public interest.

To explain these ideas, here is another story. The story involves Jean, so at this point Jean assumes her 'I' voice.

While writing this book in draft, I was invited to be a presenter at a research school in South Africa. I had visited South Africa on two previous occasions, and had at that time begun probably the most painful but exciting learning journey of my life. I had learned about the need to interrogate my own whiteness. I appreciated that I was at the beginning of this task, and had a long and probably disturbing path ahead. I shall say more about this shortly.

At the same time as I received the invitation, I was contributing to an e-seminar. Jack convened the British Educational Research Association Practitioner Research Special Interest Group e-seminar of 2005, and he had invited all members of the group to post their brief position papers, outlining how they were articulating the standards of judgement they used to judge the quality of their own ongoing action enquiries. I sent in my paper, explaining also that I was off to South Africa, and was looking forward to connecting with colleagues at the Nelson Mandela Metropolitan University, in our small project 'Interrogating our Colour'. From another member of the SIG community, I received a response that challenged me even further to interrogate my whiteness, on the grounds that, while I was clearly demonstrating support for democratic ways of working, I was still not actively getting to grips with how my whiteness represented and also itself constituted an imperialistic stance. From his perspective, I was moving towards fulfilling my own rhetoric about dismantling colonialism, but I was not yet living it out. I found the episode profoundly disturbing, and I went off to South Africa in a troubled frame of mind. The trouble was further intensified by the fact that I could not understand why I was troubled. I had at the back of my mind the idea that my critical colleague was actually right in his assessment of my state of transformation, and I was probably resisting his rightness, but I could not identify the reasons why I was resisting it. I decided that I had to do something about this, to try to re-establish my ontological security and get back onto stable ground.

My first action was to talk with people and ask their help in understanding what was going on. Colleagues of all colours were only too glad to help. I explained sincerely my view that I regard any human encounter as a meeting of persons, at an ontological level. When I meet a person I meet them, not their hairstyle or their clothes or their colour. My colleagues responded kindly, pointing out that this may be my genuine ontological standpoint, but, by virtue of the fact that we all live in socio-economic historically constituted situations, as soon as we open our mouths to say, 'Hello', we are in a context of using the norms of whiteness. These are not necessarily indigenous norms. They are the norms of the historical colonizer. The language we use is English, which is the language of the colonizer. English has its own epistemological structures. We speak a language of 'you and I', which is a European construct, informed by the binary divides of propositional logics. Some African epistemologies work in terms of 'you-I-we', a transformation of the African concept *ubuntu*, which is a view of humanistic living together.

I came to realize, with little intellectual but major emotional difficulty, that I had not interrogated my own whiteness. Having started this journey I am committed to continuing it. Any process of turning the lens back onto oneself is perhaps painful, but it is also probably a necessary condition for coming to understand the other's point of view from their colonized positioning as a historically and socio-politically constituted subject. My aim from now on is to use my own learning to influence the learning of others about how they also need to understand how and why they are positioned as historically and socio-politically constituted subjects, and use their knowledge and inherent capacity for the exercise of their originality of mind and critical engagement to change their situations.

However, yet another anomaly presented itself. I already understood the underlying principles involved in processes that position people as historically and socio-politically constituted subjects. I had learned both through my study of feminist literatures, and from practical experience, how as a woman I had been 'othered' by people who had not turned the lens on their own capacity critically to examine their own prejudices around how women are perceived. Here is a brief example from Robbins, who offers a quotation from Roberts to explain how women are 'othered'.

> W is certainly for Woman and Witch. She picked up a nineteenth-century reprint of an old herbal in a bookshop once ... She cradled it between her hands, and then opened it, leafing idly through the index. The male author's entries for W rivet her: warts; weevils; white, women's whites, how to control; witches, how to guard against; wolfbane; womb: women's weeping therefrom; women in childbed; women's complaints, how to soothe; women's courses, how to stop, how to bring on; women's diseases; women's longings; women's pains; words in the ears. When she turns the leaves of the index back to M, she finds no corresponding entry for Man. (Roberts 1983, cited in Robbins 2000: 1)

I knew this. I knew how people used 'othering' categories in order to position themselves as the inviolable norm. I had known it for a long time. Why, then, did I not make the connection with issues of race and colour? Why had I not seen the same principles underpinning issues of race and colour? Had I been blinded by my whiteness? Could it be that the category of gender meant a lot to me, because I had been othered in terms of my gender, but the category of race had not meant anything because I had never been othered in terms of my colour? Was this the meaning of racism, which I had always combated intellectually but never stopped to consider ontologically? Could I be racist by negligence?

Perhaps, perhaps. Yet, if I was, I am no longer so. I say I am no longer so because I have learned from the work of Memmi (1974) the difficult idea that colonizer and colonized are mutually reciprocal participants in a larger normative system, in this case, the system of colonization. Neither party questions the system that contextualizes and dictates the parameters and practices of their lives. This is how I was positioned. I challenged racism at an intellectual level, yet never stopped to think about how I was inevitably part of an overarching racist system, and, because I willingly bought into the system, I inevitably positioned myself as perpetuating both it and my part in it.

Now I question. I have understood for a long time that social systems are neither inviolable nor stable. Transform participants' attitudes, and you can transform the system. I have made myself critically aware. I have become acutely aware and discerning in my social and mental life. I now try to problematize everything I had previously seen as unproblematic, including how I define my identity in relation to others who may define their, and my, identity in ways different from my own.

I believe the kinds of experiences and learnings I am describing here could be included in what counts as ethical validity, an agreement by all participants that certain conducts may be seen as ethical, in terms of what ought to be done. Kant suggested that the way to ethical conduct is to do unto others as you wish they would do unto you, but achieving Kant's theoretical principle has to involve a form of real-life practical critical reflection that is rooted in the personal experience of how being the recipient of discrimination enables one to understand oneself also as a perpetrator. When Eichmann said (in Arendt 1994) he was not involved in the executions but only made sure that the trains ran on time, he was profoundly mistaken. All who are involved in the discourses are also potentially complicit in discriminatory practices. Even to speak in the terms of othering is to engage in processes of othering. Here I recognize myself as a living contradiction. I have to engage with the issues, such as othering, at the level of critical analysis, in order to transform them into a situation that is a realization of my own commitments to recognizing each person as unique in their individuality, and who is ready to share their uniqueness with unique others (see Kristeva 2002, cited on page 52 of this book), and work through and beyond the discourses of othering to discourses of shared uniqueness.

What has this to do with educational action research? Everything, I believe. The same colonizing principles permeate the field. Throughout the book we have explained how practitioners' work has been delegitimized by the colonizing impulses of the establishment of orthodox educational researchers. Colonization is premised on the desire to oppress and dominate (Young 1990), usually in the interests of established elites. In this case the Marxian concept that colonization is largely to do with economic wellbeing is also relevant. By subjugating dissenting voices, and reinforcing their own positions as knowers and theory generators, research elites ensure that any money available comes to them, and does not go to 'ordinary' practitioners.

How then to ensure that the processes of validating and legitimating practitioners' knowledge claims themselves demonstrate a postcolonial critical awareness, an awareness of the critical capacity of all to interrogate their own positioning within the encounter and to understand their encounter as conducted within a historical and socio-political context in which certain forms of educational research are seen as superior to others? How to make judgements about the ethical validity of our own decision-making processes? If we say we are engaging in democratic processes, how do we ensure that we are not making decisions that are rooted in the uncritical stance of identifying oneself, albeit unconsciously, as a norm, as a colonizer, while not appreciating how the positioning of self as a colonizing norm automatically positions the other as a non-normal subject? How to appreciate that a social or discursive action is never innocent, but is always located within a historical, social and political context, which itself is the product of non-innocent normative social and discursive practices?

Establishing the moral validity of democratic decision-making processes

We, Jack and Jean, return to our 'we' form.

We have maintained throughout that to stay consistent with the idea that all participants should live in the direction of their democratic and egalitarian values in processes of validating and legitimizing claims to knowledge, all need to interrogate their own perceptions of how they are positioned in historical and socio-politically constituted situations. This is a first step, as noted earlier. A second step is then to articulate their ontological values, so that the status of the values transforms from ontological to epistemological. This implies that concepts such as Habermas's criteria of social validity (that a person's account is comprehensible, truthful, sincere and appropriate), which can be understood as grounded in ontological values such as freedom, respect and valuing the other, need to emerge as the epistemological standards whereby participants make judgements about their social practices. This element of critical self-reflection and critical self-interrogation transforms the process of establishing social validity into a process of establishing ethical validity. From this perspective, making judgements in a democratically constituted encounter is a profoundly moral undertaking, a realization of an ethical impulse as a moral form of living.

We believe that this is a most important area for future scholarship, for it implies not only agreeing to the standards of judgement of social validity, but finding appropriate standards of judgement whereby people are prepared to arrive at agreed standards of judgement in the first place. Alasdair MacIntyre hinted at this when he spoke about the rival claims to truth of contending traditions of enquiry:

> The rival claims to truth of contending traditions of enquiry depend for their vindication upon the adequacy and explanatory power of the histories which the resources of each of those traditions in conflict enable their adherents to write. (1988: 403)

If each tradition has validity in its own right, and some are in contention with others, not as rights and wrongs, but as competing rights, how do the members of those traditions manage to suspend their judgements about their own 'rightness' and enter the other's house, albeit temporarily, as a guest who is aware of their provisional status, not as an invader who wishes to take over the territory?

In this area, the research community can learn much from the procedures of the Truth and Reconciliation Commission in South Africa, which takes as some of its core organizing principles the values of integrity, forgiveness and commitment to transformation. Throughout, the commitment to truth requires a determined engagement with what has been done in the past, which demands the openness of all to engage with their own historically and socio-politically constituted identities as participants in egregious forms of social practices. The commitment to forgiveness is grounded in a capacity to love, to be prepared to see the other as a person rather than an object, and to recognize that forgiveness is possible only when one forgives oneself as much as the other, so that new identities may emerge. A sense of a valued self is a core condition for a sense of a valued other. The commitment to transformation enables participants to plan imaginatively for new forms of social orders that are grounded in those same values of truth and reconciliation, recognizing and incorporating the past within the present, as the grounds for a new future.

For us authors, these principles need to be lived in the evolution of social formations that carry hope for the future of humanity in their judgements about what constitutes a good social order. The standards of judgement need to be lived in a realization of the values of truth, in understanding the normative contexts of practice; of forgiveness, in a readiness to extend understanding from one valued self to another; and of commitment to transformative communicative action, to transform the normative conditions of current social formations into new, compassionate and equitable social formations. To establish their own moral authority, social formations, including the social formations whose duties involve making judgements, need to be grounded in a view of communities of valued singularities, each of whom recognizes the other as of equal status and value, and to accept these values as their regulating and binding principles. Nothing less will do.

So, how do we show that we are fulfilling our own rhetoric? We do so in the following ways. We try to maintain a caring and respectful attitude in our personal and professional relationships. We aim to show our respect for those whose opinions we do not share, while explaining carefully our points of disagreement. We demonstrate care throughout our pedagogical relationships while demanding the kind of rigorous discipline we know is required in the submission of scholarly reports. In our writing we try to maintain a balance, and we evaluate our work consistently, as demonstrated in Chapter 9. We are however human, which means that we do not always achieve our own high principles of conduct, but we try, and we are prepared to make our work open to the critical scrutiny of others, and modify our ways in the light of their evaluation. We also maintain our own integrity, by staying true to ourselves in our stance of claiming originality and expressing our own point of view with universal intent, and by offering explanations for all aspects of our lives, especially in terms of how we are trying to exercise educational influence, which is the focus of the next chapter.

SUMMARY

In this chapter we have shown how we take care in supporting our conclusions by submitting our research findings to the critical scrutiny of others. This, we say, is an epistemologically and methodologically rigorous research process, as well as one that shows our own epistemological, methodological and moral accountability. We explain how we take our interpretation of Habermas's (1987) criteria of social validity as the core criteria we use in judging the quality of evidence of the educational nature of our relationships with others. We explain how the criteria contain linguistic descriptions of our values, and we go on to explain how we transform those linguistic criteria into our living critical standards of judgement. This process, we claim, helps us to achieve necessary ethical and moral validity in the production of our research account, which we believe is a core standard of judgement by which to demonstrate the ethical and moral nature of validation and legitimation processes.

7 The potential significance of our research

How do we show the potential significance of our research?

We understand action research to be about both action and learning. It is about taking action in the world, and it is also about learning, which enters into the action, so that the action is informed and not indiscriminate. The process of action learning then needs to be theorized and transformed into action research by gathering data and generating evidence to test the practitioner's claim that they have improved both their action and their learning. Furthermore, the learning of one practitioner action researcher can in turn influence the development of their own and other people's learning. In this chapter we speak about how especially research-based learning can influence other learning, and we explain how, by telling research-based stories of learning, practitioners can influence the learning of others, even when they are absent in space and in time. This, we believe, also addresses what we consider the main significance of our own action research, which we understand as the capacity to influence learning in the interests of good social orders.

Research is about learning in a focused, informed way. Earlier we noted that it is of course possible to act without learning, such as when we blink or smile, or when people think and act in a way that shows they have not thought about what they are doing. Thoughtless action, in terms of what is done and said, can often result in harm. David Peat (1995) explains how, in some indigenous North American societies, no collective action is undertaken without first considering the implications for the next seven generations (see McNiff 1997). The question then becomes, what kind of action is most appropriate for influencing learning, and how should it be exercised?

The chapter is organized in three sections to address these issues:

1   Educational influence in our own and each other's learning
2   Educational influence in the learning of others
3   Educational influence in the education of social formations

1   Educational influence in our own and each other's learning

At this point, we, Jack and Jean, wish to outline how we believe we have influenced learning. We begin by saying how we believe we have influenced our own and each other's learning, and we then go on to consider how we may have influenced others' learning.

The story of our learning

Here we tell the story of our individual and shared learning. This is not simply a story, where we tell of events in narrative form, but is also a story about influence, which is a tansformative process. Because the content of the story is about transformation, the form of the story also needs to show its transformative quality. We say more about this shortly. In the following sections we explain how the story transforms into a story of an increasing ambit of influence.

Our story begins in 1980. Jack had been a teacher of science in a London comprehensive school, and was now working as a lecturer in education at the University of Bath. Jean was a deputy head teacher in a Dorset comprehensive school, and had the responsibility for introducing in-service provision for the then new curriculum area of personal and social education (PSE). Jack had gone to Bath because he had become aware of how dominant forms of propositional theory were distorting educational practices. He wanted to research his own understanding of educational theory, and contribute to debates about how it could be reconceptualized. Jean wanted to study for her doctorate as she worked out the nature of personal and social education and how it should be taught in schools. Jack became Jean's supervisor in 1981.

Our relationship remained fairly formal for the next eight years, until 1989, when Jean graduated (she took a year's suspension and a year's extension to the usual five/six years that part-time postgraduate reseachers are permitted). During that time, we focused on our own learning, Jean on her studies in PSE and what became increasingly widening related fields, and Jack on developing his ideas about living educational theory. Occasionally we shared our learning, but our social and learning relationships tended to remain separate, as we stayed in our separate roles.

In the 1990s, Jean went to Ireland to support professional learning programmes for teachers using an action research approach. She learned a great deal from the experience of supporting professional education, and about engaging with the politics of knowledge. Jack had already learned a great deal about these issues when, during the 1980s, his two doctoral theses were rejected, and he was disciplined on the grounds that his activities and writings were a challenge to the present and proper organization of the university and not consistent with the duties the university wished him to pursue in teaching and research. This was also the beginning of the widespread use of e-mail communication, so it was easier to stay in touch, and we did so, possibly out of our wish to share our successes as we managed to support professional workplace learning and, in Jean's case, secure the award of masters degrees for Irish teachers, and, in Jack's case, secure the award of doctoral degrees in the University of Bath. The nature of our relationship also changed, as we moved out of a student–supervisor relationship into one of a dialogue of equals, as we offered each other mutual support, critique and affirmation, and began actively to share our learning. It was also the beginning of our collaborative writing programme. Jack's writings were already well known to an academic public, and in 1988, the first edition of *Action Research: Principles and Practice* (McNiff 1988) was published, which was to prove a seminal text in the more popular field of practitioner enquiry. Since then we have pursued a vigorous publications programme, writing separately and jointly for academic and practitioner audiences, always acknowledging the contribution of the other in our learning. In 2000, Jean moved back to England, and this saw the beginning of an intensified effort in relation to exercising our influence, and to producing texts and other resources to support the learning of others. You can read more detailed stories at Whitehead (1993) (http://www.bath.ac.uk/~edsajw/bk93/geki.htm) and McNiff (2005) (http://www.jeanmcniff.com), and you can see many of our publications on our websites.

At this point we return to the idea of the nature and form of educational relationships, that is, what shape they take and how they develop. Here we also draw on the ideas of Alan Rayner at the University of Bath.

The nature and form of educational relationships

Like many writers in the field of the new science (for example, Kauffman 1995; Wheatley 1992), Rayner (2004; 2005) sees all phenomena as in intimate relation with one another, and uses metaphors of networks and labyrinthine channels to describe the nature of these relationships. He understands networks as dynamic and fluid (see also Capra 2003; O'Donohue 2003). He is also interested in developing the kind of metaphors that can communicate the ideas of dynamic fluidity most appropriately, and he communicates those metaphors through artwork (see Rayner 2004, retrieved 11 August 2005 from http://www.bath.ac.uk/~bssadmr/inclusionality/placesspaceevolution.html). Jack is interested in showing how these metaphors can in turn transform into the demonstration of social practices also as dynamic and fluid, and he is currently exploring the use of multimedia to communicate the interrelational processes of educational relationships. Multimedia lend themselves to this task because, while dynamic fluid networks can be represented visually on paper (see McNiff 1984; McNiff and Whitehead 2002: 57), they are restricted to the two dimensions of up–down and left–right, whereas digitally computerized images can show the multidimensional nature of the networks as they move and re-form themselves in every direction. Furthermore, the mental form of up–down and left–right is evidence of the normative assumptions of the binary divides of western forms of thinking, where everything tends to be thought of as 'either–or'. To communicate 'both–and', which is an inclusional way of thinking, as set out on page 39 of this book, it is important to develop forms of representation that are commensurate with the nature of what they are supposed to be communicating. Rayner understands everything as in flow, so, although local networks may appear as clusters, or nodes, the nature of those nodes is that they also are dynamic local channels, that have the potential to spill over into wider channels (see McNiff and Whitehead 2000: 9). These channels connect with one another through their labyrinthine form, and, as noted by Keiny (2002), develop a rhizome-like action where the roots spread and metamorphose into new extended roots that will generate new growth.

Rayner links these images with ideas to do with the nature and form of space and boundaries, and how these reflect images of the trajectories of human enquiry. In the western intellectual tradition, boundaries are usually thought of as fixed demarcation barriers, often deliberately erected to keep things in and shut off outside intrusion. They are impenetrable firewalls, and enclose a finite space. Space on this view is empty, so fixed boundaries enclose an empty space. Rayner says that this tends to be a preferred metaphor of dominant western epistemologies, which aim for the certainty of closure, because of fear of the unknown, uncertainty in all its forms. Forms of action and forms of thinking are organized in terms of finding specific answers to questions. For Rayner, this view actually distorts a representation of human enquiry, which is spontaneous and open, and demonstrates a genuine love of life and learning. The desire for closure represents the anxiety of avoiding uncertainty. He says:

> For thousands of years, faced with the variability of our surroundings and needing to secure our own survival, we human beings have made an enemy out of uncertainty. The principal combative tactic that we have brought to bear on this enemy has been to try to *exclude* or *confine* it by *imposing closure* on it. That is, we have tried mentally and/or physically to box uncertainty inside or outside absolutely fixed and sealed boundaries. In this way we have consciously or unconsciously sought the security system by means of which we can wield control over the wildness that we perceive both in nature and, if we allow it free access and expression, within ourselves. And as we do this, we invest hugely in what my colleague, Ted Lumley, has aptly described as the 'objectifiction' and attachment of name labels to 'things' out there in nature, whose independent existence we talk ourselves into believing, at the same time as reinforcing our egotistical self-boundaries against the possibility of assault. We build ourselves up as we reduce others down to a scale we feel we can cope with, just as we do in our abstract representations of networks. (2005: 2, emphasis in the original)

For Marcuse (1964), this same anxiety can lead people to commit to using technology as instruments that, rather than serving and promoting human understanding, are used instead to control and subjugate human freedom through the very institutions of a technocratic society. Jack on the other hand is using technology to communicate the idea of free-flow relationships that are grounded in relationships that show love and respect for the other.

To overcome the fear of uncertainty, akin to what Fromm (1941) calls the fear of freedom, we need, says Rayner, to appreciate ourselves as 'complex selves', and to understand space not as empty but as teeming with life and the further potentialities of life, so that we come to see ourselves as living spaces within broader living spaces. The relationships we develop with ourselves, with others, and with our environments can be understood as 'inclusional communication networks'.

> From this inclusional perspective, effective *communication* networks are understood to be very different in form from the space-excluding artefacts of thread-like links and knot-like nodes that we currently tend to envisage as 'webs' ... Inclusional communication networks can be thought of as '*communities of common space*' and they characteristically have the form, explicitly or implicitly, of interconnected *riverine* or *labyrinthine channels* or *tubes* with variable permeable and deformable inner-out boundary linings and internal partitions. In other words, they are what my research colleague, Karen Tesson, has described in her PhD thesis as *flow-form networks*, which emerge as both manifestations and facilitators of energy flow in dynamic relation with physical space. (2005: 3, emphasis in original)

Educational influence and educational relationships

We return to the ideas in Chapter 2, where we discussed the nature of logics. We spoke about inclusional logics as incorporating propositional and dialectical forms within themselves, and we explained how inclusional forms are generative and transformational in nature.

We think of influence not as a solid entity, but as incorporated within human relationships. Foucault (1980) spoke about power like this. He said that power was not a thing, but was within human relationships, and operated via a kind of capillary action. What would be the kind of relationships that encourage the free-flow exercise of influence so that the free-flow potentials of ourselves as living spaces can be realized? We said in Chapter 5 that people can choose whether or not to be influenced, that is, people mediate one person's influence through their own capacity for choice. Learning that takes place can therefore be seen as a transformation of mediated influence. The influence can be from one person to themselves, from one person to another, and from many persons to many others.

These ideas are, we believe, important for original scholarship about processes of educational leadership and change management, and their accompanying literatures, as well as the literatures of professional education. All too often, change is communicated in the dominant literatures as something done to someone else. The phrase 'the spread of influence' is commonly understood as the spread of a thing, like the spread of a disease or a rumour, or perhaps it happens like casting seed to the wind. This may be the reality of the model, but it is not a model of reality (Bourdieu 1990). Learning does not happen only because one person gives another a template, but is more often a matter of personal choice. We choose whether to learn, and what to learn. Habermas (1975) says that it is part of the human condition that we cannot *not* learn. What is learned, and how it is learned, therefore becomes the issue. Dewey (1916) speaks of learning as a form of growth, and learning how to influence others' learning as a form of collective and mutual growth. The kind of learning that influences further learning has to be a matter of influence, and influence happens through free-flow interpersonal and intrapersonal relationships which respect the other's capacity for choice in choosing whether or not to be influenced, and to use the learning in ways that are right for them.

Returning to and continuing our story of learning, then, during the 1990s Jack and Jean began to theorize the nature of their educational influence, in terms of how they were enabling themselves and each other to learn, through establishing the kind of free-flow intrapersonal relationships within themselves, and interpersonal relationships with each other, as the kind of relationships that would help them realize their potentials for further learning, and how this learning may be understood as having the potential to influence the learning of others. Our written works are full of these emerging understandings, which also provide evidence for the provisional claims we are making here about the nature of our educational influence in our own and each other's learning.

2   Educational influence in the learning of others

From the beginning of our shared work with others, and separately before that time, we had always aimed to influence other people's learning in a way that they could decide for themselves how they wished to proceed with their enquiries as they asked, 'How do I improve what I am doing?' We also encouraged them to show how they held themselves accountable for what they were doing and thinking. We never set out to 'change' people and their circumstances, because, as noted, we have always understood the idea of 'changing' people as the imposition of one person's will on another, and the enforcement of particular ways of thinking and acting. The ideas of force and imposition are alien to our own values of freedom and the right of all people to make up their own minds about what they choose to think and do. We did however quite deliberately set out to exercise our influence in people's learning in what we understand as an educational way, by offering ideas about what they could do, helping them to develop insights about the nature of their own ideas and practices, and offering resources that would help them to create their own ways forward. These ideas included advice on where people could go to access the literatures and the other intellectual resources they would need in their action enquiries.

Over time, quantities of practitioners' research accounts have appeared. Many of them are on our websites, publicly available, from which others can learn if they wish. These accounts are special, in several ways:

- They show how practitioners have been able to come to understand their practices more adequately, and to theorize those practices in terms of how they can offer descriptions and explanations for what they are doing.
- The stories are not only accounts of action, but also accounts of learning, that is, they are explanatory accounts that show how practitioners have intervened in their own learning, and how that learning has influenced their practices.
- The stories themselves are accounts of processes of theorizing, and as such can be seen as the articulation of practitioners' own living educational theories.
- Further, the accumulation of the stories is significant, in that they comprise a body of knowledge that has future implications for influencing new directions in educational research and educational practices.

These points are discussed below, in terms of the transformational nature of stories, and the development of collections of stories as a knowledge base for educational enquiry and educational practice.

The transformational nature of stories

Todorov (1990) speaks of two principles of narrative. The first, he says, is the principle of propositional form. A text can be a 'sequence of propositions that is easily recognized as a narrative' (1990: 27). The second principle shows how narratives can have transformational quality. Each episode of the text contains the potential to generate the next, which turns into a transformation of the previous form. These ideas are expressions of the basic principles of generative transformational potential that we outlined in Chapter 3. They show how episodes of practice lead to episodes of thinking, which in turn lead to new insights that inform new episodes of practice. Nor are these episodes linear or separate from their contexts. Action, reflection and learning can go on virtually simultaneously, as a person does something, and in the doing thinks, 'I should be doing this differently', and swerves immediately to a new form of action, which, they think as they are doing it, is better than the previous one. Sometimes reflection follows action, as when we sit quietly at home watching television, and go through the events of the day, like an action replay, and comment mentally on what we have done. These times of reflection can generate important new learning, when we say, 'I should have done that differently. Next time I will, and I will check how the modified practice may be better.' A distinctive feature of the living educational theory studies that we support is that practitioners both show how their learning influences new learning and new action, and also are able to stand back and offer their own critical commentaries as they go.

The practitioners' stories of practice that we have collected, systematized and published, many of which are on our websites (see also in the next paragraph), all reveal this quality of generative transformation. Further, these stories themselves constitute a knowledge base that also has the generative transformational capacity to influence new thinking and new practices for new communities of enquiry.

A knowledge base for communities of enquiry

In 2001, Catherine Snow, then President of the American Educational Research Association, called for the development of a knowledge base that would collect and systematize the stories of practitioners' research, and make those stories available to the rest of the teaching community. This, she said, would provide a solid base from which teachers could learn and develop their own practice in light of others' experiences. We support this idea. We have been creating such a knowledge base since the 1980s, which is now widely available to the teaching and other professions.

A knowledge base can be found in the discourses of a profession or a community, and is perhaps most prominently displayed in the publications of the community. The idea of publication and dissemination is central to contributing to new practices and new theory. It is also essential to contributing to policy formation and implementation. The two main ways in which the developing knowledge base does this is to show how practitioners' research stories can contribute to new practices and to new theory.

Contributing to new practices

Many masters dissertations and doctoral theses are now available to show how practitioners contributed to new practices.

From Jean's website you can read the following:

- Siobhan Ní Mhurchú developed a portfolio-based approach to helping her students monitor and evaluate their own learning. She found that students became more involved in their own learning when compiling their own narratives of learning than when engaging in teacher-set learning tasks (Ní Mhurchú 2000, retrieved 11 August 2005 from http://www.jeanmcniff.com/siobhan.htm).
- Marian Nugent found that a caring approach in classrooms encouraged learning more effectively than a more structured disciplinarian approach. She explains how her modified attitudes towards her children manifested as new practices that also set new precedents for organizational practices (Nugent 2000, retrieved 11 August 2005 from http://www.jeanmcniff.com/marianabstract.htm).

- Thérèse Burke moved from the normative concept of 'children with special educational needs' to develop her own theory of learning difference. She developed new conceptualizations of herself as a teacher who was learning with her students. From her own critical stance, she was able to develop new communities of critically oriented practice (Burke 1997, retrieved 11 August 2005, from http://www.jeanmcniff.com/tereseabstract.html).

From Jack's website you can read the following:

- Terri Austin developed a supportive approach to encouraging the formation of educational communities. Her thesis shows an alternative to traditional forms of criticism frequently found in academic work related to the growth of knowledge. 'Set in a narrative context, I present a living picture of helping to form and work with communities of students, parents, teachers and teacher researchers which provides the life-situations in which I created my own knowledge and strive to identify and live out my values' (Austin 2001, http://www.bath.ac.uk/~edsajw/austin.shtml).
- Marian Naidoo demonstrated how the ontological value of passion for compassion could be transformed into a living critical standard of judgement. (Naidoo 2005, retrieved 11 August 2005 from http://www.bath.ac.uk/~edsajw/naidoo.shtml).
- Madeline Church writes, 'Through questioning myself and writing myself onto the page, I trace how I resist community formations, while simultaneously wanting to be in community with others. This paradox has its roots in my multiple experiences of being bullied, and finds transformation in my stubborn refusal to retreat into disconnection' (Church 2004, retrieved 11 August 2005 from http://www.bath.ac.uk/~edsajw/church.shtml) (see also page 148 of this book).

From Margaret Farren's website you can read how a pedagogy of the unique and a web of betweenness can influence the creation and testing of the living educational theories of practitioner researchers (Farren 2005, retrieved 11 August 2005 from http://webpages.dcu.ie/farrenm/dissertations.html).

From Jackie Delong's website you can read four volumes of 'Passion in Professional Practice' (http://schools.gedsb.net/ar/passion/index.html) that have emerged from the generation of a culture of inquiry promoted by Jackie Delong and researched in her doctoral thesis (Delong 2002, retrieved 11 August 2005 from http://www.bath.ac.uk/~edsajw/delong.shtml).

These bodies of knowledge contribute to a validated and legitimated knowledge base that has implications for new policies and practices (see Section 3).

Contributing to new theory

What is special about these stories of practice is that they show the processes of how their authors came to understand their practices, and express their understandings as their own theories of practice. The theories are located within and generated from within the practice, and influence the development of new practices, which in turn act as the grounds for the development of new theory and new practices. While the narratives you read are narratives of practice, they are also narratives of theorizing, that is, what the person has come to know and how they are thinking differently about their work and themselves.

Major implications reside in these ideas, including the following:

- One implication is about the nature of theory and practice. From an externalist perspective, theory and practice are seen as objects of enquiry, fields of activity to be studied by a spectator researcher. The researcher offers theories about theory and practice, in an abstract way. You can go to the library and find books on theory, and books on practice. The assumption is that you will read the books, and apply what they say to your practice. If you do this, you will supposedly become a better practitioner.
- A second implication is about the public positioning of practitioners. We have noted throughout that practitioners are not generally considered by the educational research community as entirely capable of theorizing. By producing their narratives of practice, and offering their own critical reflection on the significance of the stories of practice as they tell them, they show how they are theorizing and potentially generating new theories. These kinds of theories, and the processes that generate them, are however different in kind from the dominant forms, where researchers generate theory, which practitioners are expected to access, internalize and apply. By positioning themselves publicly as theorists, as well as practitioners, professionals in all professions are able to reclaim their professions as their own, and exercise their authority in making decisions about the future of the profession and their own lives.
- A third implication is about the future of educational research and educational theory. We have said throughout that a current weakness in the field of practitioner-based research is the lack of adequate theorizing about how quality can be assessed in personal narratives. We are not claiming to have concrete answers to the issue. We are however showing how we are prepared to put forward our own ideas and theories, to have them tested in the public domain against the responses of practitioner researchers and the higher education community of researcher practitioners. We also believe it is essential not only that practitioners show how they are expressing their insights about how they are refining their ideas about the nature of standards of judgement and the need to articulate them and show how they form an integral part of their own accounts, but also that the higher education community do the same. We repeat our belief in the elementary moral principle that one cannot expect others to do something which one is not prepared to do oneself. For their processes of assessment to be seen as grounded in the criteria of social and ethical validity (Chapter 6), higher education assessors must themselves articulate the standards of judgement they use in validation and legitimation processes, and justify them by showing how they apply their own standards of judgement to their own practices.

This brings us to the next section about influencing the education of social formations.

3   Educational influence in the education of social formations

The idea of higher education researcher practitioners studying their practices as evaluators is already happening, although it needs to happen much more. In this chapter we give examples of initiatives on the ground. In the next chapter we give two examples of how the education of social formations works. In Chapter 10 we speak of the implications of our research, and how the focus of our research and practices is changing accordingly.

Before we go on to describe what is happening, it may be helpful to revisit the idea of the education of social formations.

A social formation is a group of people who come together with a common focus. It could be a football team, a board of directors, or a government. The usual way to conceptualize a social formation, from the dominant externalist perspectives in the mainstream literatures, is to think of it as an object of enquiry, that is, something 'out there' to be studied from an outsider's position. This means the social formation would be observed and analysed in terms of its structures and configurations. People would be identified in terms of their designated roles and specific responsibilities. Many organizational flow charts appear on office walls or in institutional handbooks to show, usually in hierarchical form, how each role is positioned in relation to other roles. The roles tend to be thought of not as people but as positions, and relationships tend to be thought of not as personal interactions but as structures. To test this idea for yourself, draw a diagram of some of your own social formations. You could draw a diagram of your family, your workplace, your church, or your sports club. Note where you allocate people and how you think of them. Note also that what you are doing is a conceptual analysis, which may reflect how you understand the formation of your social grouping, but does not necessarily reflect the realities of the social formation. You may for example have located a patriarchal father figure at the top of your diagram, such as the priest or the manager of the club, which may not be the actual reality of the relationships in the group. The priest may be influenced by his wife, and the manager by the team members. Conceptual analyses and two-dimensional models seldom represent the realities of real life or how influence really works.

An understanding that is grounded in real-life experience shows that a social formation is organized in terms of its relationships and discourses, and these relationships and discourses are premised on certain rules. These rules tend to become normative, that is, they go unseen and unquestioned. Members of the social formation often do not appreciate that rules exist in the first place. In many power-constituted contexts, those in power often discourage people from being aware, so that they do not question or even think of questioning, and so the status quo is protected. People in power tend to work hard to reinforce the normativization of rules, and they go to considerable lengths to develop strategies of persuasion to reassure people that the way things are is the way they should be. However, once people do become aware of the fact that rules underpin their practices, and that they can and should question the rules, and see the need to evaluate practices which are built on the rules, they then have an opportunity to change things. They begin to intervene in their own learning, and begin to influence their existing practices in terms of their own learning. In other words, they begin to educate themselves. This is the core purpose of action research, which is a form of enquiry that encourages people to ask, 'Am I living in the direction of my own values, or someone else's? Who writes my script, me or someone else? What really makes my life worthwhile, and how do I realize my values?'

This view of course can get people into trouble. Sometimes they blow whistles and are punished (Alford 2001). Sometimes they question managers and begin what are seen as subversive conversations with colleagues, and are silenced. Sometimes they question rules, and the rules that keep the rules in place. Many people, ourselves included, can tell stories of voices and work suppressed, of publication refused, and of punishments designed to deter freedom and democracy. Sometimes the strictures are so severe that a culture of servitude and silence is imposed to stop the potential emergence of a culture of enquiry and dissent. Many current and historical episodes around the world attest to this situation. Even action researchers are sometimes prevented from undertaking studies in their workplaces that involve other people. This is one of the reasons why the social sciences remain the favoured paradigm in educational research. It is safe to have an external researcher enquire into others' practices, through a relationship of dominance, especially when the researcher receives their brief and funding from policy makers who wish to ensure that their own policies are implemented.

Fortunately, although these issues should definitely not be ignored or downplayed, there are also positive signs that show how practitioners are conducting their enquiries, within a supportive organizational culture that actively encourages the work to go ahead.

Here are some examples to show this in practice:

- Jane Spiro, Head of the Department of Applied Linguistics at Oxford Brookes University, is encouraging the sharing of teachers' stories. These can be accessed from http://www.bath.ac.uk/~edsajw/monday/jsTeacherStories.htm. This practice is a new departure in the cultures and literatures of teacher professional education, and shows a distinct development from the disciplines approach of the 1960s, and the competencies approach of the 1990s, to a new approach, where teachers are seen as reflective practitioners and theorists of their own practices.
- Margaret Farren, working as a lecturer in e-learning in Dublin City University, has generated and sustained a creative space that has supported practitioner researchers in the creation of their own living educational theories. Holding open such a creative space requires energy, sustained commitment and an understanding of power relations that legitimates what counts as valid knowledge in a particular context. The learning resources available at http://webpages.dcu.ie/~farren/ demonstrate all of these.

Three striking examples are the following.

Work at St Mary's University College, London, England

St Mary's College, which is a college of the University of Surrey, aware of the need to provide systematic professional support in raising research capacity in their own bid for university status, put in place a one-year series of seminars that were designed to develop the academic staff's knowledge of educational research and the skills to carry it out. Jean was invited to present the seminars. About thirty members of faculty attended, but attendance was intermittent because of the demands on faculty of other institutional work. A group of seven however formed themselves into a research group, with the intent of investigating their practices. They did this in their own time, supported by Jean. They began to publish their work, and it was accepted as part of a prestigious international research symposium (see Johnson 2005; Moreland 2005; Moustakim 2005; Renowden et al. 2005). The work of the group was watched with interest by senior management, who also read participants' evaluations of their learning experiences. The senior management saw this kind of organic development as appropriate to achieving the institutional aims of growth and change of status, and consequently set in place a regular programme of professional academic staff development. This meant that all academic staff would have the opportunity to study current and new issues in educational research, evaluate and improve their practice at an informal level, and achieve their higher degrees if they wished. While the aims of the programme are ambitious, it actually is working well in action, grounded as it is in the capacity of all to theorize their practices in ways that are right for them, to have that capacity formally acknowledged, and to change their practices accordingly. Because of the influence of the small group, and the influence of the evidence of its influence, new institutional practices and epistemologies are being developed. Once such new epistemologies begin to develop, they do not go away easily. Precedents are established, and new forms of standards of judgement are developed (see McNiff 2005). The initiative will be closely monitored, evaluated, and made public.

Work at the Nelson Mandela Metropolitan University, Port Elizabeth, South Africa

Following presentations by Jean of Jack's ideas about living action research, and led by Professor of Education Ana Naidoo, some members of the Faculty of Education at the Nelson Mandela Metropolitan University formed themselves into an action research group with the intent of studying their practices, with a special focus on how they were democratizing education within the new post-apartheid South Africa. They also saw it as an opportunity to democratize their own practices of doing educational research. Their work is having significant influence in developing new practices. Tilla Olivier and Lesley Wood, both professors in the faculty, are evaluating their practice of supporting teachers in townships (Olivier and Wood 2005). In turn they are linking with Joan Whitehead, who is doing significant work in reconceptualizing traditional power relationships between higher education personnel and classroom-based teachers (see Joan Whitehead 2003; Joan Whitehead and Bernie Fitzgerald 2004). Drawing on Joan's work, Tilla and Lesley are repositioning themselves as practitioner researchers, alongside the teacher researchers whom they support. This work is receiving some attention (see McNiff and Naidoo 2005; Naidoo and McNiff 2005). As well as the work in workplaces, some members of faculty, and faculty from other universities, are developing an unfunded research programme on 'Interrogating our Colour', by means of which they hope to address issues of how the hegemonizing discourses of colour and race are used systematically as strategies for the perpetuation of regimes of colonization. This work is in its infancy but holds much promise for the future development of educational research in South Africa.

Work at Guyuan Teachers College, Ningxia Province, People's Republic of China

In 2001, Moira Laidlaw went as a volunteer with Voluntary Services Overseas to Guyuan Teachers College, which is in Ningxia Province, one of the most economically deprived areas in China. Moira, who had been a secondary school teacher and later a lecturer at the University of Bath, had studied for her doctorate with Jack (Laidlaw 1996), and now wished to bring her expertise to other, less privileged contexts. Her work was officially to teach English as a foreign language, and she began working in the Department of Foreign Languages at the college. However she also introduced action research methodologies to the college, and enabled teachers and professional educators to appreciate that they also could come to theorize their work in ways that encouraged their personal evaluation and actions to improve what they were doing. As a volunteer, Moira had gone to China as part of the new Open Door policy, which also generated other initiatives such as the New Curriculum. It had been recognized by the authorities that, to ensure its own economic and cultural sustainability, China could usefully draw on work being done in the west, including work in education and educational research. Moira therefore had an opportunity to develop living action research methodologies, that themselves demonstrated an openness to enquiry learning, within a new culture of openness to new opportunities. Over the last four years, Moira has succeeded in developing what has now come to be recognized nationally as a form of professional education and of educational enquiry that has profound significance for the future of China. Her work has been reported on at national level (see Perrement 2005, retrieved 11 August 2005 from http://www.jackwhitehead.com/china/cdbmay05), and she and colleagues are now focusing on disseminating the work through a systematic publishing programme (Tian and Laidlaw 2004; 2005).

These are just some examples of how social formations have come to educate themselves by intervening in the established norms of educational practices, and also of how we, Jack and Jean, believe we have influenced these developments. We are not claiming in any way to have caused them. That is simply untrue, nor would we see organizational growth in cause-and-effect terms. We are delighted to say that we have had an influence, perhaps in a generative and transformational capacity, and so encouraged what was already latent there to emerge and reach its realization of potential in ways that are life-affirming for all.

The next chapter contains two further case studies of people who have had significant influence in the education of social formations. These are Dean Tian Fengjun in China, and Branko Bognar in Croatia. In Chapter 10 we explore further some of the significant implications of the work for the development of future practices and the development of educational theory.

S U M M A R Y

In this chapter we have outlined what we consider to be the potential significance of our research for education and educational research. We explain how we have influenced our own and each other's learning, and also the learning of others, specifically as they are members of social formations in education. The kind of influences we aim to exercise, we say, are those that encourage others to exercise their capacity for freedom and creativity. We explain that the examples we produce as evidence for these claims show how people are contributing both to new educational practices in their own settings, and also to new forms of educational theory, by showing how the practice itself can contribute to a form of practical theorizing in action. We choose specific examples of work in the UK, South Africa and China, to show how the work has implications at global level, and how this supports our own stance as making our evidence-based claims to personal knowledge with universal intent.

PART 4

Implications, Evaluation and Dissemination

This part deals with some of the implications of the research, how research can be evaluated, and how its influence can be extended through the production and dissemination of practitioners' stories. *It contains the following chapters:*

8 Case studies
 How do we show the implications of our research?

9 Evaluating the account of our research
 How do we evaluate the evidence-based account of our learning?

We explain how the dissemination of the stories of practitioner action researchers can contribute to new learning and practices that have the potential to inform the education and practices of social formations.

8 Case studies

How do we show the implications of our research?

This chapter contains the case studies of two educational leaders who have done much to promote action research in their own countries. They are Tian Fengjun in China and Branko Bognar in Croatia. The stories show what can happen when people of vision exercise their educational influence in the learning of others in organizational contexts. Their original vision can lead to personal, organizational and cultural transformation. In these stories, the authors show how they are contributing to the education of their own social formations, with wider implications. By presenting these case stories, we believe we are, through the authors, showing some of the implications of our own work.

A dean's educational story

Tian Fengjun

This report tells my story of how, as a dean in the Guyuan Teachers College, in the People's Republic of China, I learned how to improve my learning and my work and come to influence the learning and work of others in my college, with the potential of informing the education of the wider social formation of educators in my country. I tell of how I developed new ideas about education and educational leadership and management, and how this was conducted in a spirit of ethical cooperation throughout my everyday professional life. Inspired by my own experience of loving family relationships, I tell how I decided to bring the same values of love and relation to my professional life, and how in so doing I am now able to work with colleagues in a way that can help teachers and their students, at local and national level, to develop the New Curriculum in China.

My background

I was born in a more turbulent time when the Cultural Revolution had just begun. My home town, a small village in a Hui area, is located in the north-west of China, which is said to be one of the three most backward western regions in China. At that time, people's living conditions were less than adequate, given that the then social order did not allow people to improve their lives, and education was thought to be 'terrible poisonous weeds', 'useless' and simply 'an excuse for revolution' (Deng Xiaoping 1989). The whole nation was urged to be more technologically productive, to be prepared for possible warfare, and to catch up with more developed countries. Consequently schools were used as camps for Red Guards, and education was filtered out. People living in rural areas had no access to education, and the situation was exacerbated for many, including us, the Hui people, living in the mountainous regions. Even if we wished for an education, we were prevented from gaining access because of the cultural tradition that sent children over twelve to work in the fields in order to provide income for their family. Most families considered education and schooling unnecessary for their children.

I was fortunate. Although I grew up in these circumstances, my parents were desperately concerned about my education. I did not know the reason for this until I recently became a father to a son. As well as working with my mother in the fields, my own beloved father conducted a small business, in secret, of course, for fear of recriminations from the authorities, and he managed to put me through school from the age of five. He did this out of his determination that I should benefit from a better chance in life than he had. I went to the village primary school and then on to Haiyuan Middle School, near Guyuan. Twelve years later I enrolled at university. My great love and admiration for my parents has led me to do what I do today, in the hope that I also can contribute to someone else's life chances through education. Many instances come to mind of the measure of my parents' devotion to me, such as when they spent five hours finding their way to where I was studying, in spite of the fact that they had never previously ventured more than a hundred kilometres away from home. Now I strive to make an equal contribution to the development of the people and our country.

In 1988 I graduated from Xi'an International Studies University and came back to Guyuan Teachers College as an English teacher in the Foreign Languages Department. From the beginning of my career I decided to try to live out my deeply held values, learned from my parents, of care, kindness and compassion, throughout all aspects of my personal and professional life.

This now brings me to a point in my story where my career began to take an important new direction.

What was my concern?

Guyuan Teachers College is the only higher education establishment in the northern part of Ningxia Province, and the Foreign Languages Department is now an established part with its own long history. The Department currently has responsibility for training well-qualified English graduates for nearly one thousand middle schools and primary schools in the province. Over the last twenty-five years, the Department has grown from three professional educators to fifty. Most are young, and their professional and teaching expertise are not always adequate for the task of training new teachers, and often not up to the standards of a qualified College teacher. It has therefore become a pressing task for me to find new ways of raising professional standards to meet increasing demands. This presents a special problematic, given that the College is seriously underresourced, because of its rural location and its currently relatively low status in public perceptions. Moreover, it has become popularly expected that the College will take the lead in finding ways of raising standards in economic and social conditions through education. However, new initiatives by the provincial Government to invest in the area have given me hope and renewed determination to turn the Department into an exemplar of good practice that can stand as a precedent for all.

This in itself presents particular challenges for me. Our student teachers come mostly from remote country regions and deprived family backgrounds. The hope of their parents is that the teachers can get a job and so support the family. Most families can support only one child through College, and this often means serious sacrifices such as selling the ploughing cattle or borrowing money from neighbours or relatives. The responsibilities for the College, and for me as a Dean, are intensified, a responsibility that I am willing to accept but need to find imaginative ways of responding to.

My responsibilities are intensified by the introduction of the New Curriculum, which, as part of China's new Open Door policy, requires all teachers to be rich in professionalism, have significant cultural character, and have an excellent sense of vocation. A Dean therefore has the responsibility of developing forms of management that will help student teachers to develop these capacities. Considerations of these factors exercised my mind considerably. How could I do this? What assistance could I find? An unexpected form of support however was suddenly to appear.

Beginning action research in Guyuan

It was a bright afternoon three years ago that Dr Moira Laidlaw walked into my office. Moira, newly arrived from England, was working with Voluntary Services Overseas. Her work would involve helping teachers develop new teaching methodologies in English as a foreign language. Her background in English teaching more than qualified her for the task, and her knowledge of action research would enable her to work with teachers in an innovative and supportive way. We cheerfully chatted over a cup of tea. I told her my worries about how I could help to improve colleagues' professional capacity. She told me about action research. She explained that action research was underpinned by clear educational values about teaching to learn and learning to teach, and the potentials of raising colleagues' capacity by working in this way. I am always interested in new ideas, and I immediately saw the potential. As time went on I asked Moira about the possibility of doing action research at the College, especially in our department. She told me about the enormous successes in other countries, so I decided to give it a try in ours. Before presenting the idea to colleagues, however, I decided to undertake my own action enquiry into how I could improve my own work, and my learning led me to believe that it would help colleagues to learn how to improve their teaching. It is partly thanks to Moira that more and more colleagues became interested in understanding their teaching as a form of research. After just two months I found myself involved in the teaching practice of many of my colleagues, and this convinced me of the need formally to organize the beginnings of educational action research at the College. In all honesty, the more I became involved in the practice, the more confident I felt that I could successfully carry this project through the Department.

I therefore systematically set about developing action research approaches, and this involved a range of strategies, which included the following.

Given that there is a new demand for qualified teachers of English, our student population had increased significantly. This in turn placed increased responsibilities on the shoulders of the academic staff. I made it my responsibility to support the staff personally. This meant creating more time for staff, talking with them and developing democratic forms of discussion. It also meant meeting with students on a personal basis, and I found informal meetings at social events or along corridors more conducive to professional talk than formally scheduled meetings. This, I felt sure, would lead to increased confidence among both the student population and the staff, and also lead to cementing relationships between them.

I paid a good deal of attention to my own learning about administrative and management matters. I drew up my own systematic action plans, and also paid attention to evaluating my own performance and my influence in the learning of others. By implementing strategies like this, I hoped to encourage a special collegial spirit, in which I became a participant rather than a manager. The values that inspired these practices were to do with paying attention to the detail of care and communicating the significance of care as an organizational ethic. Everything I asked the staff to do, I first did myself. I invited peer observation of my teaching, and invited critical feedback from all members of staff on how I was influencing their learning and their work.

Working collaboratively with individuals and groups

I spent considerable amounts of time with more senior colleagues, discussing pedagogical and administrative matters, and in turn we senior colleagues spent time with more junior colleagues, supporting them as we worked together on developing their action plans for improving their practice. I provided material resources in the form of books and resource banks.

In particular I consistently promoted a view of practice as systematic enquiry, and encouraged all to maintain records of their own learning and the learning of their students. I encouraged all members of staff to undertake their action enquiries, and to regard professional development as an ongoing enquiry. To encourage and support their writing, I provided writing workshops, and arranged for inexperienced colleagues to receive critical feedback from the more experienced ones. This has enabled many to write papers for publication and apply for funding for their academic projects (see the extensive case study material on http://www.bath.ac.uk/~edsajw/moira.shtml). I arranged for different groupings among the staff to promote their collaborative research activities. Consequently, different subject areas such as pragmatics and sociolinguistics have been studied and developed to a high level of expertise. This has led to planning for the systematic development of new classes that will both benefit individual students and also contribute to the wellbeing of the institution.

Of special importance is the fact that I have negotiated with the Xi'an International Studies University to create a postgraduate course for young colleagues in my Department. Staff may now raise the status of their professional development. The educational value of this initiative has been recognized by the President of the College, who confirms that I am contributing to the development of teacher professional education at the College, by setting precedents from which other departments can learn.

In summary, I can say that I have deliberately tried to exercise my capacity for transformative leadership and educational influence throughout the College. I now turn to how I can evaluate the quality of my educational influence.

How do I evaluate my educational influence?

When I reflect on my life's work, and given that I have not enjoyed perfect health for some years, I sometimes catch myself wondering why I do not devote more time to myself and my wife and son. Yet when I walk through the College gates or open my office door I find that such self-indulgent thoughts rapidly dissipate, to be replaced by the overwhelming sense of love I have for the College, my colleagues and my work. It is this sense of love that inspires me. I often invite other senior colleagues from my own and other Departments to work with me in planning for improved administration and for the renewal and enrichment of my colleagues' educational ideas. I also invite head teachers to work with me in evaluating the quality of our education programmes.

To evaluate the quality of my educational influence I have developed a range of strategies. I maintain regular evaluation documents, from various sources. For example, here is an excerpt from an evaluation report by a senior management colleague.

> The English Department has become one of the best Departments at the College for its great care of its students, and especially for the contributions to their vocational training and character building.

Another comment from a Department colleague acknowledged my personal contribution to her wellbeing:

> We appreciate the Dean's love and care for us. His kind-heartedness helps make us stronger as teachers.

I maintain a regular diary. I keep records of my activities and learning, and also note contributions from colleagues. I especially note the educational influence of my own open door policy, where all are welcome to drop in for a chat about their work. How I judge the quality of my educational influence is to note those occasions when I appear to have realized my educational values in my practice, as when, for example, colleagues work together in a collegial manner. This is especially noteworthy in our action research initiatives. Before action research the then thirty colleagues who made up our staff acted as individuals, pursuing their own agendas and programmes. Now they work collaboratively, and present a unified front on educational matters. The contributions at our weekly action research meetings can often be startling, when a colleague will share their insights on learning and their own improvement in practice, and invite critical feedback from others to test their claim to knowledge. Such innovative forms of working have attracted the attention of the senior management of the College, who attest to the success of our Department. Information received through informal channels is reinforced by regular yearly assessments that provide formal feedback to the College management. It is pleasing to note how well we are held in public perceptions. I take consistently as my standard of judgement the idea that I am realizing my value of love in my practice, and its practical manifestation of whether or not I contribute to the educational and spiritual wellbeing of my colleagues and the institution.

Gaining legitimacy

I am aware of the need to raise the profile of our Department and so gain further legitimacy for what we are doing. This has involved several key innovations.

Over the last two years I have arranged for visits by prominent educational researchers such as Jack Whitehead and Jean McNiff. These visits have lent status and profile to our work. In 2004, we were transformed into a new Experimental Centre for Educational Action Research. Such a centre has never existed before in China, and attests to the quality of what we are doing as an organization through the publication of papers and monographs (see Tian and Laidlaw 2004). I have also developed a systematic publishing programme, through which the significance of our work can be communicated to a national and international audience. Moira Laidlaw, my ever-present friend and support, has further supported in producing a text to be published by a major Chinese publisher (Tian and Laidlaw 2005). This book contains an account of our organizational practices, and the case studies of many of my colleagues, to show how their capacity for collaborative research has enabled them to improve the quality of their practice. Over the last two years I have arranged two large-scale conferences in our College. These have further served as a platform from which we can disseminate our work and shows its significance at national and international level.

At the heart of all this work are some core features. The values underpinning the work are those of love and care. The methodological uniqueness of the work is that all colleagues study their work and produce their accounts to show the generation of their own living educational theories. Yet this is action research with Chinese characteristics, those characteristics being the traditional values of the love and care that is found in our culture of extended families and close ties of relationship. I return to my love for my parents, the original inspiration for my life work. Given that we now have a New Curriculum in China we are using action research approaches to help us make sense of our work as we hold together new ideas within a traditional context. The practices of action research are evident however not only in our College, but also in the schools where our student teachers work. Those teachers also undertake their action enquiries, as they find the most appropriate ways of implementing the New Curriculum.

My latest endeavours have been to begin discussions with the University of Bath on developing postgraduate programmes for practising teachers and staff who wish to gain accreditation for their work. These discussions are going well, and I am hopeful that the profile of our College will aspire to international status, and consequently attract students of talent on a national basis.

Conclusion

I hope through this report to have set out how I perceive my contribution in transforming the Department and making it a centre of excellence from which others can learn. It has taken more than two years for colleagues to transform their thinking and themselves as the embodiment of new pedagogical ideas and professional practices, always with a vision of educational improvement. This has shown itself in their capacity to work collaboratively, to participate actively in discussions and research, and to conduct their enquiries into their classroom teaching. I believe I have improved my own ability to work with colleagues in creating a teaching and research platform for the sharing of ideas and values. I have helped younger colleagues to have the courage to take risks in their teaching practice, and to find their own solutions to practical dilemmas. With experienced colleagues I have encouraged ways of working that have helped us deliberate on our different values in our educational development, such as problematizing the degree of autonomy or self-motivated participation in collaborative teaching. We are still very much in progress. We acknowledge that we have travelled considerable distances, and still have far to go. We are inspired by the thought that we are on this never-ending learning journey together.

Action research in Croatia

Branko Bognar

Having worked for six years as a primary school teacher in the small Croatian town of Čazma, and then later as a pedagogue in the Primary School 'Vladimir Nazor' in Slavonski Brod, I have now taken up a post in the Faculty of Philosophy at Josip Juraj Strossmayer University of Osijek, where I have responsibility for the professional education of pedagogues and teachers. In this account I set out how I have worked with others to develop action research approaches to teacher professional education, and how teachers are now developing the same action research approaches in their classroom teaching. Over recent years I have become increasingly interested in developing my work as a form of research-based practice, which enables me systematically to reflect on my work and the degree to which I am exercising my educational influence in my own learning, and in the learning of students and colleagues. Here, I outline the story of my learning from the experience of doing action research, and I also say how I believe I am contributing to the education of the social formation of teachers in schools, by encouraging them to reflect critically on their practice and show how they are improving it in relation to their own and their students' learning. I point to evidence of my learning, and to evidence that shows that students' and colleagues' learning has also improved.

First, let me sketch in a brief background to my research.

Background to my research

My research was inspired by the experience of undertaking my Master of Science degree five years ago at the University of Zagreb. I already held deep commitments to philosophical ideas about the inherent human capacity for creativity and passionate engagement in living itself. These ideas however could not be located satisfactorily within the dominant scientific approach that provided the framework for my studies. However, in spite of the prevailing epistemological assumptions of the dominant approach and the demands of the academy, I succeeded in achieving my degree as a form of creative practice. This was made possible because I experienced the academy not simply as a rigid mechanism but as a living institution, full of people who were willing to learn and to experiment with new approaches. My professors were supportive and encouraged me to try out new ideas, including action research. This proved problematic for me, because at the beginning of my research I was confronted by a serious lack of action research literature, and had no access to anyone who had done action research. To resolve my dilemma, I searched the Internet to find others who perhaps thought the same as me.

My search proved fruitful. I came across the living theory approach to action research, which seemed to fit well with my philosophical ideas. I was especially inspired by the validated dissertations and theses on Jack Whitehead's web pages (http://www.bath.ac.uk/~edsajw/). They helped me to understand the principles and practices of action research as a living practice, and encouraged me to try something similar in my own educational contexts. I became aware that this way of doing action research is in fact a more difficult and problematic methodology than traditional forms of social scientific enquiry, but my aim at this point was not only to submit my account for further accreditation but also to find my way within this new area. Therefore, even when I had been awarded my masters degree, I immersed myself in studying my practice, and discovered that, despite initial problems, I rapidly learned how to swim, and even to fly.

I said that I worked as a pedagogue. A pedagogue in Croatia has special responsibilities, which include advising students, parents and teachers, and also leading professional development initiatives. Inspired by my involvement in action research, which I saw as a powerful means of professional education, I widened my search for likeminded colleagues who would understand the importance of improving learning for improving practice, and would be prepared to work with me on developing this idea, and testing it in the public domain. In the beginning I found seventeen colleagues in six different schools who were prepared to join with me. We rapidly established a professional learning community. The main aim of our community was our own continuing professional development. We decided from the beginning to evaluate our work through doing our individual and collective action research projects.

Before I go on to describe how we developed as a group of practitioner researchers, I first need to outline why I found traditional research approaches inadequate for my practical needs.

Why I work with action research

Throughout my work as a teacher I have been concerned to evaluate and improve my practice on an ongoing basis. In spite of the fact that I have always considered myself a passionate and committed teacher, I was aware in the early days of my career that this was not enough to satisfy my understanding of the characteristics of a professional. I knew that I needed to develop a greater awareness of the need for rigour for testing the appropriateness of my teaching methodologies, and make my findings available through the professional literatures. Until recently, the main way available to teachers in my country for establishing rigour was to resort to the precise statistical methods of traditional science, with the aim of finding a perfect picture of an imperfect reality. My aim however was not to serve science, with its emphasis on finding a perfect 'truth', but to find ways of improving my practice, which, by its nature, was, and probably always will be, imperfect. I especially wanted to find ways of realizing my educational values and visions through the development of critical self-awareness and through cooperative communication with others. I came to the understanding that discovering the truth about practice is not only a question of epistemology but also an ontological issue of finding ways of transforming inappropriate practices into new ones, which may be more adequate for realizing still unrealized potentials. I grounded this desire in my reading of the philosophy and practice of modernity. For example, in his demand for the primacy of practical reason, Kant says as follows:

> When Galileo caused balls, the weights of which he had himself previously determined, to roll down an inclined plane; when Toricelli made the air carry a weight which he had calculated beforehand to be equal to that of a definite volume of water; or in more recent times, when Stahl changed metals into oxides, and oxides back into metal, by withdrawing something and then restoring it, a light broke upon all students of nature. They learned that reason has insight only into that which it produces after a plan of its own, and that it must not allow itself to be kept, as it were, in nature's leading-strings, but must itself show the way with principles of judgment based upon fixed laws, constraining nature to give answers to questions of reason's own determining. (1965: 20)

More to the point, Marx expressed his view in his eleventh thesis on Feuerbach when he stated that 'the philosophers only interpreted the world in various ways; the point is to change it' (Marx and Engels 1989: 339).

My search for an appropriate form of practice led me, as noted, to the work of Jack Whitehead and Jean McNiff, who maintain that it is not enough to proclaim practice as good simply by reflecting on what we have done and showing how we have changed it in light of what we have learned, although this is an important beginning. We also need to explain our work as a systematic, informed way of public acting, for which we hold ourselves accountable by producing our explanatory accounts. Although I agreed with this perspective, I later discovered that it was extremely difficult to fulfil in a school context. At this point therefore I will say what I did, as I tried to develop this perspective for myself.

Developing action research in my context

In my role as a pedagogue, as I have described, I began to develop good working relationships with colleagues in neighbouring schools. My aim was to encourage teachers to develop new professional self-perceptions as reflective practitioners and action researchers. Although we had no financial or practical resources, or institutional support, we decided from the start that we would form ourselves as a research group, drawing on one another as intellectual and emotional resources. Over time we have developed what could be seen as a networked learning community. We did this primarily through developing our e-communication. I was fortunate in this regard, because my hobby is computer programming and technology usage in general, so although my colleagues did not initially know very much about e-systems, I was able to teach them. I helped them to learn how to use computer technology and, with the help of a friend who is an engineer of informatics, and who agreed to support the efforts of our small community without any charges to us, we developed a virtual cooperative space (see http://mzu.sbnet.hr). We decided that we should focus on showing the nature of what we were doing as teachers in school contexts who wished to show the practical realization of their values of care, friendship, creativity and hard work. We also began to understand these values as the basis of how we could communicate the ontological rigour of our own action research processes.

The case study of my colleague Marica Zovko is a good example of the results of our efforts to improve our educational practice (see Zovko 2005). Marica is a teacher working in a primary school. With my support, she introduced her ten-year-old children to action research. She worked systematically with them, helping them to work through their own processes of identifying their concerns and addressing them in a way that showed their capacity for self-reflection and practical intervention in their own learning. Evidence for her success can be seen in two videos of practice, which can be accessed at http://www.e-lar.net/videos/AI2_0002.wmv and http://www.e-lar.net/videos/Validation.wmv). In spite of her ultimate success this proved to be a difficult task for her because she felt insecure and she needed the support of critical friends.

Marica writes in her research report:

> Each day I kept detailed accounts in my diary and sent my postings to the web forum. Branko and my teacher colleague Vesna commented on my accounts. It was very important to me that they gave me feedback, and their support meant a lot to me. I wrote in my diary, 'Right through the process of doing this research I found I needed the support of critical friends almost as much as in the beginning.' This was a surprise because I thought I was already reasonably experienced in doing action research. I have learned that an action researcher needs a reflective friend regardless of amount of experience.

Interestingly Marica explains how she used to feel insecure about trying to work in a way that honoured her own educational values, while also having to address the requirements of traditional forms of schooling:

> Probably my insecurity arose because I did not know enough about action research, and also because of the fact that my daily work often looked less and less like ordinary teaching practice, because of the demands of the official curriculum. In my classes, each day children were actively implementing their own action plans or carrying out their own critical analyses, and at the same time as helping them to do this, I also had to fulfil the required curricular teaching contents. Consequently the discrepancies between what I was doing and the official 'system' were often considerable. I worked with these tensions for a long time. I often ask myself why we teachers spend such a long time planning everything that we think children should learn and do, when to them the most interesting things are what we negotiate together or what they plan to do alone.

She did however persist, and the evidence of her students' learning vindicates her decisions. This is what her students have to say (Zovko 2005):

- What children find useful about action research:

  I can help and improve myself. I liked keeping a diary.

  My family give me more time when I am doing my research. I like it when they compliment me and see that I am doing something important.

  It is great because you entertain yourself and improve, and even learn something.

  Everyone ought to do action research. People would get to know themselves and find out how they can be better.

- What children learned from doing action research:

  I learned that I can learn through action research.

  It is possible to improve a lot of things when you want to.

  I thought that I was helping my mum too much with the housekeeping, but when I was preparing lunch as part of my action research project, I realized that the amount of work my mum does in looking after all of us is killing. I used to help my mum all right, but now I do so much more than before.

  How to live better.

In relation to Marica's tensions about the discrepancies between her practice and the wider system of schooling, my own view is that Marica overcame the external 'system' by overcoming the degree to which she had internalized the values of the 'system'. When she succeeded in changing her assumptions, she succeeded in changing her educational practice. Evidence for this change is clearly visible on the videos, where children engage in their own learning in a way that far exceeds my own expectations. Just a few days ago, Marica told me that she intends to continue working with a new generation of students. She is further inspired by the fact that several girls, who had been brought up in an extremely traditional and patriarchal way, had become active action researchers and had begun to express their understandings of how they could create their identities in ways that were right for them. From our conversations, we have come to the understanding that action research processes do not begin with fixed action steps, but start by asking how we can liberate children's potentials in ways that encourage them creatively to express themselves as unique persons and rich social beings.

I bring this understanding with me also to my work with teachers. I cannot teach teachers to do action research in terms of a set of methods. Doing action research is more of a living philosophy, a form of artistry, which requires us to change ourselves if we want to help others to become participants in processes of change. It also requires a complete commitment to the colleagues with whom we cooperate. In some ways, the quality of communication and relationship is much more important in the practical realization of our values, with both children and adults, than achieving rigour. Realizing our educational values with others cannot be forced, but requires the development of confidence and trust in one another. These early efforts are now being systematized through the formal teacher professional education programmes for which I am responsible in my new role at the university.

I have to note that encouraging teachers to record their investigations of their practices was far from easy. I experienced a distinct block to my efforts in terms of our cultural traditions, in relation to teachers' self-perceptions. Teachers are not encouraged to perceive themselves as researchers. Teachers like to talk and even to write about their experiences but they do not see the evaluation of their practice as particularly important, especially when the evaluation involves systematically gathering data. This is where my role was important. I helped the teachers to gather data and analyse them. We jointly prepared action research reports and presented them at meetings of our learning community. Recently we have placed them on our workspace (http://mzu.sbnet.hr), and I have published them in the educational research literature (Bognar 2003; 2004).

However, I still experienced a tension. In spite of the fact that the teachers were participating in all aspects of their action research projects, they were still not independent of me as their leader. Although several authors do not perceive anything untoward in this situation (for example Stenhouse 1975; McTaggart 1997), it was definitely not what I wanted. I wanted the teachers to be independent of me, and to make their own professional decisions, based on their own knowledge of practice. In future action research projects I fully intend to find ways of realizing my values of the exercise of free and independent thinking, and I hope to draw on the insights of, for example, Sagor (1992), who speaks of collaborative action research, and McNiff and Whitehead (2002), who speak of collective community enquiries. I am hoping that a further twenty teachers from five schools will soon undertake their cooperative action research projects. For this we are planning to use the Moodle system for e-learning and network cooperation (http://www.e-lar.net/moodle). We already use our web portal (http://mzu.sbnet.hr) for publishing our action research accounts. The main idea is that action research should not be an activity undertaken by lone researchers, independent of their colleagues. I am convinced that cooperation is a much better way to conduct action research because of the synergetic influence between participants that enables each individual to get back as much as, if not more than, they contribute. Although our cooperation will be mostly realized through our e-communications, it is perhaps easier to produce written reports of our learning from the experience of the research. Community enquiries can become networked enquiries, where 'network' refers not only to the use of technology but also to cooperation between action researchers from several different action research communities.

I said earlier that I consider care and kindness as of greater importance in the conduct of action research, when the aim is to develop communities of practitioner researchers and to encourage them to have confidence in their own capacity as researchers. However, demonstrating rigour is of vital importance in the production of our accounts of practice, so I turn to that aspect now.

Demonstrating the rigour and the validity of my work

Without doubt, I consider Habermas's contributions of the criteria of social validity as very important in developing new scientific approaches, especially in action research. Throughout his work, Habermas has emphasized the difference between strategic (manipulative) acting and communicative action, whose aim is to reach agreement through mutual understanding (Habermas 1979). In this way he has opened the door to small-scale research, where the quality of research depends not on already existing methodological approaches, but on communication between participants of their research findings that emphasize that accounts should be truthful, understandable, sincere and appropriate.

However, I find his approach problematic, because it is still rooted in cognitive understanding and expressed in a propositional form. It seems to me that he has the same moral commitments as Kant, who expressed those commitments as a universal moral imperative. My own view is that by trying to establish a universal moral principle, or law, or imperative, we actually militate against a lived form of life which cannot be bounded by any universal principle. Life should have its own free space, not only for formal communication but also for any form of its creative expression. On this view, when we say we wish to validate the form we give to our lives, we need to develop living, demonstrable criteria rather than only linguistic ones (McNiff and Whitehead 2002). If we try to find universal validation procedures, we make the same mistake as many others, who may have had good intentions, but did not appreciate the fact that each person is a unique identity who is capable of making judgements about their own lives, in terms of what they understand as good. However, even though each practitioner may be entitled to find their own original approach to improving their practice, and showing why this should be agreed as improvement, practitioners still have to subject their accounts to the public scrutiny of others, to reach the kind of intersubjective agreement that Habermas was speaking about. Each of us, as practitioner researchers, needs therefore to set out our original contribution about how we are establishing the validity of our claims to knowledge, drawing also on the insights of others who are involved in the same processes, and, where appropriate, on the insights of established forms of scientific enquiry, and then make our findings available for public scrutiny and critique.

Conclusion

I am offering my account here as a way of validating my research claim that I have improved my own learning and contributed to the learning of others. I claim that I have improved my own learning in the sense that I enquired into my practice and found ways of improving it, and I have helped others to improve their learning by encouraging them to become critical and to find ways of practising that are educational for themselves and their students. Further, I am claiming that I am contributing to the education of the social formation of teachers, in that my work with Marica and others shows a pattern of mutual mentoring influence between myself, a teacher, and her students. Such forms of learning and professional education have until now been relatively unavailable in my country, although they are widely accepted and practised in international contexts. I believe our small-scale action research projects carry considerable significance for others who may wish to learn from our work. We have much to learn from one another and, by the publishing of the accounts of our continued collaborative research, we hope that the international research community may also soon have something to learn from us.

SUMMARY

The two case stories in this chapter contain ideas about how practitioner educational researchers can contribute to new social practices through undertaking their action enquiries. Working with limited financial and practical resources, both researchers show how, through their struggles to realize their educational-values-based visions, they have managed to inspire others in turn to achieve their own educational values. They have both managed to encourage a culture of enquiry within the social contexts of their countries' educational and cultural transformation. These stories also show the deep implications for new practices at global level. Because the stories are about managing cultural renewal through educational action research, they also demonstrate the potential contributions of action research for the creation of sustainable social orders.

9 Evaluating the account of our research

How do we evaluate the evidence-based account of our learning?

In Chapter 7 we claimed that we are having some educational influence in our own and other people's learning. We went on, in Chapter 8, to produce examples of how we believe our learning is influencing the learning of other people in different social formations. We now have to ask whether we are exercising our educational influence in the learning of you, our reader. To influence the learning of readers, who are absent in space and time, however, means communicating the work through a text of some kind, which is a mediated form of communication rather than face-to-face communication.

Doing research, and writing a text about the research, are entirely different activities and involve different sets of skills. Doing research involves the systematic development of learning by investigating practice, which is a largely social practice. Writing involves the systematic development of language as a form of textual communication, which is a largely individual practice. Writing action research accounts, therefore, involves two things: it involves writing in a way that communicates the processes of the research, and it also involves writing in a way that maintains the reader's attention throughout and speaks to their own experience. Doing this is crucial because, like it or not, the quality of the research is judged first in terms of the research account and second in terms of the quality of the research process. While both elements have to be included, the first thing a reader encounters is the text, and, unless the text is accessible and inviting, the reader will not read it or, worse, will read someone else's that looks more appealing.

This challenge faces us in this book. We have to communicate the processes of our research through a text that is inviting and appealing, and still shows rigorous scholarship. We also have to communicate the story of the research in a way that shows the quality of that scholarship. We would like to claim validity and legitimacy both for our research and also for our account of learning. The way to claim validity for the *research* is by showing how it has been legitimated in various critical forums. The way to claim validity for the *text* is by showing that readers have accessed it and produced evidence-based accounts of its usefulness in their own learning.

This chapter addresses these two concerns. It is organized as follows:

1 Evaluating our account
2 Explaining how the account is grounded in evidence of learning

1 Evaluating our account

The account you are reading is a text, in linguistic form. We are communicating with you via the medium of written language. Our account is about presenting our provisional claim to knowledge, so that you may judge whether the account shows that we are doing what we say we are doing. If you and others in the practitioner researcher community agree that we are doing what we are claiming, we will feel confident in continuing to develop the work on a properly legitimated basis. This means that you are both our reader and our evaluator, and this means that you need to have clear criteria and standards of judgement to guide your reading and help you make judgements. In this section therefore we make suggestions about what these might be, and show how we are claiming to be meeting them. You may of course disagree, and prefer to judge the text using criteria and standards of judgement of your own.

So to be clear about this: we will adopt the same strategy as Mary Hartog (see page 104), and set out some of the normative criteria and standards of judgement by which texts are usually evaluated, and then go on to articulate criteria and standards of judgement of our own, which we would like to be used to evaluate our work.

First we offer criteria for evaluating the form and content of a text. We then go on to comment on how we transform these criteria into our standards of judgement, and the significance of the standards of judgement we are using.

Criteria for evaluating the form and content of our text

To judge the form and content of our text, we return to Habermas's criteria for social validity. We do this because writing and reading a text are a form of socially oriented communicative action, in Habermas's terms. We incorporate into these social criteria other criteria for textual validity. We therefore ask these questions in relation to these criteria:

- Is the account comprehensible?
- Is the account truthful?
- Is the account sincere?
- Is the account appropriate?

Is the account comprehensible?

Have we used a form of language throughout that is accessible and unambiguous? Have we attempted to mislead through the use of inappropriate techniques such as innuendo? Have we clarified our own position and spoken to your experience? Have we respected the academic conventions of correct referencing (Woods 1999), of grounding our work in appropriate literatures (Wilkinson 2000), of correct grammar and punctuation (Marggraf Turley 2000)? Have we structured the report coherently (R. Murray 2002)? Have we allowed our passion to show through (Dadds 1995), while not using it to reinforce our prejudices? Have we channelled our outrage at injustice in disciplined ways, so that our messages have not been distorted by outbursts of anger and wild language? What we have tried to do in presenting this account is to move beyond writing a text, which is comprehensible only in terms of its lexical and syntactic structures, and allow the meanings to emerge from within the text. This is what Barry says is the proper business of stylistics: 'Stylistics moves beyond "sentence grammar" to "text grammar", considering how the text works as a whole to achieve (or not) its purposes (for instance, to amuse, to create suspense, or to persuade) and examining the linguistic features which contribute to those ends' (2002: 215). Do we do this?

Is the account truthful?
Do we make unwarranted claims and statements without supporting them with authenticated evidence? Have we clearly explicated the nature of the evidence, and shown it to be authentic by including real names and locations? Do we contradict our own espoused values of social justice by communicating our opinions through the creation of our own propaganda, while critiquing the unjustified use of propaganda as a method of persuasion? Do we make our use of language clear on these issues? 'There are also many techniques for penetrating the veil of propaganda that should become second nature in dealing with the output of doctrinal institutions (media, journals of opinion, scholarship)', says Chomksy (1999: 1). Do we put out our scholarship as doctrine? Do we demonstrate that it is second nature to us to penetrate the veil of propaganda, and encourage you to do the same, to the extent of critiquing ours? Chomsky goes on to say:

> There's no way to be informed without devoting effort to the task, whether we have in mind what's happening in the world, physics, major league football, or anything else. Understanding doesn't come free. It's true that the task is somewhere between awfully difficult and utterly hopeless for an isolated individual. But it's feasible for anyone who is part of a cooperative community – and that's true about all of the other cases too. Same holds for 'intellectual self-defense'. It takes a lot of confidence – perhaps more confidence than one ought to have – to take a position alone because it seems to you right, in opposition to everything you see and hear. (1999: 1)

Have we encouraged you throughout the book to build up your intellectual self-defence by challenging givens and normative assumptions, including our own? Have we offered resources and advice that enable you to do so? Have we encouraged you to become a member of a cooperative community? Later in this text we produce examples of what can happen when people do become members of cooperative communities, how they can influence their own learning, and how they learn to transform their circumstances and even to engage in processes of cultural transformation.

Is the account sincere?
Have we shown sincerity throughout? Have we respected the views of researchers working in other traditions, while showing clearly our own points of disagreement? Have we used a respectful, albeit sometimes critical, tone throughout? Have we interrogated

our text, as Derrida (1976) says authors should, avoiding the temptation to present the text as the only reality, and so disguising the reality of the life stories of the people whose stories make up the text? Barry says that the work of poststructuralists includes the following:

- They 'read the text against itself' so as to expose what might be thought of as the 'textual subconscious', where meanings are expressed which may be directly contrary to the surface meaning.
- They seek to show that the text is characterised by disunity rather than unity.
- They look for shifts and breaks of various kinds in the text and see these as evidence of what is repressed or glossed over or passed over in silence in the text. These discontinuities are sometimes called 'fault-lines', a geological metaphor referring to the breaks in rock formations which give evidence of previous activity and movement. (2002: 73)

We have tried to do this. Further, we have tried to show the realization of Lyotard's views about the nature of postmodern works of art:

A postmodern artist or writer is in the position of a philosopher: the text he (or she) writes, the work he produces are not in principle governed by pre-established rules, and they cannot be judged according to a determining judgement, by applying familiar categories to the text or to the work. Those rules and categories are what the work of art itself is looking for. The artist and the writer, then, are working without rules in order to formulate the rules of what will have been done. (1984: 81)

We have deliberately chosen to present our story in a living form, commensurate with the ideas we are expressing about the need for living forms of communication to express living forms of theory. We have interspersed episodes of our own narrative with episodes of propositional theorizing, and we have pointed to the interrelated and intertwined relationship between them in the process of theorization. On occasion, we have become quite dogmatic, as Polanyi (1958) and Feyerabend (1975) say is the way with generating theories, where it is often necessary to stop and consolidate, in order to test out the provisional ideas so far, and gather confidence sufficient to warrant continuing (see our next point about the writing of pedagogical texts). Do we show the unfolding nature of our own narrative, and the narratives of the people whose work we are reporting, and offer critical reflection throughout on what we are doing?

Is the account appropriate?
We are writing a pedagogical text on action research in education. In doing so, we bear in mind, as Habermas (1987) said, that we, and you, our reader, are working against a recognized normative background, that is, we are inevitably positioned as occupants of a culture whose norms are established and, by and large, go unquestioned, or are held in place by often invisible regimes of power. Specifically, we, and you, are located within the cultures of the educational research community, whose norms are agreed (frequently by those whose voices are loudest in the communities of ordered academies) in terms of dominant assumptions about the nature and growth of knowledge and of the positioning of those who claim to be knowledge workers. These dominant assumptions permeate all areas of the culture. The dominant assumption in relation to knowledge

is that propositional knowledge is more appropriate for scholarly enquiry than practitioners' knowledge; and that the task of knowledge generation should be allocated to established researchers rather than to practitioners. Further, it is assumed that, in the writing of textbooks, writers may offer new ideas, but should remain within the boundaries of the established form of logic and the established form of representation. By and large, writers conform. Thayer-Bacon (2003) for example writes a superb book on relational epistemologies, without bringing her own story into the text or showing how she actually engages with the idea of relational epistemologies through her own lived experience. Perhaps for some it is even a case that they have not interrogated the norms underpinning the forms the culture takes, such as how textbooks should be written. They do not address the issue because for them the issue itself has been trivialized to the extent that it does not exist.

We understand such norms as contradictory, and designed to perpetuate the existing contradictions of forms of logic and forms of representation among the community of scholars. The contradictions lie in the fact that theories are spoken about, as Rawls (1971) does, when he proposes a theory of justice or a theory of justice as fairness (Rawls 2001), without showing how their authors live justice. Pedagogical texts tend to talk about their subject matters only, but the authors do not show how the abstract subject matters are interwoven in the reality of their own lives. We are not saying that pedagogical texts should avoid presenting subject matters. On the contrary, we believe they should. The theories however do need to be grounded somehow in the living reality of people's lives, in order to avoid the contradiction of offering prescriptions about human living, relying on the justification of abstract theoretical engagement but without the justification of the realities of experience. For texts, including pedagogical texts, to claim ethical validity, they need to communicate through both their form and their content the moral authority of the author and the ethical validity of the text.

In writing this book we have challenged the norms of pedagogical writing (as we do in all our writing), and in so doing we are hoping to influence scholarly and cultural change, where artists and writers gain confidence in contributing to an emergent literary genre of living texts as they communicate the stories of practitioner researchers as they show how they have generated their own living educational theories.

Transforming the criteria into living critical standards of judgement for assessing the quality of our text

In the chapter so far, we have focused on evaluating our capacity to tell a story, and, in its written communicable form, to write a good text. For that we have set out the kinds of normative criteria used for judging this capacity. Now we want more. We want the quality of our story itself to be judged, and, because living stories are never separate from their tellers, we want the quality of ourselves as storytellers to be judged. We are not satisfied that our work should be judged only in terms of the fairly technical exercise of telling a good story, which involves criteria and standards of judgement of a more technical rational nature. Reviews of books in journals do this. We want our stories to be judged also in terms of what we do and how we are, so that the meanings of our lives emerge through the stories, which incorporate the stories of those we work with, so that others can learn not only how to tell a good research story but also how to live a life of good scholarship, which, for us, means living a life of community enquiry about how to exercise educational influence in learning.

To review so far. First we have set out the kinds of criteria that we consider useful in judging the technical excellence of writing, in order to assess whether the account is accessible and clear. We have interrogated the validity of the writing, which is about establishing technical textual validity. Now we focus on how we can transform those criteria into the kinds of living critical standards of judgement that we consider useful in judging the quality of a story, and thereby the quality of the work that the story communicates, in order to judge whether the story can be believed. We interrogate the validity of the claims made within the text, which is about establishing content validity. These kinds of criteria and standards of judgement can also be considered useful in judging the quality of the storyteller, in order to assess whether the person who is telling the story can be believed, which is about establishing moral validity. These are different order truth claims. In this book we are making all kinds of truth claims about the quality of our research and how it can be assessed. The issue is: for you to believe our claims, you have to have trust in us, as people. If we are to show how we have influenced learning, and how we hope to influence future learning, it is a question not only of how believable our story is, but also of how believable we are. Can we be trusted? How do we understand trust? How can trust be established?

Understanding and developing trust

To communicate our understanding of trust, and how it can be established, we draw on the work of truth and reconciliation commissions, especially in South Africa.

The aim of a truth and reconciliation commission is twofold. The first aim is to confront acts of social injustice perpetrated in the past, to engage with them and come to terms with the hurt in order to move on (Minow 1998; Chapman 2001). The second aim is to find ways of moving on, which means coming to terms, through forgiveness, with the pain that has been inflicted. The Truth and Reconciliation Commission in South Africa was set up to allow persecutors to confess to what they had done, safe in the knowledge that a full confession would lead to amnesty, and to allow the persecuted to challenge them face to face, and hopefully achieve some kind of catharsis through engaging with the telling of crimes. Together, it was assumed, persecutor and persecuted would achieve redemption by confronting their pain, forgiving the abuse and the capacity to give and receive abuse, and so move on.

Some critique has been offered of this perspective, in relation to practice and theory. The practice of reconciliation often takes the form of a practical distributive justice, where reparations are made through the provision of pensions, counselling, and other supports of a compensatory kind (see Gibson 2004). There is little mention in the mainstream literatures, and this includes the mainstream psychology literatures, of whether or not forgiveness actually can lead to a commitment to establishing new relationships of trust. Most people would have the experience, whether personal or professional, of some kind of betrayal by a close and valued other. In the best circumstances, these acts of betrayal are ameliorated by apology, a seeking of forgiveness. However, while forgiveness is relatively methodologically straightforward, it is not so easy emotionally to transform forgiveness into new acts of trust. Trust, along with a constellation of other fragile capacities, is like breath on frozen air, impossible to capture and easily dissipated. Trust involves the full mental and emotional commitment of one person to another, and a betrayed lover may often find it difficult to commit to a new relationship as fully as before the act of betrayal. Once trust is betrayed, it can be difficult to restore it to its full original form. This is not to say that deep learning cannot arise from the experience of betrayal, or the struggle to renew trust, but it is to say that finding trust is, by and large, an elusive and problematic experience.

What then does it take to establish trust, as much as possible, in relationships? What does it take to demonstrate the worthiness of people to be trusted, to be entrusted with others' emotional wellbeing? In relation to social transformation, how can trust be established among people in social formations and among the social formations themselves, in order to move from reconciliation through forgiveness to a transformation of the social order through the establishment of trusting relationships? In relation to our claims to be doing this, what do we do that shows we are to be trusted when we claim we are competent to be make these kinds of judgements? We leave the question of the transformation of social orders through trusting relationships for future research. We deal with the issue of how we show ourselves to be competent in making judgements by demonstrating our own trustworthiness now.

We understand that establishing the truth about socio-political and historical experiences rests on the premise that participants need to engage with the issues of how they have been positioned, or have positioned themselves, within situations of social justice or injustice. This would involve interrogating their own mental stance as well as their historical and socio-cultural positioning. Some would perceive themselves as persecuted and persecutors. It would also involve their appreciating whether they had been forced into these positions by others, physically or mentally, or whether they had willingly entered these positions by believing what they were told and not questioning their own entrenched assumptions, or the norms of the culture or the regime in power (see the story on pages 106–9). These ideas about questioning givens and norms constitute a major issue in the literatures of postcolonialism (for example Young 2001; Chowdhry and Nair 2003; Murray Y.P. 2005).

Reconciliation is premised on the idea of engaging with the truth, in order to come to a point of forgiveness, of self and others, in order to create a new distinctively justice-oriented social order. The practices of arriving at the truth and point of reconciliation can be achieved by a critical interrogation of present circumstances, including the ontological and epistemological assumptions underpinning the practices and discourses of the present social order, that is, people interrogating their own perceptions of their identities, and how they have come to form those identities, in relation to what counts as knowledge (in this case, what counts as the truth), and who should be regarded as knowledgeable (in this case, who is capable of telling the truth and to whom). Showing how truth can inform reconciliation in order to inform new social action constitutes a transformational process of improved ontological and epistemological wellbeing that can transform into improved social and institutional wellbeing. In other words, having a secure sense of one's own self-identity and worth as a human being has to be an essential grounding for the development of new social and institutional practices, if those practices also are to be grounded in a sense of people's personal worth as the basis of the development of human capacity for organizational growth, on an understanding of development as freedom (Sen 1999).

This is where the theoretical base of the literatures of truth and reconciliation commissions could be developed, we believe, in terms of their articulated reasons and purposes. The situation is reminiscent of the methodological brief of critical theory. Critical theory can be seen as the methodological orientation of initiatives such as truth and reconciliation commissions, because it aims to interrogate the socio-cultural and historical factors that have led to the current situation, but does not go beyond. Although critical theory may speak of the need for political action, in order to transform the current social order, it does not make any practical recommendation about what kind of action is necessary, whose action it may be, and how the action may be implemented. Equally it has little to say about how transformative social action may be judged to have transformed the social order in question.

This, for us, is the province of action research. We believe that the practice of transforming the existing social order into a new distinctively justice-oriented social order can be achieved by practitioners as they ask, 'How do I improve what I am doing?', and disseminate their accounts of learning and practice in order to inform the learning of others, especially within the social formations of state institutions. By showing how they have engaged with the socio-political and historical antecedents of their own situations, practitioners can explain how they have come to a situation in which they feel impelled to take political action. Taking political action involves first acquiring a critical understanding (establishing the truth), which is the grounds for coming to terms with the present situation (personal and social reconciliation), and then, on the basis of the capacity for forgiveness, finding ways of renewing trust to the extent that people are prepared to work together, from the grounds of their own understanding and commitment to communicative action, to transform the social order.

This now brings us to the second section of this chapter, which focuses on our explanations for why we believe we should be trusted in offering stories of learning that constitute claims to knowledge, so that they can be tested in this public forum. Our explanations revolve around how our account is grounded in evidence of learning, and how that learning can be understood in relation to free, loving and inclusive practices.

2   Explaining how the account is grounded in evidence of learning

Our data archives are full of the stories of practitioners who have critically engaged with their past in order to achieve reconciliation with themselves and others. Having achieved reconciliation, they now decide to take action to improve their own situations. Furthermore, many go on to influence the education of social formations. A significant feature of the stories is how practitioners are able to identify their values as the living standards by which they judge the quality of their work.

One of the most beautifully written stories is by Madeline Church, whose studies Jack supported. Some extracts from her PhD thesis appear below. You can download Madeline's entire thesis from http://www.bath.ac.uk/~edsajw/church.shtml.

Madeline Church

Madeline begins her thesis with these words:

> This doctorate is the product of five years of intensive reflection, conducted while working. This written document combines two areas of inquiry. One, an internal focus, what Marshall (1995, 2001, 2004) refers to as 'self-reflective inquiry' or Whitehead (2004a) calls 'self-study', what can be thought of, as Winter et al. (1999) do, as living within the reflective practitioner paradigm initiated by Schön (1983). This involves a series of reflections on simple questions such as 'Who am I? What am I doing? How do I do these things? What do I know?', or a combined global question, 'What is going on here?' Second, a work focus, a process of collaborative action research with international social change networks, looking at what criteria might be most appropriate for evaluating them and the work we do in and through them. The combined force of these two sets of questions leads me to ask myself, 'Why do I find myself in networks?' Through a process of writing, asking myself 'what is going on here?' and writing again, I have developed a process of calling myself to account, using the standards of love, compassion, fairness and art as those most important to me to be judged by. These 'living standards' (Whitehead 2003) are, I believe, a potential contribution to the call for establishing appropriate criteria for judging such self-study, reflective practice accounts. I start from an understanding that it is through unfolding knowing of myself that I become a knowledgeable practitioner (Kushner 2000), thus confirming Bullough & Pinnegar's (2004) hunch that it is essential to consider the ontological when creating such living standards. 'The consideration of ontology, of one's being in and toward the world, should be a central feature of any discussion of the value of self-study research' (Bullough & Pinnegar 2004, p. 319).

Madeline goes on to tell her story of being bullied.

> When I was eleven, we moved to London. I was a new girl in a big comprehensive school, hopelessly unfashionable and 'too bright for my own good'. A boy whose friendship I rejected decided to *teach me a lesson*. I emphasise that because it is a phrase often used by those intending to make others alter their behaviour through intimidation and violence. I certainly learned several 'lessons' during that time, but I don't believe that any one of them was the 'lesson' he wanted me to learn. For six months I was treated like a pariah by my class. I was subjected to the usual repetitive intimidating behaviour of following, tripping, threatening to get me after school … But the one that sticks with me is the way my name, Madeline, disgusted them. Our French books starred Suzanne and Philippe, and their friend, Madeleine. We had to read aloud in classes with Mr Liebrecht, himself a consummate bully. Any child who was forced to read a sentence with the name Madeleine in it would spit on the floor. I remember thinking impotently that it wasn't even spelt the same, mine only has two e-s. It was intensely painful and humiliating. It helped me to develop a keen sense of self-disgust.

Later,

> When I was nineteen, a young actress and doing a prestigious job, which I had fought hard to get, a theatre director used me as his 'whipping boy'.

He was renowned for picking on one person and deriving pleasure from humiliating them. Everyone else in the company watched, but did nothing. My confidence fell apart, so easily, and my sense of self-disgust returned.

And later still,

The last experience [I recount] is of someone trying to bully me at work but not succeeding. I regularly tackled her about the way she treated me, although it had little lasting effect. I had made a conscious decision that I would tolerate some of her behaviour as I knew that she was on her way out. And I was prepared to work for her to get what I wanted. But I was shocked to learn later that everyone else in the organisation thought she was bullying me. And again, no one did anything about it. And I vowed that I would never stand around while someone disintegrated under my watchful eye; I would never grant someone the space to publicly humiliate another; I would never respect the culture of 'teaching someone a lesson'.

Madeline articulates her reasons for action.

I am fired by anger, and a commitment to fairness. This determination has found expression in almost everything that I do. My commitment to fairness did not start here however, with this bullying. This is not a story of revelations, or of personality transplant. This is what I mean about bullying and my experiences of it providing definition, shape. I recall an event in my early school life, probably aged nine. I had a fight at school with a girl called Wendy. I know it is an important memory because I am not usually good at retaining names. I can even still see her face, and remember feeling sort of absurd wrestling with her in the playground. I don't remember what the fight was about. I do remember that we were punished in very different ways. I was a bright, popular and middle-class girl, normally well-behaved, if precocious and big-headed. Wendy was working class and not very good at handing in her homework, getting things right in class, and she definitely got into more trouble. I was reprimanded, and she was banned from going swimming for the next week. No one tried to resolve what the fight was about. And my memory of this is that I complained because the punishments weren't fair. Looking back now I was probably pretty priggish about it and I am sure some of my motivation was even then driven by a feeling of superiority, a snobbishness based on my class. And there was certainly a bit of me that wanted to be more severely punished to show what a rebel I could be. If I am honest I still have to check myself for my motives with regard to the work I do now, to be sure that I am not motivated by an out-dated do-gooding, helping-those-who-can't-help-themselves sort of mentality. The repeated cycle of bullying in my life has been a reminder that it is for me that I do these things, just as much as for others.

When I started this research, I wrote in bold letters 'I loathe being asked questions about myself.' I also wrote this line: 'I am a sophisticated questioner.' In asking myself questions about what had happened to me, what meaning to make of it, I started to inquire into my self as a question-former, or rather one who responds in conscious and also embodied ways to her environment by asking questions. I have come close to understanding that my inquiry-filled response to my environment, my nosey curiosity, was probably something feared by those who bullied me. Also that being bullied led me to resist being seen, inspected too closely, and I began resisting others' questions about me by using questions of them as a defence. One outcome of this is that my own capacity for bullying others finds easy expression in interrogation or berating, and that I have to work hard to see that my anger does not corrupt my intention to connect with others, through questioning activity. And I have also come to see that my commitment to asking the important questions is a way of refusing to accept the dominant accepted reality, resisting easy explanations that can make us lazy, hazy, docile and complicit. 'A person who possesses the "art" of questioning is a person who is able to prevent the suppression of questions by the dominant opinion' (Gadamer, 1975, p. 330). So, this is also a story of refusing to be rejected or disconnected, of a dogged determination to be a force for good through the power of human connectivity, despite my fear of exposure.

Throughout her thesis, Madeline tells of experiences that impelled her to resist bullying, and to transform unsatisfactory situations into one in which love could be seen at work. When she concludes her thesis, she writes:

In the meantime, I use my voice to talk about love, as I have always used my voice as my centre. This voice is a powerful characteristic of mine; it is something that expresses an essence of me. My voice is unmistakable, people say. They recognise me through my voice. I have taken to saying the word LOVE out loud when in meetings about evaluation or about projects. People's eyes light up and they gasp as if I have just said I am a Martian. Then people start to flutter, and their hearts beat hard, their palms sweat a little and a little sensual rush flits round the room, and they begin to tell stories and uncover something that they had forgotten. LOVE. They talk about why they wanted to do this work, and their big dreams of making the world a better place burst from their pent up breasts, and they begin to gush and gust and garble and shudder nervously as if touched by a strange and affecting hand. LOVE. I say I believe in the transforming power of LOVE.

It seems that I have used my voice for years to speak out, yet have found the speaking out lacking in love, growing rigid and repetitive, and hard. The struggle is to find a way to speak out in defence of justice, and maintain my belief in forgiveness and love as a tempering, merciful and essential component. This of course is not just a personal struggle, it is one that many have faced with the techno-rational world we live in. It feels irresolvable and probably is. It is simply a dynamic tension of our lives. So, as part of learning to breathe again, I am working with art as a source of inspiration (in-breath) and an expression of love. The thing I hold in mind is that inspiration, that in-breath, brings me closer to the world. And that connection is secured through love. For me that inspiration comes largely through engagement with the artistic endeavour of another – Antony Gormley, Louise Bourgeois – and finds expression through my writing. For instance, the poem I wrote for Alice and James transforms our individual and collective experience. I write as a way of transforming our conversational experience into an aesthetic one. I sense Alice's pain, feel my own despair, and want to offer something up, something of beauty, something healing, something that takes us beyond. Jointly and separately we created the conditions for the poem. It is an expression of love.

So, what has Madeline's story to do with our claim that we believe we should be trusted when we say that our account is grounded in evidence of learning, and that the learning can be understood in relation to free, loving and inclusive practices? We believe that our claim is justified, because Madeline's story, and many like it, clearly articulate their commitment to free, loving and inclusive practices. The internal validity of the story is clarified. Furthermore, statements such as the following from Madeline serve to consolidate the evidence to support the claim that Jack had some influence in Madeline's thinking and practice, and lend external validity to the evidence-based claims to learning.

Madeline says:

> Jack was my supervisor for five years. What he knows about, and unhesitatingly touches when he sees it, is authenticity. Jack can read a piece of work and see the truth in it. He can spot the core phrase in any piece I write, and say, this is where the truth of this story lies, this is the important claim you are making, now where is your evidence? It took me years and much questioning really to understand the discipline he was demanding, and we spent many an hour with me saying, Jack, I don't understand, and he would say it again, and I would reply, you need to say it another way, say it differently to me, so that I get it, and we would swing back and forth, and I would take it away and ponder upon it, and re-search for my evidence, and bring it back. And again he would spot the authentic moment and the new hole in the story. As such I think we undertook a process of co-investigating my account, and reconciling his demand for clarity and authenticity as a 'reader' and my determinedly opaque and subtle aesthetic as writer.

By their deeds you shall know them. We get to know practitioners through their stories. These stories combine into a knowledge base such as that which Catherine Snow spoke about (page 118). You, our reader, get to know us through our stories. We, and those whom we support, form a narrativized community. Our stories act as evidence for the claims of the others that we have all influenced learning. We are a community of learners who are influencing learning.

How should our trustworthiness be judged? It should be judged by the existence of the stories of learning that we help others produce and have validated. That stories appear at all has been influenced by our intervention. That they are stories of learning is testimony to the quality of that intervention. That hundreds and perhaps thousands of practitioners are now also able to tell their stories of their 'I' enquiries of the kind, 'How do I improve what I am doing?', as evidenced in our books, papers and websites, is testimony to the quality of our influence. The free and spontaneous sharing of thousands of stories of learning does not happen by accident, but is an ongoing process of unflagging encouragement and commitment, what we and Madeline Church call love, a love that is free and inclusive and expressed as a life-affirming energy.

SUMMARY

Here we have returned to the theme of demonstrating the validity of our work, where we focus on issues of social validity, and we now introduce the theme of demonstrating the validity of the account of our work, where we focus on issues of textual validity. Again we draw on Habermas's (1987) social criteria of comprehensibility, truthfulness, sincerity and appropriateness in judging the validity of our evidence-based account of our own learning. As before, we explain how we transform these criteria into our living critical standards of judgement to assess the quality of our text. We go on to explore the idea that by demonstrating our capacity to make these processes transparent we are aiming to develop trust between ourselves and our audience, so that our scholarly and moral credibility can be validated and acted upon. At this point we appeal to you, our reader, to be aware of how you are exercising your own originality of mind and critical engagement as you make judgements on the validity of our account.

PART 5

Testing our Claims to Educational Knowledge

This part deals with how we test our claims to educational knowledge. *It contains one chapter:*

10   Into new research
How do we modify our concerns, ideas and practices in the light of our evaluations?

We explain how conducting our research, and testing its evidence base in terms of the learning of practitioner action researchers, has enabled us to claim with some confidence that we are achieving our values-based aims of contributing to the education of the practitioner educational research community, and possibly also to the education of the academic educational research community.

10 Into new research

How do we modify our concerns, ideas and practices in the light of our evaluations?

This book is one of several current texts that represent for us a transition point in our lifelong action research. We are aware that the focus of our research has changed over recent times. We have developed new interests that, although latent during the lifetime of our research, have recently assumed a new urgency, and demanded attention. In our previous books, which always took the form of progress reports of our research so far, we have focused more on the practicalities of action research, offering advice and guidance to practitioners on how and why to do action research, so that they can improve their professional practice. While we have always made the point that practice is a form of theorizing, in the past we deliberately focused more on practice, out of an awareness that we were writing mainly for practitioners, who needed guidance about how to conduct their action enquiries and produce a report of their work as a credible form of evidence-based practice. In this book we have reversed the focus, and we have talked more about the generative potential of action research to transform theory, explaining specifically that theorizing should be understood as a form of practice. We have tried to communicate throughout the idea of theory and practice as integrated, and as a generative transformational cycle that has the potential for infinite self-renewal. This idea of the integrated nature of living practice as a form of ongoing action–reflection has, we believe, profound implications for new perspectives in human enquiry, including the future of educational research. One of those implications is about realizing the potentials of educational research for the creation of more just and equitable societies, a point that we develop later in this chapter (see also Reason and Bradbury 2001).

At this point therefore we review the current phase of our research, which began in recent times and continues into the present, as we have reported it in this book. We set out our provisional claims to knowledge, and explain how we hope to test these claims against the critical feedback of the community of practitioner researchers. We also set out some new directions that we believe may be some of the most important next steps. Later in the chapter we speak about recent gains, and outline some of the potentials for their development. We also set out our anticipated action plans for the coming time.

We organize the chapter as follows to address these issues:

1   Summary and implications of our research so far
2   New directions for our research: setting out our action plans

1   Summary and implications of our research so far

We said in Chapter 1 that we had two specific sets of concerns. The first was in relation to the continuing focus of the social sciences as the recommended form of educational research. The second was in relation to the appearance of a new form of performance-management-type action research. Both initiatives represented a deep concern, because they appeared to be grounded in the values of control and domination. These values manifested themselves in the sense that an external person, either a researcher who takes a spectator stance, or an author who takes a directive stance, gives instructions to practitioners on what to do and how to do it. The inherent colonialist assumptions of these stances are directly contradictory to our own values and philosophies of education. Our values and philosophies are to do with the freedom of individuals to think for themselves and to make their own decisions about how they should act in the world. The colonialist assumptions also deny our understanding of people as moral beings, who have the capacity to make decisions about what they should do, and to justify why they should do it. The matter becomes especially serious in relation to how educational research in general and action research in particular should be conducted.

We have also made the point throughout this book that many other educational researchers, including those outside the practitioner research community, share the same views as ourselves about these things. Many educational researchers would in fact like to see a change in the current epistemological base of educational enquiry, and would welcome greater participation in public debates by the practitioner researcher community. However, it is publicly acknowledged that the practitioner researcher community is generally lacking in awareness about the need for rigour in establishing procedures for judging quality and validity in research (see Furlong 2000; 2004). By not raising their awareness of such matters, the practitioner researcher community is colluding in its own subjugation. By maintaining the lack of awareness that is keeping them out of the debates, they are lending increased legitimacy to the claims of those in the mainstream educational research communities who maintain that practitioners are not able to take part in the debates because of lack of knowledge of the issues and, by implication, lack of capacity to get to grips with the issues. On this matter we have taken to heart Donald Schön's (1995: 33) point that the problem of introducing and legitimizing in the university the kinds of action research associated with the new scholarship is one not only of the institution but of the scholars themselves.

Consequently, while practitioner action research is generally admired by the educational research community, and indeed by many policy makers, for its contributions to practice, practitioner researchers are seldom acknowledged in the research literature as having made original, significant and rigorous contributions to educational theory. Responsibility for this state of affairs has to be acknowledged by the practitioner researcher community itself, for not giving sufficient attention to these issues within its own discourses and debates, and hence giving little reason to the academic research community to have faith in practitioners' capacities to generate educational theories that can explain educational influences in learning. This is a serious matter, given also that it is the responsibility of the academic community to sit in judgement on practitioners when masters and doctoral reports are submitted for validation to the academy. In this case, the academic research community has no option but to fall back on whatever established criteria and standards of judgement are available, and these tend to be the traditional criteria and standards of judgement of the social sciences and other disciplines of education.

The matter has been made even more pressing with the recent publication of the criteria that will be used to judge practitioner research in the UK 2008 Research Assessment Exercise (2005), with indicated star ratings as follows:

4*   Quality that is world-leading in terms of originality, significance and rigour.
3*   Quality that is internationally excellent in terms of originality, significance and rigour but which nonetheless falls short of the highest standards of excellence.
2*   Quality that is recognized internationally in terms of originality, significance and rigour.
1*   Quality that is recognized nationally in terms of originality, significance and rigour.

These criteria have been set out mainly to establish where funding goes in the highly competitive context of securing money and prestige through the research output of universities. In our view, the criteria are in fact eminently useful for the practitioner research community. Practitioners can see easily what is expected of them in terms of producing research reports that will stand the test of public critique. But practitioners also have a unique opportunity to be creative, and to develop ways that are appropriate for themselves to achieve these criteria. It is in fact up to the practitioner research community to specify their own standards of originality, significance and rigour by which they wish their work to be judged, and show how they are fulfilling those standards in their scholarly reports, and so produce the quality that is looked for. This has implications for research in international contexts, too, because practitioners now have a clear indication of what is required of them if they wish their research to be deemed as equal to the best anywhere in the world. We understand education as perhaps the most important domain for influencing actions that will determine the future of humanity. Therefore we do not see the future of education or educational research in the hands of practitioners who understand their main responsibility as implementing policy, or who are not particularly passionate about articulating why their research is meeting standards of originality, significance and rigour. Nor do we see the educational professions as divided between researchers who generate theory and practitioners who implement theory-informed policies. We believe education to be a domain for the critical engagement of all participants, who wish to learn and to influence the learning of others, and hold themselves accountable for their learning and influence. In our view, practitioners in all educational settings need to work collaboratively, regardless of status or positioning, to find the best way of living that ensures the future sustainability of humanity.

This then is what led us to begin the current phase of our research some little while ago. In this book, we have articulated the main aim of our research as the need to raise awareness and capacity in addressing the issue of what counts as quality action research in the generation of educational theory, and therefore by what standards quality is to be assessed. We have also articulated the need for practitioners to engage with these issues, for reasons already stated, first so that they can show how they take responsibility for their work by explaining how it is to be judged, and second, so that they be appreciated as members of the academic community of researchers, who are contributing to the generation and testing of educational knowledge.

Jack Whitehead has been addressing these issues for some time now (see Whitehead 1989; 2004a; 2005a). This book sets out the issues in a coherent way, and also offers advice to readers on how they may wish to take their own ideas forward. We have also produced evidence to show that we have already had some influence in the community of practitioner action researchers, who are now producing quality reports that clearly meet the criteria of the 2008 Research Assessment Exercise related to originality, significance and rigour. We are summarizing all these issues here. Our claims to knowledge are therefore about how we have begun to articulate the kinds of standards of judgement that are appropriate for judging quality, and how we have had some influence in the work of practitioner researchers in focusing their attention on the need to develop and articulate their own standards of judgement and helping them raise their capacity to do so.

The views we are expressing here carry deep implications both for the community of practitioner action researchers and also for the community of traditional academic educational researchers. All need to accept responsibility for what should be done now. While we acknowledge that not all may wish to become action researchers, we do believe that it is important that all at least indicate their awareness of these matters, to the extent that those who do not wish to become activists will support, in practical and emotional terms, those who do. Above all, those who do not wish to become involved should not stand in the way of those who do, and those who remain stuck in outmoded forms of thinking, such as beliefs that the practical principles used by practitioners to explain their lives and learning should be replaced by principles with more rational justification from the traditional disciplines of education, should resist the urge to promote their own self-interests at the expense of support for practitioner researchers.

Here then is what we believe needs to be done.

For the community of practitioner researchers

The community of practitioner researchers needs to think about the following.

Practitioners as educational activists in contexts of practice and theory

Practitioners need to become educational activists (Sachs 2002) if they wish to take control of their own lives and professions, and not let others impose on them rules and values that are incommensurate with their own. Education remains one of the most exacting and stimulating disciplines, and its constitutive professions such as teaching and counselling need to be reclaimed as passionate and compassionate fields of enquiry. An activist workforce needs to be active in making contributions to new practices, and also to new theory. Good practice is informed by a theoretical base, and, in the case of activist professionals who wish to realize their humanitarian educational values in their practices, this means the generation of theory from within the practice, as well as in relation to theories from the traditional disciplines of education, to show how good quality practice can act as the grounds for the generation of good quality theory. Therefore, practitioners need to enter the domain of theory generation and testing.

Practitioners as theorists

Practitioners need to raise their sights from a self-perception as competent practitioners to become also competent researchers and generators of educational knowledge and theory. If an aim of research is to generate new theory, this means they also have to perceive themselves as competent theorists, and take pains to equip themselves with the appropriate scholarly and intellectual supports. Up to the 1980s, action research was seen by and large as a form of professional development that could help practitioners to be better at their job. This was the dominant message, even in the scholarly literatures. Some lone voices were heard (for example Whitehead 1985; 1989; 2000), maintaining always that practice should be seen as the grounds for theory generation, and that action research should be seen as a form of research, not simply as a form of improving action. Those lone voices have proved highly influential, and have now been joined by other voices. Yet if they are to educate themselves as theorists, practitioners need to work hard to skill themselves in the procedures of doing research, and also in the theoretical underpinnings of research, with a view to demonstrating the internal validity and legitimacy of their research. This means, perhaps above all, articulating what they understand as the means by which they judge the quality of their own work, and how they wish other people also to judge it. This view is now being taken seriously, and work of quality is emanating from those universities who are prepared to endorse such a view, such as the University of Bath, whose Education Department received a 5 rating in the previous three Research Assessment Exercises. The mission statement of the University of Bath claims that it has a distinctive academic approach that emphasizes the education of professional practitioners. We are suggesting that the approach presented in this text is contributing to such a distinctive approach to the education of professional practitioners.

Practitioners as professional and academic writers

Furthermore, teaching and other professions need to be seen as research-based professions. This means that practitioners need to undertake their own action enquiries, in which they ask questions of the kind, 'How do I improve my practice? How do I assess the quality of the improvement? How do I demonstrate the validity of my claims to knowledge through their evidence base?' They need to produce their scholarly accounts to show how they have engaged with these issues, and made their contributions both to new practices and to new theory. These accounts should go into the public domain, in the form of scholarly professional papers and accounts, from which other educational researchers can learn, regardless of the nature of their workplace. Such publication and dissemination are crucial if other professions and the general public are to learn. Through the systematic publication and dissemination of their work, practitioners can build up a coherent knowledge base that will serve to contribute to the education of social formations and in turn to the development of sustainable societies.

Practitioners as qualified professionals

Professional qualification is essential, for several reasons. Qualification is of course a marker of success. Just as important, it is a marker of recognition. Work that has been accepted by the academy is deemed valid and legitimate. Once the work has been accredited, academic and social authority is established. A sign of legitimacy by the highest authority goes far in activist initiatives. While those who wish practitioners to be silent may try to trivialize their efforts, that mark of approval by the academic community goes far in maintaining credibility and securing future legitimacy. From time to time, funding is awarded to practitioners to conduct their research in their workplaces. Such provision tends to be inconsistent however. It is as much up to the community of practitioners to demonstrate their worth, and to demand funding to support their work, as it is to policy makers to make such decisions, informed, as policy makers tend to be, by what sometimes turn out to be inaccurate or misleading assumptions about what kind of knowledge is valuable and who counts as a knower.

Practitioners as exercising public influence

Practitioners need deliberately to set out to exercise their educational influence in the public sphere. They can do this in relation to their own learning, the learning of others, and the learning of people in social formations. By producing their accounts of practice they are able to show how they have improved their practice by taking informed and principled action, and offering their explanations for why they did so and what they hoped to achieve. They show the processes of disciplined enquiry in arriving at informed practice. Many people can learn from these stories of disciplined enquiry, not least in terms of how they might do the same and what may be some of the consequences for their own learning and the learning of those in their contexts. Practitioners in all professions can and should show how they engage with their own positioning as public intellectuals who have worthwhile things to say about what counts as a good society and how it may be achieved.

Practitioners as collaborative communities of educational enquiry

Perhaps one of the greatest opportunities for practitioners currently is to form themselves into collaborative communities of educational enquiry. This means they need to find ways of working with other like-minded people in their local, national and international contexts, whichever is right for them, with a view to exercising global influence. The opportunities for networking have never been greater, with the widespread use of electronic technology that enables people to stay in touch anywhere in the world. Practitioners have untold opportunities for influence by sharing their stories of theorizing practice, and showing the implications of their learning in their own developing learning and the learning of others. Given the potentials of such networking, practitioners need to think imaginatively about how to connect with like-minded colleagues to develop ways and means of influencing those not of a like mind, in a way that respects rival traditions yet shows the value of practitioner enquiry. Especially, through their networks of communication and the systematic development of a knowledge base, practitioners stand a real chance of influencing the future of educational research in their own countries and internationally, and also influencing policy formation and implementation for education.

Implications for the community of academic educational researchers

The community of academic educational researchers needs to think about the following.

Academic researchers as practitioners

Perhaps the greatest challenge for the academic educational research community is to question and destabilize their own hegemonizing discourses about their professional roles and responsibilities. Currently academic educational researchers are positioned as having the responsibility to generate 'pure' kinds of theory, on the basis that dominant forms of propositional knowledge and theory should continue to provide the epistemological base for educational research, and point the way to correct policy. Increasing numbers of academic researchers however reject this view, on the grounds that its colonialist impulses lead towards intellectual and social apartheid, where they are positioned as superior to those whose studies they are supporting and assessing. In the struggle for academic and epistemological supremacy, abstract knowledge is still held to be the best kind of knowledge, over and above the practical knowledge of practitioners. Many academic researchers now regard themselves as practitioners, but equally and legitimately many do not. The question becomes how the epistemological struggle within the academy itself will influence the learning of practitioners in the social formations of their educational communities. The academy has become a strategic site in the struggle for contested epistemological legitimacy, and it bears repeating that we recognize the importance of MacIntyre's insight:

> The rival claims to truth of contending traditions of enquiry depend for their vindication upon the adequacy and explanatory power of the histories which the resources of each of those traditions in conflict enable their adherents to write. (1988: 403)

Academic researchers as participants

We have noted throughout that the social sciences position researchers as spectators of other people's practices, in the sense that they produce explanations for the practices and influences of others rather than explain their own. Given that educational research originally took its lead from the physical and then the social sciences, it is not surprising that spectator forms of research were from the beginning held to be the correct approach here, too. In action research however the individual practitioner researches their own practice. It can be difficult for academic educational researchers who wish to engage in action research to let go of their spectator stance, especially when their institutions expect this of them, but it has to be done if they are to engage in action research.

Academic researchers as supporters

Academic researchers who wish to continue to generate explanations for the lives of others could however adopt a new stance as supporters. This means that they could provide emotional and intellectual support to practitioners as necessary, not aim to impose their knowledge on them, and encourage the emergence of their latent personal knowledge. Being a supporter means adopting a stance similar to what Buber described (page 91) as an attentive attitude and a readiness to listen. This can be particularly difficult for academic researchers who have developed a self-perception as holders and creators of knowledge, whose responsibility it is to pass on that knowledge to others who do not yet know. Traditional practices of transmission modes of teaching are well ingrained in the cultural psyche. It can also be difficult to dislodge the assumption that practitioners' knowledge is of a lesser order and inferior in value to abstract knowledge. Such disruption of the current epistemological order can be achieved only through a critical interrogation of one's own stance in relation to others, which is an ontological and epistemological commitment that raises questions about how the other is perceived and what they are valued for. Some especially significant work has been undertaken recently by Joan Whitehead and Bernie Fitzgerald (2004), who have developed school – university partnerships on the basis of shared dialogue and mutual professional and epistemological regard. These kinds of partnerships focus on how work should be assessed and presented as quality theorizing, and also how the quality of the relationships that sponsor the work should be assessed and theorized.

Academic researchers as activist intellectuals

Those in the academy are in positions of extraordinary power and privilege. Given that they have the intellectual and personal freedom largely to negotiate their work hours, and given that they are financially secure, compared to other social groupings in the world, it seems sensible to believe that they should devote their best energies to using their scholarly activities on behalf of others, to combat ills and alleviate suffering. These efforts can take many forms, yet all can show how social orders are grounded in specific intellectual and epistemological traditions, sourced in, authorized by and legitimated by the academy, some of which need to be disrupted if the social order is to be reconceptualized and transformed to meet the interests of all citizens. Given also that it is the responsibility of academics, and a fulfilment of their professional duties, to generate knowledge, it would seem sensible that they should generate the kind of knowledge that will help others and not only themselves. This is a basic moral principle. Achieving this principle means, however, again disrupting traditional institutional epistemologies that focus on producing propositional theory of a kind that is often irrelevant to the practical needs of much of humanity (Schön 1995). Disrupting the social order can of course be a frightening experience, especially when an intellectual activist is alone or made to feel isolated, and it takes a particular kind of courage to challenge the epistemological authority of an institution as powerful as the academy. It is common knowledge, however, that it is easier to launch a challenge in solidarity with other like-minded colleagues than to do it alone, and most academic researchers can now find colleagues who will form activist groupings, to challenge colonialist practices within the daily life of the institution and through the dissemination of their scholarly publications. This has to be a new mandate for academic researchers, and a new focus for their scholarly enquiries, to understand both what kind of knowledge will best serve the whole of humanity, and what kind of relationships can best foster the formation and communi-cation of that knowledge.

This is a core aspect of the task that we, Jack and Jean, have set ourselves. Our broad research interests are to do with how we can learn to influence the learning of people in different social formations, such as schools, workplaces, and the academy. A special focus of this work is on how we can encourage them to evaluate their work and say how and why they understand their work as worthwhile, as they produce their living educational theories of practice. This inevitably involves their identifying and articulat-ing their values as their living standards of judgement, as the evaluative principles of their personal and professional lives.

We explore these ideas further in Section 2, as we set out new directions for our research.

2   New directions for our research: setting out our action plans

A considerable amount has already been achieved in this regard, and significant numbers of validated dissertations and theses are in the public domain, all of which explain clearly how their authors give meaning to their lives in terms of what they passionately believe in, so that what they value becomes their guiding evaluative principles. Here are some of the accounts, all of which can be downloaded by accessing their accompanying URLs. Many more are in preparation, and will be made available as soon as they are ready.

Work that Jack has supported:

Eames, K. (1995) 'How do I, as a teacher and educational action-researcher, describe and explain the nature of my professional knowledge?' PhD thesis, University of Bath. Retrieved 19 February 2004 from http://www.actionresearch.net/kevin.shtml.

Evans, M. (1995) 'An action research enquiry into reflection in action as part of my role as a deputy headteacher'. PhD thesis, Kingston University. Retrieved 19 February 2004 from http://www.actionresearch.net/moyra.shtml.

Laidlaw, M. (1996) 'How can I create my own living educational theory as I offer you an account of my educational development?' PhD thesis, University of Bath. Retrieved 19 February 2004 from http://www.actionresearch.net/moira2.shtml.

Holley, E. (1997) 'How do I as a teacher-researcher contribute to the development of a liv-ing educational theory through an exploration of my values in my professional practice?' Mphil thesis, University of Bath. Retrieved 19 February 2004 from http://www.actionre search.net/erica.shtml.

D'Arcy, P. (1998) 'The whole story...'. PhD thesis, University of Bath. Retrieved 19 February 2004 from http://www.actionresearch.net/pat.shtml.

Loftus, J. (1999) 'An action enquiry into the marketing of an established first school in its transition to full primary status'. PhD thesis, Kingston University. Retrieved 19 February 2004 from http://www.actionresearch.net/loftus.shtml.

Whitehead, J. (1999) 'How do I improve my practice? Creating a discipline of education through educational enquiry'. PhD thesis, University of Bath. Retrieved 19 February 2004 from http://www.actionresearch.net/jack.shtml.

Cunningham, B. (1999) 'How do I come to know my spirituality as I create my own living educational theory?' PhD thesis, University of Bath. Retrieved 19 February 2004 from http://www.actionresearch.net/ben.shtml.

Adler-Collins, J. (2000) 'A scholarship of enquiry'. MA dissertation, University of Bath. Retrieved 19 February 2004 from http://www.actionresearch.net/jekan.shtml.

Finnegan, J. (2000) 'How do I create my own educational theory in my educative relations as an action researcher and as a teacher?' PhD submission, University of Bath. Retrieved 19 February 2004 from http://www.actionresearch.net/fin.shtml.

Austin, T. (2001) 'Treasures in the snow: what do I know and how do I know it through my educational inquiry into my practice of community?' PhD thesis, University of Bath. Retrieved 19 February 2004 from http://www.actionresearch.net/austin.shtml.

Mead, G. (2001) 'Unlatching the gate: realising the scholarship of my living inquiry'. PhD thesis, University of Bath. Retrieved 19 February 2004 from http://www.actionresearch.net/mead.shtml.

Bosher, M. (2001) 'How can I as an educator and professional development manager working with teachers, support and enhance the learning and achievement of pupils in a whole school improvement process?' PhD thesis, University of Bath. Retrieved 19 February 2004 from http://www.actionresearch.net/bosher.shtml.

Delong, J. (2002) 'How can I Improve my practice as a superintendent of schools and create my own living educational theory?' PhD thesis, University of Bath. Retrieved 19 February 2004 from http://www.actionresearch.net/delong.shtml.

Scholes-Rhodes, J. (2002) 'From the inside out: learning to presence my aesthetic and spiritual being through the emergent form of a creative art of inquiry'. PhD thesis, University of Bath. Retrieved 19 February 2004 from http://www.bath.ac.uk/~edsajw/rhodes.shtml.

Roberts, P. (2003) 'Emerging selves in practice: how do I and others create my practice and how does my practice shape me and influence others?' PhD thesis, University of Bath. Retrieved 19 August 2004 from http://www.bath.ac.uk/~edsajw/roberts.shtml.

Punia, R. (2004) 'My CV is my curriculum: the making of an international educator with spiritual values'. EdD thesis, University of Bath. Retrieved 19 August 2004 from http://www.bath.ac.uk/~edsajw/punia.shtml.

Hartog, M. (2004) 'A self-study of a higher education tutor: how can I improve my practice?' PhD thesis, University of Bath. Retrieved 19 August 2004 from http://www.bath.ac.uk/~edsajw/hartog.shtml.

Church, M. (2004) 'Creating an uncompromised place to belong: why do I find myself in networks?' PhD thesis, University of Bath. Retrieved 24 May 2005 from http://www.bath.ac.uk/~edsajw/church.shtml.

Naidoo, M. (2005) 'I am because we are (a never-ending story): the emergence of a living theory of inclusional and responsive practice.' See abstract at http://www.bath.ac.uk/~edsajw/arsup/mnabsok.htm.

Work that Jean has supported:

Cluskey, M. (1997) 'How can I facilitate learning amongst my Leaving Certificate Applied students?' MA dissertation, University of the West of England, Bristol. Retrieved 3 August 2005 from http://www.jeanmcniff.com/Moira%20Cluskey%20dissertation.htm.

Burke, T. (1997) 'How can I improve my practice as a learning support teacher?' MA dissertation, University of the West of England, Bristol. Retrieved 3 August 2005 from http://www. jeanmcniff.com/tereseabstract.html.

Glenn, M. (2000) 'How can I improve my practice as co-ordinator of Schools Integration Project 062?' Progress Report. Retrieved 3 August 2005 from http://www.jeanmcniff.com/mairinsip.html.

McDonagh, C. (2000) 'Towards a theory of professional teacher voice'. MA dissertation, Dublin, University of the West of England, Bristol. Retrieved 3 August 2005 from http://www.jeanmcniff.com/caitriona.pdf.

McGinley, S. (2000) 'How can I help the primary school children I teach to develop their self-esteem?' MA dissertation, University of the West of England, Bristol. Retrieved 3 August 2005 from http://www.jeanmcniff.com/sallyabstract.html.

Ní Mhurchú, S. (2000) 'How can I improve my practice as a teacher in the area of assessment through the use of portfolios?' MA dissertation, University of the West of England, Bristol. Retrieved 3 August 2005 from http://www.jeanmcniff.com/siobhan.htm.

Nugent, M. (2000) 'How can I raise the level of self-esteem of second year Junior Certificate School Programme students and create a better learning environment?' MA dissertation, Dublin, University of the West of England, Bristol. Retrieved 3 August 2005 from http://www.jeanmcniff.com/Marian%20Nugent%27s%20Dissertation.htm.

Roche, M. (2000) 'How can I improve my practice so as to help my pupils to philosophise?' MA dissertation, Cork, University of the West of England, Bristol. Retrieved 3 August 2005 from http://www.jeanmcniff.com/maryma.htm.

Lillis, S. (2001) 'An inquiry into the effectiveness of my practice as a learning practitioner-researcher in rural community development', PhD thesis, Dublin, National University of Ireland. Retrieved 3 August 2005 from http://www.jeanmcniff.com/SeamusLillis.htm.

The accounts contain some significant features:

- They all explain how their authors undertook their action enquiries from the perspective that their values were being denied in their practice. Each author worked systematically to find ways of realizing their values in their practice. Each account contains the story of the struggle to do so, and shows the transformative process of the establishment of truth, the transition phase of reconciliation with self and sometimes others, and the strategic stage of moving into transformative political action.

- They explain how the authors identified what was worth fighting for in their personal and professional lives. Each author articulates their wish to realize their values as the guiding principles for their work, and how those values come to act as the living standards of judgement they use as they assess whether or not they have achieved their research purposes.

- The accounts come from a range of educational constituencies. The stories are located in schools and workplaces, and also in higher education settings. The idea of realizing one's educational values in one's practice is clearly appropriate in all contexts, and is available to practitioner researchers and academic researchers alike. What is also significant is that those who may formerly have identified themselves as 'just a teacher' now regard themselves as a practitioner scholar, and, by the same token, those who may have been identified as 'an academic' now identify themselves as an academic practitioner. All show how they are contributing to new practices and new theory, and thereby reconceptualizing practice as a form of theory and theory as a form of practice.

We said earlier that several key points need to be addressed in the current awareness of assessing quality in action research. These are as follows:

- Standards of judgement need to be identified and articulated as such, so that it is clear how living accounts are to be judged.

- These standards of judgement need to be understood and used within the living theory accounts of practitioners.

- Those positioned in the academy also have to understand and use those same standards of judgement as they make judgements about the validity of the accounts they assess.

This is happening. In work submitted in recent years, since the need for appropriate standards of judgement became clear and pressing, researchers have made a point of explicating how they wish their work to be judged. Examples of such accounts are Holley (1997), Hartog (2004), Church (2004) and Naidoo (2005). The accounts have been approved and validated by examiners who are willing to engage with these important new scholarly developments. Significantly, many of those who have submitted their work are already positioned in the academy, and have themselves had to go through the same rigorous procedures as other colleagues in schools and workplaces of demonstrating the validity of their own personal knowledge and their capacity to make scholarly judgements on the quality of their work. Consequently, new forms of standards of judgement are rapidly entering the entire community of educational researchers, and are being acknowledged as such.

The work continues. A new focus also is developing, that shows how relationships between those currently positioned as practitioners and those currently positioned as academics are systematically breaking down false barriers that have in the past led to a kind of ontological and epistemological separatism. The values that inspire our commitments to keep this work going are to do with our own desires to challenge colonialist discourses and practices, and to show the kind of life-affirming communities of enquiry that can arise from such collaborative working. Our view is that the trajectories of social orders are largely influenced by what is happening in the epistemological base of the social order. If we can work towards transforming the epistemological base, and show how that has the transformative capacity to influence the development of new social practices, we shall feel our work is worthwhile. We judge our work in terms of the extent to which we can encourage others also to judge theirs in relation to the kind of values that can contribute to the wellbeing of humanity. We have made our account available, and we leave it to you to judge whether or not our account is trustworthy, whether our claims to knowledge should be validated, and whether you have been inspired sufficiently to take up some of the ideas in this book for your own practice.

Setting out our action plans

Finally, we set out how we hope to develop our own research programmes over the coming time. First we set out our individual action plans. We then say how we hope to continue working together.

Jack identifies his future work with the mission of the University of Bath in terms of the further development of a distinct academic approach that emphasizes the education of professional practitioners. His immediate research programme will continue to clarify and legitimate the living critical standards of judgement in educational theories that carry hope for the future of humanity. These educational theories take the form of living theories that are influenced by inclusional, responsive and postcolonial values, understandings and practices. With the help of government funding for the continuing professional development of teachers, he hopes to continue to work and learn with local practitioner researchers in Bath about the possibilities of strengthening the educational influences of their communities of enquirers. With the help of the world wide web he hopes to continue to act locally and publish globally. Jack gives a special thanks to Peter Reason for Peter's influence as Director of the Centre for Action Research in Professional

Practice (CARPP – see http://www.bath.ac.uk/carpp/) for enabling Jack's supervision of living theory doctoral research programmes.

Jean sees her future work with groups of practitioner researchers in several locations: with academic staff in St Mary's University College London; with teachers working in local contexts in South Africa; and internationally with groups of academic practitioners who as educational activists wish to influence debates about the direction of educational research in their contexts, with a focus on social and epistemological justice. She aims to encourage all to produce their scholarly reports, as they build collaborative action research networks on a local and international basis, and as they enquire into how they can contribute to new forms of social justice that are grounded in the values that give meaning to their lives.

We hope our work together will continue. Life would be almost unthinkable without it, given that we have been working together for twenty-five years. During that time we have critiqued, learned from, and inspired each other, out of an understanding that we both have a shared sense of mission, that we have something useful to do, and that neither of us wishes to die disappointed. These same commitments should keep us going for the next little while at least.

SUMMARY

In this final chapter we have explained how we are modifying our concerns, ideas and practices in the light of our evaluation of our research so far. We explain how we are moving into new research areas of encouraging others to show how they judge the quality of their work in relation to their identified standards of judgement. We also explain how the ideas we are exploring here are already having some influence among the practitioner action research community and in the community of academic educational researchers. While we do not ask all completely to embrace our ideas, we do ask all to give attention to the crucial issue of how they meet the standards of originality, significance and rigour as they offer their own accounts of practice. Without such attention, we believe, practitioner action researchers will continue to be relegated to the ranks of good practitioners but not good theorists. With such attention, we are convinced that practitioner action researchers will demonstrate their capacity to contribute, through educational theory, to the formation of the kind of societies that are the manifestation of the values that honour and sustain humanity. With collaborative attention by both communities of practitioner and academic educational researchers, we believe that all can show the transformative potentials of the communicative action of the social formations of educational researchers who are committed to social renaissance.

References

Alexander, R. (1995) *Versions of Primary Education*. London, Routledge.

Alford, C.F. (2001) *Whistleblowers: Broken Lives and Organizational Power*. Ithaca, NY, Cornell University Press.

Arendt, H. (1958) *The Human Condition*. Chicago, University of Chicago Press.

Arendt, H. (1994) *Eichmann in Jerusalem*. London, Penguin.

Austin, T. (2001) 'Treasures in the snow: what do I know and how do I know it through my educational inquiry into my practice of community?' PhD thesis, University of Bath. Retrieved 6 January 2004 from http://www.bath.ac.uk/~edsajw/austin.shtml.

Bachelard, G. (1969) *The Poetics of Space*. Boston, Beacon.

Barry, P. (2002) *Beginning Theory* (2nd edn). Manchester, Manchester University Press.

Bassey, M. (1999) *Case Study Research in Educational Settings*. Buckingham, Open University Press.

Bataille, G. (1987) *Eroticism*. London, Marion Boyars.

Bateson, G. (1972) *Steps to an Ecology of Mind.* New York, Dutton.

Bateson, G. (1979) *Mind and Nature: A Necessary Unity*. New York, Dutton.

Berlin, I. (1969) *Four Essays on Liberty*. London, Oxford University Press.

Bernstein, R. (2000) *Pedagogy, Symbolic Control and Identity: Theory, Research, Critique*. Lanham, MD, Rowman & Littlefield.

Bognar, B. (2003) 'School in transition from industrial to post-industrial society', *Metodicki ogledi*, Zagreb, 10 (2): 9–24.

Bognar, B. (2004) 'Inspiring creativity in the school environment', *Napredak*, Zagreb, 145 (3): 269–83.

Bourdieu, P. (1990) *The Logic of Practice*. Cambridge, Polity.

Bourdieu, P. and Passeron, J.-C. (1977) *Reproduction in Education, Society and Culture*. London, Sage.

Buber, M. (1937) *I and Thou*. (trans. R. G. Smith) Edinburgh, Clark.

Bullough, R. and Pinnegar, S. (2004) 'Thinking about thinking about self-study: an analysis of eight chapters', in J.J. Loughran, M.L. Hamilton, V.K. LaBoskey and T. Russell (eds), *International Handbook of Self-Study of Teaching and Teacher-Education Practices*. Dordrecht, Kluwer.

Burke, T. (1997) 'How can I improve my practice as a learning support teacher?' MA dissertation, Dublin, University of the West of England. Retrieved 27 November 2004 from http://www.jeanmcniff.com.

Capra, F. (2003) *The Hidden Connections*. London. Flamingo.

Carr, W. and Kemmis, S. (1986) *Becoming Critical: Education, Knowledge and Action Research*. London, Falmer.

Chapman, A. (2001) 'Truth commissions as instruments of forgiveness and reconciliation', in R. Helmick and R. Petersen (eds), *Forgiveness and Reconciliation: Religion, Public Policy and Conflict Transformation*. Philadelphia, Templeton Foundation Press.

Chomsky, N. (1986) *Knowledge of Language: Its Nature, Origin and Use*. New York, Praeger.

Chomsky, N. (1999) 'On staying informed and intellectual self-defense'. Retrieved 3 August 2005 from zmag.org/ZSustainers/ZDaily/1999-03/mar_8_1999.htm.

Chowdhry, G. and Nair, S. (2003) *Power, Postcolonialism, and International Relations*. London, Routledge.

Church, M. (2004) 'Creating an uncompromised place to belong: why do I find myself in networks?' PhD submission, University of Bath. Retrieved 24 January 2005 from http://www.bath.ac.uk/~edsajw/church.shtml.

Clandinin, D.J. (in production) *A Handbook of Narrative Inquiry*. New York, Sage.

Clandinin, D.J. and Connelly, F.M. (2000) *Narrative Inquiry*. San Francisco, Jossey-Bass.

Collingwood, R.G. (1939) *An Autobiography*. Oxford, Oxford University Press.

Comey, D.D. (1972) 'Logic', in C.D. Kernig (ed.), *Marxism, Communism and Western Society*, vol. 5. New York, Herder and Herder.

Connell, R.W. (1993) *Schools and Social Justice*. Philadelphia, Temple University Press.

Corey, S. (1953) *Action Research to Improve School Practices*. New York, Teachers College Press.

Dadds, M. (1995) *Passionate Enquiry and School Development: A Story About Teacher Action Research*. London, Falmer.

Dadds, M. and Hart, S. (2001) *Doing Practitioner Research Differently*. London, Routledge.

De Botton, A. (ed.) (1999) 'Phaedrus', in *The Essential Plato*. London, Softback Preview.

Delong, J. (2002) 'How can I improve my practice as a superintendent of schools and create my own living educational theory?' PhD thesis, University of Bath. Retrieved 26 November 2004 from http://www.actionresearch.net/delong.shtml.

Deng Xiaoping (1989) *Selected Works of Deng Xiaoping*, vol. 2. Beijing, People's Publishing House.

Derrida, J. (1976) *Of Grammatology*. Baltimore, Johns Hopkins University Press.

Derrida, J. (2003) 'Following theory', in M. Payne and J. Schad (eds), *life.after.theory*. London, Continuum.

Dewey, J. (1916) *Democracy and Education*. New York, Free Press.

Farren, M. (2005) 'Developing my pedagogy of the unique as a higher education educator. How can I co-create a curriculum in ICT in education with professional educators?' Draft PhD thesis, University of Bath. Retrieved 3 August 2005 from http://www.webpages.dcu.ie/~farren/research.html.

Feyerabend, P. (1970) 'Consolations for the specialist', in I. Lakatos and A. Musgrave (eds), *Criticism and the Growth of Knowledge*. Cambridge, Cambridge University Press.

Feyerabend, P. (1975) *Against Method*. London, New Left.

Foucault, M. (1980) 'Truth and power', in C. Gordon (ed.), *Power/Knowledge: Selected Interviews and Other Writings, 1972–1977*. Brighton, Harvester.

Fromm, E. (1941) *Escape from Freedom*. New York, Holt, Reinhart & Winston.

Furlong, J. (2000) *Higher Education and the New Professionalism for Teachers: Realising the Potential of Partnership*. London, CVCP/SCOP. Retrieved 26 November 2004 from http://www.edstud.ox.ac.uk/people/furlong.html.

Furlong, J. (2004) 'BERA at 30. Have we come of age?', *British Educational Research Journal*, 30 (3): 343–358. Presidential address to the British Educational Research Association, 2003.

Furlong, J. and Oancea, A. (2005) *Assessing Quality in Applied and Practice-Based Educational Research: A Framework for Discussion*. Oxford, Oxford University Department of Educational Studies.

Gadamer, H.G. (1975) *Truth and Method*. London: Sheen and Ward.

Gibson, J. (2004) *Overcoming Apartheid: Can Truth Reconcile a Divided Nation?* New York, Russell Sage Foundation.

Gladwell, M. (2005) *Blink: The Power of Thinking without Thinking*. London, Penguin.

Glenn, M. (2004) 'How am I enhancing inter-connections with ICT?' Paper presented at the British Educational Research Association symposium 'Have We Created a New

Epistemology for the New Scholarship of Educational Enquiry through Practitioner Research? Developing Sustainable Global Educational Networks of Communication', UMIST, Manchester, September. Retrieved 26 November 2004 from http://www.action-research.net/bera04/bera5.htm.

Goldstein, H. (2002) 'Designing social research for the 21st century'. Inaugural professorial address, University of Bristol, October.

Gorard, S. (2004) 'Sceptical or clerical? Theory as a barrier to the combination of research methods', *Journal of Educational Enquiry*, 5 (1): 1–21.

Goyen, W. (n.d.) *House of Breath*. New York, Random House.

Grandi, B. (2004) 'An action research expedition: how can I influence my students in developing their creativity and critical thinking? A self study'. MA dissertation, University of Bath. Retrieved 16 January 2005 from http://www.bath.ac.uk/~edsajw/grandi.shtml.

Habermas, J. (1975) *Legitimation Crisis* (trans. T. McCarthy). Boston, Beacon.

Habermas, J. (1979) *Communication and the Evolution of Society*. Boston, Beacon.

Habermas, J. (1987) *The Theory of Communicative Action. Volume Two: The Critique of Functionalist Reason*. Oxford, Polity.

Hartog, M. (2004) 'A self-study of a higher education tutor: how can I improve my practice?' PhD thesis, University of Bath. Retrieved 26 November 2004 from http://www.bath.ac.uk/~edsajw/hartog.shtml.

Hirst, P.H. (1983) *Educational Theory and its Foundation Disciplines*. London, Routledge & Kegan Paul.

Hirst, P. and Peters, R.S. (1970) *The Logic of Education*. London, Routledge & Kegan Paul.

Holley, E. (1997) 'How do I as a teacher-researcher contribute to the development of a living educational theory through an exploration of my values in my professional practice?' MPhil thesis, University of Bath. Retrieved 14 January 2005 from http://www.bath.ac.uk/~edsajw/erica.shtml.

Husserl, E. (1931) *Ideas: Pure Phenomenology*. London: Allen and Unwin.

Ilyenkov, E. (1977) *Dialectical Logic*. Moscow, Progress.

Johnson, C. (2005) 'Drama in primary teacher education: fostering critical reflection and metacognition'. Paper presented at the Invited Symposium for the Special Interest Group Teaching and Teacher Education 'Demonstrating Accountability Through our Self-Study Practices as Teacher Educators', EARLI, Nicosia, August.

Kant, I. (1965) *Immanuel Kant's Critique of Pure Reason* (trans. N.K. Smith). New York, St Martin's.

Kauffman, S. (1995) *At Home in the Universe*. London, Viking.

Keiny, S. (2002) *Ecological Thinking: A New Approach to Educational Change*. Lanham, MD, University Press of America.

Kenny, M. (1997) *The Routes of Resistance: Travellers and Second-Level Schooling*. Aldershot, Ashgate.

Kristeva, J. (2002) 'Interview', reproduced in J. Lechte and M. Margaroni (eds), (2004) *Julia Kristeva: Live Theory*. London, Continuum.

Kushner, S. (2000) *Personalizing Evaluation*. London, Sage.

Lagemann, E.C. (2000) *An Elusive Science: The Troubling History of Education Research*. Chicago, University of Chicago Press.

Laidlaw, M. (1996) 'How can I create my own living educational theory as I offer you an account of my educational development?' PhD thesis, University of Bath. Retrieved 3 August 2005 from http://www.actionresearch.net/moira.shmtl.

Lakatos, I. and Musgrave, A. (eds) (1970) *Criticism and the Growth of Knowledge*. Cambridge, Cambridge University Press.

Lather, P. (1994) 'Textuality as praxis'. Paper presented at the American Educational Research Association annual meeting, New Orleans, April.

Lechte, J. and Margaroni, M. (2004) *Julia Kristeva: Live Theory*. London, Continuum.

Lohr, E. (2004) 'Love at work'. Draft prologue to PhD submission to the University of Bath. Retrieved 16 January 2005 from http://www.jackwhitehead.com/elFront%202.htm.

Lynch, K. (1999) *Equality in Education*. Dublin, Gill and Macmillan.

Lyotard, J.-F. (1984) *The Postmodern Condition: A Report on Knowledge*. Manchester, Manchester University Press.

MacAongusa, M. (1993) 'Travellers and schooling: value systems in conflict', in Parish of the Traveller People (ed.), *Do You Know Us At All?* Dublin, Parish of the Traveller People.

MacDonald, B. (1987) *The State of Education Today*. Record of the First CARE Conference. Norwich, University of East Anglia.

Macdonald, B.J. (ed.) (1995) *Theory as a Prayerful Act: The Collected Essays of James B. Macdonald*. New York, Lang.

MacIntyre, A. (1988) *Whose Justice? Which Rationality?* London, Duckworth.

MacLure, M. (1996) 'Narratives of becoming an action researcher', *British Journal of Educational Research*, 22 (3): 273–86.

Marcuse, H. (1964) *One-Dimensional Man*. Boston, Beacon.

Marggraf Turley, R. (2000) *Writing Essays*. London, RoutledgeFalmer.

Marshall, J. (1995) *Women Managers Moving On: Exploring Career and Life Choices*. Europe: International Thomson.

Marshall, J. (2001) 'Self-reflective inquiry practices', in P. Reason and H. Bradbury (eds), *Handbook of Action Research, Participative Inquiry and Practice*. London: Sage. pp. 433–9.

Marshall, J. (2004) 'Living systemic thinking: exploring quality in first-person action research', *Action Research*, 2 (3): 309–29.

Marx, K. and Engels, F. (1989) *Early Writings*. Zagreb, Naprijed.

McDonagh, C. (2000) 'Towards a theory of professional teacher voice: how can I improve my teaching of pupils with specific learning difficulties in the area of language?' MA dissertation, Dublin, University of the West of England. Retrieved 26 November 2004 from http://www.jeanmcniff.com/caitriona.pdf.

McDonagh, W. (2000) 'A Traveller woman's perspective of education', in E. Sheehan (ed.), *Travellers: Citizens of Ireland*. Dublin, Parish of the Traveller People.

McNiff, J. (1984) 'Action research: a generative model for in-service support', *British Journal of In-Service Education*, 10 (3), Summer.

McNiff, J. (1988/1992) *Action Research: Principles and Practice* (1st edn). Basingstoke, Macmillan and London, Routledge.

McNiff, J. (1997) 'Seven generations on', *Journal of Professional Studies*, 4 (2): 8–14.

McNiff, J. (2005) 'Pedagogy, theory of mind, and educational influence: how do I contribute to the education of sustainable social formations?' Paper presented at the Invited Symposium for the Special Interest Group Teaching and Teacher Education 'Demonstrating Accountability through our Self-Study Practices as Teacher Educators', EARLI, Nicosia, August. Retrieved 3 August from http://www.jeanmcniff.com.

McNiff, J. (2006) 'My story is my living educational theory', draft chapter submitted for D. Clandinin (ed.), *A Handbook of Narrative Inquiry*. In production. New York, Sage.

McNiff, J. and Collins, Ú. (eds) (1994) *A New Approach to In-Career Development for Teachers in Ireland*. Bournemouth, Hyde.

McNiff, J. and Naidoo, A. (2005) 'How do we develop inclusional epistemologies for a new scholarship of democratic educational enquiry?' Paper presented at the conference '(In)equality, Democracy and Quality', Kenton, October.

McNiff, J. and Whitehead, J. (2000) *Action Research in Organisations*. London, Routledge.

McNiff, J. and Whitehead, J. (2002) *Action Research: Principles and Practice* (2nd edn). London, RoutledgeFalmer.

McNiff, J. and Whitehead, J. (2005a) *Action Research for Teachers*. London, Fulton.

McNiff, J. and Whitehead, J. (2005b) *All You Need to Know about Action Research*. London, Sage.

McNiff, J., Whitehead, J. and Laidlaw, M. (1992) *Creating a Good Social Order through Action Research*. Bournemouth, Hyde.

McNiff, J., Naidoo, A. and Naidoo, A. (2005) 'Interrogating our Colour'. Working paper, in preparation, Port Elizabeth, Nelson Mandela Metropolitan University.

McTaggart, R. (ed.) (1997) *Participatory Action Research: International Contexts and Consequences.* New York, State University of New York Press.

Medawar, P. (1996) *The Strange Case of the Spotted Mice.* Oxford, Oxford University Press.

Memmi, A. (1974) *The Colonizer and the Colonized.* London, Souvenir.

Minow, M. (1998) *Between Vengeance and Forgiveness: Facing History after Genocide and Mass Violence*. Boston, Beacon.

Mitroff, I. and Kilman, R. (1978) *Methodological Approaches to Social Science.* San Francisco, Jossey-Bass.

Moreland, J. (2005) 'How do I improve my practice as a lecturer working with a group of trainee primary teachers to develop their science subject knowledge using a virtual learning environment (VLE)?' Paper presented at the Invited Symposium for the Special Interest Group Teaching and Teacher Education 'Demonstrating Accountability through our Self-Study Practices as Teacher Educators', EARLI, Nicosia, August.

Moustakim, M. (2005) 'Theorising educational practice'. Paper presented at the Invited Symposium for the Special Interest Group Teaching and Teacher Education 'Demonstrating Accountability through our Self-Study Practices as Teacher Educators', EARLI, Nicosia, August.

Murray, R. (2002) *How to Write a Thesis*. Buckingham, Open University Press.

Murray, Y.P. (2005) Welcome to my multiracial and inclusive postcolonial living education: Theory – practice, research and becoming. Retrieved 7 October 2005 from http://www.rac.ac.uk/rpaul_murray/default.htm.

Naidoo, M. (2005) 'I am because we are (a never ending story): the emergence of a living theory of inclusional and responsive practice'. PhD thesis, University of Bath. Retrieved 1 August 2005 from http://www.bath.ac.uk/~edsajw/naidoo.shtml.

Naidoo, A. and McNiff, J. (2005) 'Managing educational change in the new South Africa'. Paper presented at the British Educational Research Association annual conference, Pontypridd, University of Glamorgan, September.

Namulundah, F. (1998) *bell hooks, Engaged Pedagogy: A Transgressive Education for Critical Consciousness*. Westport, CA, Bergin and Garvey.

Ní Mhurchú, S. (2000) 'How can I improve my practice as a teacher in the area of assessment through the use of portfolios?' MA dissertation, Cork, University of the West of England, Bristol. Retrieved 3 August 2005 from http://www.jeanmcniff.com/siobhan.htm.

Nugent, M. (2000) 'How can I raise the level of self-esteem of second year Junior Certificate School Programme students and create a better learning environment?' MA dissertation, Dublin, University of the West of England, Bristol. Retrieved 30 November 2004 from http://www.jeanmcniff.com/theses.

O'Donohue, J. (2003) *Divine Beauty*. London, Bantam.

Olivier, T. and Wood, L. (2005) 'How do we encourage teachers to develop self-efficacy?' Working paper, Port Elizabeth, Nelson Mandela Metropolitan University.

Ó Mhurchú, D. (1997) *Quantum Theology: Spiritual Implications of the New Physics*. New York, Crossroads.

Orwell, G. (1990) *Nineteen Eighty-Four*. London, Penguin.

Owen, H. (1996) *Open Space Technology: A User's Guide*. San Francisco, Berrett-Koehler.

Peat, D. (1995) *Blackfoot Physics*. London, Fourth Estate.

Perrement, M. (2005) 'Action research revolutionises the classroom', Beijing, China Development Brief, 10 May 2005. Retrieved 3 August 2005 from http://www.jackwhitehead.com/china/cdbmay05.

Peters, R.S. (1966) *Ethics and Education*. London, Allen and Unwin.

Polanyi, M. (1958) *Personal Knowledge*. London, Routledge and Kegan Paul.

Popper, K. (1959) *The Logic of Scientific Discovery*. London, Hutchinson.

Popper, K. (1963) *Conjectures and Refutation: The Growth of Scientific Knowledge*. London, Routledge & Kegan Paul.

Popper, K. (1972) *Objective Knowledge: An Evolutionary Approach*. Oxford, Oxford University Press.

Prasad, P. (2005) *Crafting Qualitative Research: Working in the Postpositivist Traditions*. Armonk, New York and London, Sharpe.

Pring, R. (2000) *Philosophy of Education*. London, Continuum.

Purpel, D. (1999) *Moral Outrage in Education*. New York, Lang.

Rawls, J. (1971) *A Theory of Justice*. Cambridge, MA, Harvard University Press.

Rawls, J. (2001) *Justice as Fairness*. Cambridge, MA, Harvard University Press.

Rayner, A. (2004) 'Introduction to the complex self'. Retrieved 8 March 2005 from http://www.bath.ac.uk/~bassadmr/inclusionality/complexself.htm.

Rayner, A. (2005) 'Why I need my space – I'd rather be a channel than a node'. Leading Article from Members of the Scientific and Medical Network. Retrieved 6 June 2005 from http://www.datadiwan.de/SciMedNet/Leadarts/Rayner_space.htm.

Raz, J. (2001) *Value, Respect and Attachment*. Cambridge, Cambridge University Press.

Raz, J. (2003) *The Practice of Value*. Oxford, Oxford University Press.

Reason, P. and Bradbury, H. (eds) (2001) *Handbook of Action Research*. London, Sage.

Reid, L.A. (1980) 'Art: knowledge-that and knowing this', *British Journal of Aesthetics*, 20 (4): 329–39.

Renowden, J., Johnson, C. and Richardson, J. (2005) 'How can we improve our effectiveness as teachers of student teachers?' Paper presented at the Invited Symposium for the Special Interest Group Teaching and Teacher Education 'Demonstrating Accountability through our Self-Study Practices as Teacher Educators', EARLI, Nicosia, August.

Research Assessment Exercise (2005) Website address http://www.rae.ac.uk/pubds/2005/04/.

Robbins, R. (2000) *Literary Feminisms*. Basingstoke, Palgrave.

Roberts, M. (1983) *The Visitation*. London, Women's Press.

Roche, M. (2005) 'Setting the what its free: critical thinking in the primary school' (working title). University of Limerick.

Royce, J. (1891) 'Is there a science of education?', *Educational Review*, 1 (January): 23–4.

Russell, B. (2002) *Education and the Social Order* (1932). London, Routledge.

Ryan, W. (1971) *Blaming the Victim*. New York, Vintage.

Ryle, G. (1949) *The Concept of Mind*. Harmondsworth, Penguin.

Sachs, J. (2002) *The Activist Teaching Profession*. Buckingham, Open University Press.

Sagor, R. (1992) *How to Conduct Collaborative Action Research,* Alexandria, Association for Supervision and Curriculum Development.

Said, E. (1994) *Beginnings: Intention and Method*. London, Granta.

Schön, D. (1983) *The Reflective Practitioner: How Professionals Think in Action*. New York, Basic.

Schön, D. (1995) 'Knowing-in-action: the new scholarship requires a new epistemology', *Change*, November–December: 27–34.

Sen, A. (1999) *Development as Freedom*. Oxford, Oxford University Press.

Slavin, R.E. (2002) 'Evidence-based education policies: transforming educational practice and research', *Educational Researcher*, 31 (7): 15–21.

Snow, C. (2001) 'Knowing what we know: children, teachers, researchers', *Educational Researcher*, 30 (7): 3–9. Presidential Address to the American Educational Research Association Annual Meeting, Seattle.

Stenhouse, L. (1975) *An Introduction to Curriculum Research and Development*. London, Heinemann.

Sternberg, R. and Horvath, J. (1999) *Tacit Knowledge in Professional Practice*. Mahwah, NJ, Erlbaum.

Sullivan, B. (2005) 'Towards a living theory of a practice of social justice'. Draft PhD thesis, University of Limerick.

Thayer-Bacon, B. (2003) *Relational '(e)pistemologies'*. New York, Lang.

Tian, F. and Laidlaw, M. (2004) 'Educational action research and foreign languages teaching', *Journal of Foreign Language Teaching*, Xi'an International Studies University Press: 6.

Tian, F. and Laidlaw, M. (2005) 'How can we enhance educational and English-language provision at our Action Research Centre and beyond?' Retrieved 5 August 2005 from http://www.arexpeditions.montana.edu/articleviewer.php?AID=87.

Todorov, T. (1990) *Genres in Discourse*. Cambridge, Cambridge University Press.

Tormey, R. and Haran, N. (2003) 'Education and Social Justice in Ireland', in R. Tormey (ed.), *Teaching Social Justice: Intercultural and Development Education Perspectives on Education's Context, Content and Methods*. Limerick, Mary Immaculate College.

Walsh, D. (2004) 'How do I improve my leadership as a team leader in vocational education in further education?' MA dissertation, University of Bath. Retrieved 16 January 2005 from http://www.bath.ac.uk/~edsajw/walsh.shtml.

Wheatley, M. (1992) *Leadership and the New Science: Learning about Organization from an Orderly Universe*. San Francisco, Berrett-Koehler.

Whitehead, J. (1976) *Improving Learning for 11–14 year olds in Mixed Ability Science Groups*. Swindon, Wiltshire Curriculum Development Centre. Retrieved 26 November 2004 from http://www.actionresearch.net/writings/ilmagall.pdf.

Whitehead, J. (1985) 'The analysis of an individual's educational development', in M. Shipman (ed.), *Educational Research: Principles, Policies and Practice*. London, Falmer. Retrieved 24 January 2005 from http://www.bath.ac.uk/~edsajw/bk93/5anal.pdf.

Whitehead, J. (1989) 'Creating a living educational theory from questions of the kind, "How do I improve my practice?"', *Cambridge Journal of Education*, 19 (1): 137–53. Retrieved 26 November 2004 from http://www.bath.ac.uk/~edsajw/writings/livtheory.html.

Whitehead, J. (1993) *The Growth of Educational Knowledge: Creating Your Own Living Educational Theories*. Bournemouth, Hyde. Retrieved 21 January 2005 from http://www.bath.ac.uk/~edsajw/bk93/geki.htm.

Whitehead, J. (2000) 'Creating our own knowledge'. Keynote address to the Act, Reflect, Revise IV Conference, Brantford, Ontario, 17 February 2000. Retrieved 7 October 2005 from http://www.bath.ac.uk/~edsajw/writings/keyarr.pdf.

Whitehead, J. (2003) 'Creating our living educational theories in teaching and learning to care: using multi-media to communicate the meanings and influence of our embodied educational values', *Teaching Today for Tomorrow*, 19: 17–20.

Whitehead, J. (2004a) 'What counts as evidence in the self-studies of teacher education practices?', in J.J. Loughran, M.L. Hamilton, V.K. LaBoskey and T. Russell (eds), *International Handbook of Self-Study of Teaching and Teacher Education Practices*. Dordrecht, Kluwer.

Whitehead, J. (2004b) 'How valid are multi-media communications of my embodied values in living theories and standards of educational judgement and practice?' Retrieved from http://www.bath.ac.uk/~edsajw//multimedia/jimenomov/JIMEW98.html. In *Action Research Expeditions*, October 2004. Retrieved 15 August 2005 from http://www.arexpeditions.montana.edu/articleviewer.php?AID=80.

Whitehead, J. (2004c) 'Do action researchers' expeditions carry hope for the future of humanity? How do we know? An enquiry into reconstructing educational theory and educating social formations'. *Action Research Expedition*. Retrieved 26 November 2004 from http://www.arexpeditions.montana.edu/articleviewer.php?AID=80.

Whitehead, J. (2004d) 'Do the values and living logics I express in my educational relationships carry the hope of Ubuntu for the future of humanity?' Paper presented at a symposium of the British Educational Research Association annual conference 'How Are We Contributing to a New Scholarship of Educational Enquiry through our

Pedagogisation of Postcolonial Living Educational Theories in the Academy?',
Manchester, September.

Whitehead, J. (2005a) 'Developing the dynamic boundaries of living standards of judgement in educational enquiries of the kind, "How do I improve what I am doing?"'
Retrieved 17 January 2005 from http://www.jackwhitehead.com/jwartl141015web.htm.

Whitehead, J. (2005b) 'Do these living educational theories explain educational influence in
learning with values of humanity?' Retrieved 15 August 2005 http://www.jackwhitehead.
com/monday/jwedth.htm.

Whitehead, J. (2005c) 'How can we improve the educational influences of our teacher-
researcher quests?' Keynote Presentation to the 12th International Conference of
Teacher Research at McGill University, 16 April 2005. Retrieved 3 August 2005 from
http://jackwhitehead.com/jwictr05key.htm.

Whitehead, Joan (2003) 'The future of teaching and teaching in the future: a vision of the
future of the profession of teaching – making the possible probable'. Keynote address to
the Standing Committee for the Education and Training of Teachers Annual Conference,
Dunchurch, October. Retrieved 23 January 2005 from http://www.bath.ac.uk/~edsajw/evol/
joanwfiles/joanw.htm.

Whitehead, Joan and Fitzgerald, Bernie (2004) 'New ways of working with mentors and
trainees in a training school partnership as practitioner-researchers'. Paper presented at
the symposium 'Have We Created a New Epistemology for the New Scholarship of
Educational Enquiry through Practitioner Research? Developing Sustainable Global
Educational Networks of Communication', presented at the British Educational Research
Association annual meeting, UMIST, Manchester, September. Retrieved 23 January
2005 from http://www.bath.ac.uk/~edsajw//bera04/bera3.htm.

Whitty, G. (2005) 'Education(al) research and education policy making: is conflict inevitable?'
Presidential Address to BERA 2005. Retrieved 28 September 2005 from http://www.
bera.ac.uk/pdfs/Microsoft%20-%20Bera2005 presidential address CircFin.pdf.

Wilkinson, D. (ed.) (2000) *The Researcher's Toolkit*. London, RoutledgeFalmer.

Winter, R. (1989) *Learning from Experience*. London, Falmer.

Winter, R., Buck, A. and Sobiechowska, P. (1999) *Professional Experience and the Investigative
Imagination: The Art of Reflective Writing*. London: Routledge.

Woods, P. (1999) *Successful Writing for Qualitative Researchers*. London, Routledge.

Yeaman, K. (1995) 'Creating educative dialogue in my classroom – my educational journey'.
Action research module, University of Bath. Retrieved 3 August 2005 from http://www.
bath.ac.uk/~edsajw/module/kathy.htm.

Young, I.M. (1990) *Justice and the Politics of Difference*. Princeton NJ, Princeton University
Press.

Young, R. (2001) *Postcolonialism*. London, Blackwell.

Zovko, M. (2005) Progress report. Available at http://mzu.sbnet.hr/files/report.zip.

Index